Forties Film Funnymen

Forties Film Funnymen
*The Decade's Great Comedians
at Work in the Shadow of War*

WES D. GEHRING

Foreword by Anthony Slide

McFarland & Company, Inc., Publishers
Jefferson, North Carolina, and London

ALSO BY WES D. GEHRING
AND FROM MCFARLAND

Mr. Deeds Goes to Yankee Stadium: Baseball Films in the Capra Tradition (2004)

Joe E. Brown: Film Comedian and Baseball Buffoon (2006)

Film Clowns of the Depression: Twelve Defining Comic Performances (2007)

Frontispiece: Charlie Chaplin as dictator Adenoid Hynkel, contemplating world conquest, *The Great Dictator* (1940).

LIBRARY OF CONGRESS CATALOGUING-IN-PUBLICATION DATA

Gehring, Wes D.
    Forties film funnymen : the decade's great comedians at work in the shadow of war / Wes D. Gehring ; foreword by Anthony Slide.
       p.   cm.
    Includes bibliographical references and index.

ISBN 978-0-7864-4257-7
softcover : 50# alkaline paper ∞

    1. Comedy films — United States — History and criticism.
2. Motion pictures — United States — History — 20th century.
I. Title.
PN1995.9.C55G4242   2010
791.43'6170973 — dc22   2010016074

British Library cataloguing data are available

©2010 Wes D. Gehring. All rights reserved

No part of this book may be reproduced or transmitted in any form or by any means, electronic or mechanical, including photocopying or recording, or by any information storage and retrieval system, without permission in writing from the publisher.

Front cover: W.C. Fields' ongoing battle of the sexes plays out here with a stranger as he throttles her bratty kid in *The Bank Dick*, 1940 (author collection)

Manufactured in the United States of America

McFarland & Company, Inc., Publishers
   Box 611, Jefferson, North Carolina 28640
     www.mcfarlandpub.com

To a lovely muse named Cassie,
my daughters Sarah and Emily,
and Anthony Slide

TABLE OF CONTENTS

Foreword by Anthony Slide   1
Preface and Acknowledgments   5
Introduction   9

1. Charlie Chaplin: *The Great Dictator* (1940)   13
2. W. C. Fields: *The Bank Dick* (1940)   30
3. Abbott & Costello: *Buck Privates* (1941)   46
4. Jack Benny: *To Be or Not to Be* (1942)   59
5. Eddie Bracken: *The Miracle of Morgan's Creek* (1944)   75
6. Bob Hope & Bing Crosby: The *Road to Utopia* (1946)   89
7. Danny Kaye: *The Kid from Brooklyn* (1946)   102
8. The Marx Brothers: *A Night in Casablanca* (1946)   115
9. Harold Lloyd: *The Sin of Harold Diddlebock* (1947) (a.k.a. *Mad Wednesday*)   133
10. Bob Hope: *My Favorite Brunette* (1947)   150
11. Charlie Chaplin: *Monsieur Verdoux* (1947)   165
12. Red Skelton: *A Southern Yankee* (1948)   179

Epilogue   192
Filmography   199
Chapter Notes   201
Bibliography   213
Index   223

FOREWORD
by Anthony Slide

The 1895 Lumière Brothers film *L'Arroseur arrosé* or *The Waterer Watered* holds a special place in film history as the first comedy — albeit only a couple of minutes in length. There are two characters: a young boy, the comedian, whose foot action prevents the hosepipe from working until the gardener, the straight man, peers down the nozzle. Not only is this a defining moment in world cinema, but also the screen's original defining comic performance. The young boy is the first in a very long line of screen comedians, only a relative few of whom can be identified as providing something unique and inceptive in their performances.

In the early years of the American cinema, comedians were many, but until Charlie Chaplin appeared on the scene, none were associated with an individual role in an individual film. The Keystone Kops, John Bunny, even Mabel Normand are judged and remembered for their representational roles and not for a personalized characterization. Even with his Tramp persona, Chaplin's work does not necessarily stand out in any particular film until the feature-length *The Kid* in 1921. It is a defining moment in Chaplin's career, bringing together all aspects of the Tramp characterization, and molding them into a single sophisticated performance.

Not surprisingly, Charlie Chaplin is represented by two films in Wes Gehring's study of a dozen comedic performances from the 1940s, whose stars were both personalities and comic actors. Chaplin is not alone among the performers under discussion whose film careers started in an earlier decade. He is but one of a number here — the others are W. C. Fields, Bob Hope, the Marx Brothers, and Harold Lloyd — whose work in the 1940s is as good, at least in my opinion, as their work in the 1930s.

Yes, other comedians were active a decade earlier, although some barely.

Bud Abbott and Lou Costello made their first film, *One Night in the Tropics*, in 1940, at the cusp of the new decade, and *Buck Pirates*, under discussion here, is only the duo's second feature. Jack Benny's film career goes back to the coming of sound and *Hollywood Revue of 1929*, but one will look in vain for any performance on screen in the 1930s that remains memorable. In fact, after *To Be or Not to Be* did Jack Benny ever do anything comparable? No, but then, he never again had a director as talented as Ernst Lubitsch.

Eddie Bracken's appearance here is something of a surprise. Like Abbott and Costello, he made his film debut in 1940. But, unlike the comedy duo, he is difficult to put into any specific category. He is as far removed from a burlesque style of comedy and fast-paced verbal humor as it is possible to be. His characterizations are usually gentle, confused and shy — somewhat in the Harold Lloyd tradition. It was Paramount who understood his capabilities and teamed him with director Preston Sturges in two major productions, *The Miracle of Morgan's Creek* and *Hail the Conquering Hero*. Wes Gehring has selected the first of these 1944 films for this book, and he gets no argument from me as to Bracken's presence here, only as to whether the chosen title is any better than the rejected one.

Danny Kaye was an all-round entertainer, both a comedian and a comic actor. If one were to judge him by the Educational comedy shorts that he made in the 1930s, Danny Kaye would have long been forgotten. Luckily, in the late 1930s and early 1940s, he was a smash hit on Broadway, leading to his first feature film role in *Up in Arms*. Wes Gehring goes out on a limb somewhat by ignoring *The Secret Life of Walter Mitty* and selecting *The Kid from Brooklyn* as the comedian's pivotal performance.

Anyone who follows Wes Gehring's career knows that he has something of a fixation with Red Skelton. He has authored two biographies and a mystery novel featuring the comedian. If Red Skelton had not made it into this book, there would have been doubt as to Wes Gehring's mental state. I am sure the major problem was not ensuring Red Skelton a place here, but restricting the choice to only one film — and then having to select *A Southern Yankee* over *I Dood It* or *The Fuller Brush Man*.

Luckily, there was not the same problem with Chaplin. His only two films of the 1940s are here. W. C. Fields had only two starring roles in the decade, in *The Bank Dick* and *Never Give a Sucker an Even Break*, and the former won out. Similarly, the Marx Brothers starred as a group in only two films in the 1940s and there is no competition between *A Night in Casablanca* and *Love Happy*. Harold Lloyd made only one film in the 1940s, *The Sin of Harold Did-*

dlebock, which harkens back to his great days in the 1920s, not least of all by including a lengthy sequence from the silent classic, *The Freshman.*

With each chapter, the reader is introduced to the star comedian, to what went towards creating a screen persona and, with a careful reading of the film, why it was important then and remains important today. Often the work of one comedian discussed in one chapter intertwines with the work of another in a further chapter. Throughout, Wes Gehring is respectful and sympathetic towards his cast of characters and the work under discussion. He never seeks to bring down the glory that was screen comedy, or to deflect from its importance in the history of American popular culture.

Forties Film Funnymen: The Decade's Great Comedians at Work in the Shadow of War reminds us of the many types of performance that fall into the category of the comedic. There is parody, used for political effect, in *The Great Dictator* and also in *To Be or Not to Be.* And, in my humble opinion, the latter is far more of a dark comedy than the work Chaplin conceived. Indeed, one might argue that the opaque side of Chaplin is better represented by *Monsieur Verdoux,* although its ending is awkward and bombastic in the censorial tone that Chaplin as the title character adopts. Some of the works here are mindful of the best of screwball comedy from the previous decade. Some signify the last great hurrahs of a career about to decline, as with Harold Lloyd, or the first flush of genius in a career expanding from strength to strength, as with Danny Kay or Red Skelton. Others demonstrate the comic genius to be found in words or situations be they from the pen of W. C. Fields or Preston Sturges. All are evidence of the brilliant comic art that existed in the 1940s and, indeed, throughout what is described as Hollywood's "golden age."

— Anthony Slide

Anthony Slide was said by the Los Angeles Times *to be "a one-man publishing phenomenon." He has written 72 books on the history of popular entertainment and edited 150 more. In 1990, he was awarded an honorary doctorate of letters by Bowling Green State University (Ohio), at which time he was hailed by Lillian Gish as "our preeminent historian of the silent film."*

Preface and Acknowledgments

We are all amateurs— none of us live long enough, or know enough, to be anything more.

— *Charlie Chaplin*

A gift from life which frequently goes unacknowledged is simply finding a positive passion which rewardingly helps pass the time. Writing about film comedy is my safety valve. *Los Angeles Times* columnist Steve Lopez, author of *The Soloist* (2008, adapted to the screen 2009), the poignant true story of the fall of a former Juilliard student to skid row musician, captures this sense of passion in his description of finding a story:

> When you're in the chase, the adrenaline pumps, minutes seem like seconds, and in your single-minded state you are for all intents and purposes a zombie, ignorant of everything around you.... I still came upon each one [story] like a kid at an Easter egg hunt, as if I wasn't certain I'd ever find another.[1]

If one can have that passion about some task, then a personal Valhalla is forever at hand, such as Noël Coward's own description of writing, where "work is more fun than fun."[2]

Coupled to this personal joy activity, sometimes a setting can be an added catalyst for creativity, either through the singular beauty or accumulated history of one place, or an artistic "well" of a broader domain. An example of the latter would be the aforementioned Lopez "mining" the streets of Los Angeles for columns. In contrast, a more ephemeral yet specific inspirational location is encapsuled in Christopher Buckley's description of the Metropolitan Museum's (New York) "Temple of Dendur," the stunning Egyptian block-long "room" with a glass back wall view of Central Park—"the coolest space on the planet."[3] While I happen to share this sentiment, a close second for this researcher-writer is the New York Public Library's main branch at Fifth

Avenue and Forty-Second Street — "the one with the stone lions," as my daughter Emily labeled it as a child.

Of the libraries to which each book takes me, I always log the most time at "the one with the stone lions." This text was no exception, with many days spent in the library's "Tombs" (dead newspaper department). Another important stop in the city is the New York (Performing Arts) Public Library at Lincoln Center, with its critical period clipping files of film artists and individual movies.

On the West Coast, a research sojourn at the Academy of Motion Picture Arts and Sciences' Margaret Herrick Library (Beverly Hills) is equally important. Another stop that must be made is the Cinema and Television Library of the University of Southern California (Los Angeles), which was especially helpful in covering this book's chapter on *A Southern Yankee* (1948). When I think of these amazing centers of learning and how they nurture me, I am reminded of legendary basketball player and passionate athletic artist Bill Russell's thoughts about departing his creative space: "Whenever I leave the [Boston] Celtics locker room, even heaven wouldn't be good enough because anyplace else is a step down."[4]

Just as friends help one through life, they obviously facilitate the creative process, too. Starting with those at the greatest distance, Joe and Maria Pacino always provide research assistance and a place to crash when I am in the Los Angeles area. Ball State teaching colleague and film author Conrad Lane offered frequent advice, as well as a close reading of the manuscript. My department chair, "Dr. Joe" Misiewicz, is a supportive friend who also orchestrates university financial support. Janet Warrner supplied valuable editorial help, while Jean Thurman was responsible for computer preparation of the manuscript.

I was pleased that one of my scholarly heroes, Anthony Slide, was able to pen the foreword. I have always admired both his work and his honesty, especially his ability to slice through the pretension which sometimes passes for academic achievement. Though our friendship has often been limited through the years to correspondence, he remains an artistic and historical compass for the direction of my "more fun than fun" work.

Ultimately, my writing comes from the comfort zone provided by family: my parents, who came of age during the 1940s; my daughters, Sarah and Emily, inundated with enough films from that decade to think maybe they came of age then, too; and my special muse, Cassie Beal, who continues to inspire. Thank you.

Before exiting this preface to another study of my personal passion, however, I feel compelled to affix a final addendum to the throwaway simplicity which has often been comedy's MO through the ages. Decades before another Hoosier-born comedian, David Letterman, announced his casual comedy style as "It ain't brain surgery," Red Skelton had embraced a similar philosophy: "Even if we fluff a few [comic lines], who cares? We aren't the United Nations in a debating session. We're just having fun."[5] I was recently reminded again of the universality of this sentiment with a revelation made by Conan O'Brien shortly before he briefly became the host of the *Tonight Show*. Showing an interviewer his new but modest dressing room, the only distinctive object in which was a framed etching of President Lincoln in death, surrounded by mourning members of his government, O'Brien, also a student of history, explained, "I've always practiced my monologue in front of this image before going on stage. Looking at that, I figure, heck, it could always be worse."[6]

This darkly comic spin on an old axiom about comedy's "aw shucks" insignificance will forever be part of the entertainment landscape, a legacy which probably dates from Aristotle's greater fascination with the flawed figures of tragedy. But personally I am not fooled. Humanity has much more to learn through laughter from the *really* flawed clowns of comedy ... because they are we. And when our favorite funny men pay lip service to that lesser state, remember, it is just a cover, in order for them to better perform their comedy reconnaissance work—"wise fools" indeed.

— Wes D. Gehring

INTRODUCTION

To borrow an insight from critic John Lahr, "[Great artists are those] whose life and work, however uneven, are among the blueprints by which future generations reconstruct the follies and the accomplishments of times gone by."[1]

This book examines a dozen defining comic performances during a volatile war-torn decade, which often seemed to operate without any "blueprints." Fittingly, most of these highlighted films traffic in clown comedy's most central message—*resilience*, the hope that one can soldier through the most slapstick of life dilemmas. Yet, given this shadow of World War II influence, some of these focus films begin to "trounce any persistent belief you may have that the world makes sense and that art should reflect that...."[2]

Each of these key comedies merits an individual chapter in which the movie is both closely critiqued and considered as a mini-microcosm of the antiheroic world of its central clown, or clowns. The dozen films are: *The Great Dictator* (1940, Charlie Chaplin), *The Bank Dick* (1940, W. C. Fields), *Buck Privates* (1941, Abbott & Costello), *To Be or Not to Be* (1942, Jack Benny), *The Miracle of Morgan's Creek* (1944, Eddie Bracken), *Road to Utopia* (1946, Bob Hope & Bing Crosby), *The Kid from Brooklyn* (1946, Danny Kaye), *A Night in Casablanca* (1946, Marx Brothers), *The Sin of Harold Diddlebock* (1947, Harold Lloyd), *My Favorite Brunette* (1947, Bob Hope), *Monsieur Verdoux* (1947, Charlie Chaplin), and *A Southern Yankee* (1948, Red Skelton).

Rare is the screen clown, or filmmaker in general, who can perform the cinematic hat trick of being the writer, director and star. Thus, with the exception of triple-threat Chaplin, and W. C. Fields (writer and clown extraordinaire), the other funny men featured herein often received major assistance from additional legendary talents. While each chapter will attempt to document the credit, three auteurs merit special notations. Writer and director Preston Sturges orchestrated the inspired antics of both *Morgan's Creek* and *Diddlebock*. Ernest Lubitsch directed and co-authored the original story for the brilliant dark comedy companion piece to Chaplin's *Dictator*, as well as being Jack Benny's greatest showcase, *To Be or Not to Be*. And Buster Keaton was forever a creative force behind the now neglected but superlative silliness of Red Skelton, especially in the watershed *Yankee*.

A clown movie is the most basic of the comedy genres. But these pictures seldom exist without ties to other genres of laughter. However, this is not usually some helter-skelter linkage. The focus clown persona provides an obvious explanation on why a compound comedy genre blossoms. For instance, even in Charlie Chaplin's earliest films, his Tramp figure forever flirted with dark comedy, from using a gas street lamp to anesthetize a nemesis in *Easy Street* (1917), to contemplating chucking an abandoned baby down a curb sewer opening in *The Kid* (1921). Consequently, Chaplin's full embrace of black humor in *Dictator* and *Monsieur Verdoux* is hardly surprising.

While the catalysts for both Chaplin pictures were real life monsters (Adolf Hitler and serial killer Henri Landru), dark comedy also frequently centers upon a leaf-in-the-wind victim, à la Chaplin's second *Dictator* role as the Tramp-like Jewish barber. Such vulnerability greatly assisted the antiheroic personae of Fields and Benny in the darkly comic *Bank Dick* and *To Be or Not to Be*, respectively. But *the* companion genre for screen clowns is parody. Fully one-third of this text's focus films also strongly operate as spoofs. Both a *Night in Casablanca* and *My Favorite Brunette* double as film noir parodies; the *Road to Utopia* and *A Southern Yankee* spoof the action adventure genre. Yet, given that the vast majority of personality comedies are predicated upon a goofy clown entertainingly *not* measuring up to an audi-

Preston Sturges and Preston Sturges (circa 1945).

ence's expectations for a traditional leading man, there is an element of parody in most screen comedian roles. For example, Danny Kaye is a reluctant boxer in *The Kid From Brooklyn*, as foreign to the ring as Chaplin's Tramp in *City Lights* (1931). But beyond the demonstrative multiple masks any clown brings to a part, 1940s audiences were undoubtedly further amused by juxtaposing the image of milquetoast man-child Kaye as a boxer, with earlier serious portrayals of fighters, such as James Cagney in *City for Conquest* (1940), or Errol Flynn in *Gentleman Jim* (1942).

For anyone piecing together a text on comedians, regardless of the moment in time, playwright and actor Wallace Shawn's one-man show, *The Fever* (1990), offers a crucial observation on the human comedy:

> A human being happens to be an unprotected little wriggling creature ... without a shell or a hide or even any fur, just thrown out onto the earth like an eye that's been pulled from its socket, like a shucked oyster that's trying to crawl along the ground. We need to build our own shells.

That protective shell can come from clown comedy—making us realize we are neither alone in our angst, nor as limited in our struggles to cope as our favorite befuddled funny men. Of course, Shawn did not limit his insights to being a wordsmith. In the United States he is better known as a comic screen actor, including his turn as the amusingly menacing kidnapping villain in *The Princess Bride* (1987), or his earlier self-exploring, philosophizing writer in the cult classic, *My Dinner with Andre* (1981), which he also co-scripted.

Laughter helps distance the viewer from personal pain, even if, as Sartre cynically suggests, "Hell is other people." But that shell Shawn suggests we build is grounded not just in the resiliency of clowns but also in our awareness that to not learn to cope exposes one to chaos—the brief bouts of comic insanity which more and more define modern comedians. In this book Danny Kaye and Eddie Bracken best represent this precursor period to the full-blown insanity shtick made mainstream with 1950s Jerry Lewis. As Conan O'Brien's physician father once told him, "You're making a living off of something that probably should be treated."[3]

Maybe, however, the best guide to embracing comedy as part of the human survival kit is found in Woody Allen's title for *Whatever Works* (2008). Fleshing this out further at the picture's premiere, he said:

> Yes, whatever works to get you through [life] is fine, and not necessarily in relation to relationships. If it's collecting stamps obsessively, or lis-

tening to ball scores, if you're not encroaching on anyone else, then that's what you have to do....⁴

"Whatever works" for me is comedy. Even if I cannot grow that shell, I will hopefully be frequently distracted from personal travail by laughter. Whatever works.

1

CHARLIE CHAPLIN
The Great Dictator (1940)

"I thought The Great Dictator *was a marvelous film. I thought it was a remarkable combination of comedy and outrage."*
— Historian Arthur Schlesinger, Jr.[1]

Fittingly, this study of twelve defining cinema comic performances from the 1940s begins with a Charlie Chaplin film. Chaplin (1889–1977) is the greatest comedy auteur in movie history. His talent to write, direct, perform, produce, and compose the music for one watershed picture after another is unprecedented. But given all of Chaplin's classics, *The Great Dictator* was the filmmaker's most controversial work. After all, the world's most beloved figure, Chaplin's "Little Fellow Tramp," was taking on the globe's public enemy number one — the quasi-look-alike Adolf Hitler! Plus, as a *New York Times* period piece (1941) noted, "Chaplin is one of the greatest artists who ever lived, and when it was first announced several years ago that he would impersonate a dictator, the anticipation of satirical enjoyment throughout the world was immense."[2]

Yet, when *The Great Dictator* came to the screen (October 1940), Europe was at war, and the picture's dark comedy overtones — an "in" genre for modern society — was much more of an iffy proposition for period viewers. As *New York Times* critic Bosley Crowther suggested in an otherwise positive review, for many people, "the subject of it [Hitler] is much too grim for jesting."[3] *The New Yorker*'s critique added, "There were never any very good Hitler jokes, and now [in the three years since the satirical story was first suggested to Chaplin by British producer/director Alexander Korda], I should say, there are none [Hitler jokes] anywhere near being good."[4] Thus, as the *Hollywood Citizen-News* later summarized, "With one or two exceptions, the [all-important] New York reviewers were what might euphemistically be called 'disappointed.'"[5] Of course, there were some 1940s critics who saw the uniqueness of Chaplin's movie. For example, the *Variety* reviewer prophetically recognized the picture's innate greatness: "Audience reaction can't help but be favorable, granting that Nazi sympathizers are not considered at all. Through the 127 minutes of the film it is virtually certain that the average customer will go out of the theatre with a feeling of having thoroughly enjoyed it."[6]

Before examining the *Dictator* production in detail, as well as additional period reviews, one needs to look at Chaplin's then recent career. *Years* were now passing between pictures. It had been four years since his last movie, *Modern Times* (1936), had been released. Meant as a swan song for the Tramp, *Modern Times* was also driven by a seminal social issue of the Depression: "I wondered what would happen to the progress of the mechanical age if one person decided to act like a bull in a china shop ... I decided it would make a good story to take a little man and make him thumb his nose at all recognized rules and conventions."[7]

As with *Modern Times*, another social issue, the rise of dictators like Hitler, once again pulled Chaplin and his little Tramp back on the screen in *Dictator*. As he put it:

> Laughter may help check the ... bad behavior in the world.... Leaders with tenth-rate minds have captured the new instruments of propaganda and are using these instruments to destroy good, civilized behavior. I'm the clown, and what can I do that is more effective than to laugh at these fellows who are putting humanity to the goose-step; who, as I say in one of my first [*Dictator*] captions, are kicking humanity around?[8]

But dusting off the Tramp for *Dictator* posed an aesthetic problem for Chaplin. The coming of sound had made the retirement of the comedian's silent screen alter ego inevitable, though he had still managed two Charlie hits during the first decade of the "talkies"—*City Lights* (1931) and *Modern Times*. But the comedian's creative close to the latter picture had painted him into an artistic corner. *Modern Times*' finale allowed the Tramp to speak briefly for the first and only time. Charlie sings an inspired gibberish song, "a sort of Katzenjammer French," whose nonsense lyrics he improvises after losing the originals.[9] Thus, director Chaplin creates a delightful device with which to preserve the formerly silent universality of Charlie's character. The Tramp is given his own language.

A gibberish language, however, is not something one could sustain for a whole feature film. So what would Chaplin do in *Dictator*? First, he defused the subject by playing two parts in the picture: the Charlie-like Jewish barber, and Dictator Adenoid Hynkel. Second, until the barber's finale speech — which is really Chaplin stepping out of character to plead for world peace — this variation on Charlie is all but silent. Third, for Chaplin's first truly sound film, he wisely throws the emphasis upon a character, the Hitler-like Hynkel, where the comedian can embellish his gibberish gift for humor with a Katzenjammer German. Fourth, by making the Jewish barber more vulnerable than the Tramp, Chaplin further redirects the viewer's attention to the more broadly comic Hynkel. While the barber is definitely a first cousin to Charlie, one could still argue that *Modern Times* is the last Tramp picture.

If the gibberish elements of *Modern Times* gave Chaplin ideas for *Dictator*, one of his earliest seminal satires, *Shoulder Arms* (1918), was undoubtedly another catalyst for his Hitler take-off. On the eve of World War II, Chaplin was sometimes encouraged to either reissue or remake this darkly comic World War I picture. Though the comedian did neither, there are several parallels between this film and *Dictator*. *Arms* has Charlie the Tramp as a fighting American soldier in Europe who comically orchestrates the capture of Germany's leader, Kaiser Wilhelm. Of course, the movie's close reveals this to be merely a dream of Charlie's doughboy. But even this plays into *Dictator*.

Consequently, here are the basic links between *Arms* and the *Dictator*, beyond their shared satirical base. First, *Dictator* begins with the Charlie-like Jewish barber as a World War I soldier, too, though now he is Tomanian (German). Second, a war-related head injury has given him amnesia, and he has no knowledge of the twenty-year flash forward which soon follows — coupled with the repressive actions taken by Hitler's Nazi party. Thus, while *Arms'* Charlie dreamed of being a hero, the *Dictator's* barber simply slept away the years. Third, just as *Arms'* Charlie gets a chance to end World War I by capturing the Kaiser, the *Dictator's* Jewish barber has an opportunity for derailing World War II by way of being mistaken for the Hynkel Hitler.

Naturally, one might segue from these *Arms-Dictator* parallels to several almost perverse dark-comedy links between Chaplin and Hitler. The ties would include having European births a mere four days apart (1889), having alcoholic fathers but mothers they worshipped, surviving childhood poverty, and fears of family histories with insanity. Most telling, both men were control freaks easily reduced to childish behavior if things did not go their way — a situation often minimized by surrounding themselves with yes-men. Ironically, at a time (1914) Chaplin was discovering international fame as a Tramp, Hitler was a real tramp in Austria. Plus, while Chaplin was an actor whose art often had political overtones (starting with the Progressive Era issues he addressed in many of his early short subjects of the 1910s[10]), Hitler was a politician who took acting lessons to better sell his politics. And both men had a natural gift for mimicry. Like Chaplin, Hitler was fascinated by

Chaplin as a World War I doughboy in *Shoulder Arms* (1918).

film and utilized arguably cinema's greatest woman director (Leni Riefenstahl) to celebrate Nazi Germany in the acclaimed documentaries *Triumph of the Will* (1935, chronicling the 1934 Nazi Party Convention at Nuremberg) and *Olympia* (1938, covering the 1936 Berlin Olympic Games).

All these parallels, however, neglect the central link between Chaplin and Hitler — the toothbrush mustache which was the central catalyst for *Dictator*. History's funniest man first wore the undersized mustache when he began appearing as Charlie in 1914. History's scariest man assumed the style shortly after the war (1919). Though there has always been speculation that the dictator copied the popular toothbrush mustache of the comedian (especially among persecuted Jews of the 1930s[11]), there is no hard evidence to support this entertaining claim. But what would have been the motive of the then wannabe leader, had he consciously borrowed Charlie's "cookie duster"? One assumes it would have been the hope that some of the Tramp's fame/recognition would have rubbed off on him. After all, to paraphrase gifted period humorist Will Rogers, "Charlie is better known in Zululand than Greta Garbo is in Arkansas." Along less amusing lines, some historians have suggested that Hitler's appropriation of Charlie's mustache caused period leaders to initially underestimate the dictator. For instance, Ron Rosenbaum argues:

> Chaplin's mustache became a *lens* through which to look at Hitler. A glass in which Hitler became *merely* Chaplinesque: a figure to be mocked more than feared, a comic villain whose pretensions would collapse of his own disproportionate weight like the Little Tramp collapsing on his cane. Someone to be ridiculed rather than resisted.[12]

Be that as it may, given the myriad of satirical swipes taken at Hitler since Chaplin's *Dictator*, one might now mistakenly assume that it was a no-brainer for the comedian to take on the Nazi leader. But given the overwhelmingly isolationist sentiment in America during the late 1930s, Chaplin's production was an act of artistic bravery. Couple this with the sad scenario that there was also a great deal of anti–Semitism in America; the celebrated comedian actually received death threats over his decision to shish kebab the director. Controversy associated with *Dictator*, besides the aforementioned pioneering dark comedy status of the film, also involved something of a rarity for a 1930s movie star — being in the public "doghouse" for taking *any* political position. That is, while embracing a stand on topical issues is now common in Hollywood — though still often controversial with the public — it was just not done in the pre-war film capital. The phenomenon might be compared to the movie industry's now legendary axiom against the problem film genre during the same time: "If you want to send a message, use Western Union" (attributed to countless movie producers).

Dictator provocativeness might also be attributed to Chaplin breaking what film historian Charles J. Maland calls an actor's "aesthetic contract" with the public.[13] Thus, while a semblance of the comedian's beloved silent Tramp remains in the Jewish barber, the *Dictator*'s focus is clearly on the comic villain title character. Historically, the public is seldom happy with personality comedians who abandon their antiheroic personae in favor of more complex dark figures, whether one is talking about Chaplin's Hynkel, or more recent creative wanderings by Jim Carrey and Adam Sandler. Moreover, besides playing a brilliantly comic but less sympathetic character, Chaplin, in his open-ended preachy *Dictator* close, steps out of character and shares his personal slant on society, contrary to the typical feel-good, definite conclusion of the standard Charlie movie.

For the 1940 public, however, the most dicey aspect of the *Dictator* still probably came down to the picture's watershed dark comedy status — this being a genre which did not move to pop culture's center stage until *Dr. Strangelove or: How I Learned to Stop Worrying and Love the Bomb* (1964). A central theme of dark comedy is portraying man as beast. What could be a more apropos example than Chaplin's darkly comic rendering of a beast-like Hitler? This is never more apparent than in the film's initial presentation of Hynkel. The scene is a delicious travesty of Hitler as an orator, with its "Demokratien shtunk!" and "Frei Sprecken Shtunk!" allowing Chaplin to showcase his exceptional talents for both verbal mimicry and pointed political satire. This acclaimed performance of German gibberish (echoed in the full name Chaplin gives the dictator — Adenoid Hynkel) is complemented by the comedian's ongoing ability to give his work numerous levels of comedy richness. Consequently, while one first laughs at Chaplin's parody of German guttural sounds (reminiscent of Mark Twain's essay "That Awful German Language"), the speech disintegrates into an angry tirade of an incoherent scene which manages to be simultaneously funny and frightening.

In a period article from the *New York World Telegram*, Chaplin said, "I listen to Hitler on the radio. The mad, bitter voice I listened [to] only a few times. Then I had it, and we worked out some ordinary German words every American could understand. The rest was gibberish."[14] As if playing off his comments on gibberish, the comedian later insightfully observed, "Mine made just as much sense as his do. It's not the words, it's the tone. [This] Makes for complete mass hysteria. That voice bangs on your brain, and before you know it you're [reluctantly] cheering."[15]

Hynkel's metamorphosis to a beast-like state during this time is punctuated by more traditional moments of visual Chaplin comedy, such as the microphone that recoils from his verbal attack or the beating of his chest like a gorilla. But even such physical comedy is not entirely divorced from Hitler. During the production of *Dictator*, Chaplin was intrigued by some newsreel footage of Hitler in which the dictator seemed to do a little dance after the signing of the French surrender. Chaplin told friend Tim Durant, "This guy is one of the greatest actors I've ever seen."[16]

At the end of Hynkel's gibberish tirade, the voiceover narrator chillingly informs the viewer that the dictator has been discussing the Jewish race. Like everything else the anonymous voice has told the viewer, this does not come as a surprise. But whereas earlier intrusions had been either comically unnecessary (such as translating "Libertad shtunk!") or a simple spoof of "diplomatic" decoding ("Demokratien shtunk!" becoming "Democracy is fragrant") — obviousness here is the message of the movie — such racist slander was the Hitler norm. Thus, even the use of the voiceover has changed by scene's end, just as Chaplin has altered one's response to the dictator from seeing a buffoon to viewing a monster. (A comically lighter variation of this scene occurs in Woody Allen's later black comedy *Bananas*, 1971, with Fidel Castro as the target dictator.)

The second basic theme of black comedy is the absurdity of the modern world, in which the individual does not count. This victimization is realized in the Tramp-like Jewish barber. Suffering from a World War I injury, the barber has been an amnesia victim until the eve of World War II. By this time the Hynkel Hitler has already established his persecution of the Jewish people. The barber's twenty-odd-year blank spot also acts as an ironic metaphor for a real world that somehow missed the ugly rise of Hitler during the same period. Regardless, the barber is constantly endangered by a Hynkel-led racism that is patently absurd. Indeed, it is the dark comedy absurdity upon which the movie is founded. As Holocaust historian Ilan Avisar has stated, with Chaplin playing both Hynkel and the barber, what better way is there to demonstrate ludicrousness — "the great [Aryan] dictator looks so exactly like the small Jew that at the end of the movie the closest colleagues and ardent admirers of the former cannot distinguish between the two."[17]

As a paradoxical aside, the little barber is even buffeted about in extrafilmic terms. At the close of the movie, when mistaken identity allows the barber to speak in place of Hynkel, one quickly realizes that the antihero has really been displaced by Chaplin the impassioned filmmaker ... calling for peace. Period critics protested this stepping out of character. The comedian replied, "The time had come when I simply had to stop kidding. They had their laughs.... But now I wanted to make them stop being so damned contented. This isn't just another war."[18] (As will be addressed shortly, the critical take on the closing speech has now assumed a 180-degree swing.)

If one, however, wanted to do a period defense of *Dictator*'s close, several other then contemporary major productions also included self-conscious conclusions. For example, director William Dieterle's controversial film about the Spanish Civil War, *Blockade* (1938), ended with Henry Fonda's character dropping any pretense of story and making an impassioned plea to the film audience, not unlike Chaplin's close to *Dictator*. John Ford's 1940 adaptation of *The Grapes of Wrath*, with Ma Joad's (Jane Darwell) uplifting final speech — tacked on by producer Darryl Zanuck to avoid a downer ending, remains a controversial contradiction of John Steinbeck's original novel — though it is perfectly consistent with Ford's populist oeuvre. And Alfred Hitchcock's stylish Nazi warning, *Foreign Correspondent* (1940), concludes with an emotional radio broadcast by title character Joel McCrea that quickly becomes a self-conscious plea to America, from the still British citizen Hitchcock, that a conflict with Germany is imminent.

While period critics were less than enthralled by *Dictator*'s close, in the early 1940s Chaplin received requests to repeat the address, both at public rallies and over the radio. What has never been discussed, though, are the dark comedy implications of the speech. Whether it is aesthetically appropriate to step out of character is not the issue here. Despite the heartfelt feelings of Chaplin, the fact that he believed the little barber was not up to the situation makes the close pure wishful thinking ... a fantasy exit. Ironically, later black film comedies often purposely and mockingly embrace an impossible fantasy close, such as Tim Robbin's film producer suddenly having the Midas touch after committing murder in *The Player* (1992). Or, closer to the subject at hand, in writer-director Quentin Tarantino's dark comedy take on Nazis, *Inglourious Basterds* (sic, 2009), this over-the-top filmmaker ultimately has Hitler and his hierarchy dying earlier and differently than the historical record. Chaplin's unrealistic segue to his final populist pitch also helps explain why the comedian's radio and rally performances of the speech, divorced from both the movie and the genre expectations of dark comedy, were popular in that Capraesque, populist time.

Returning to the second theme of black humor, absurdity, this phenomenon is usually presented in two ways — through the chaos of an unordered universe and through the flaws of mortal man. Both are found in *Dictator*. The first and most fundamental simply has man being victimized for merely trying to exist. One has only to think of the World War I scenes that open the film, in which the barber has the most frustratingly dangerous time playing soldier. An example would be his attempts to get away from the misfired cannon shell that anticipates his every move. Of course, the mere fact that he is reminiscent of the Tramp adds empathy and connects the viewer to an earlier body of work often grounded in comic chaos. In fact, this cannon shell which forever manages to point at the barber reminds one of *The Gold Rush* scene in which Charlie is trying to get away from the rifle over which Big Jim McKay (Mack Swain) and Black Larson (Tom Murray) are fighting. No matter where Charlie goes, this weapon only has "sight" for him.

For all the comic frightfulness of an unordered universe, man has been a strong contributor to the absurdity of the dark comedy world. Manmade absurdity is the result of both general species incompetence and its perpetuation in human institutions. Hynkel the dictator is black comedy's most basic example of a derailed humanity— the crazed person in power playing God. Fittingly, the aforementioned scholar Charles J. Maland reminds us that Hynkel is from Tomania, "a blend of the word for food poisoning and the suffix 'mania'— madness."[19]

Despite the physical resemblance between Hitler and Chaplin's Tramp, the filmmaker was not just playing one crazed leader. At the time Chaplin said, "I tried to make [Hynkel] a composite of all dictators ... every actor has

Chaplin's title character, with Jack Oakie's (right) scene-stealing takeoff on Mussolini, and Henry Daniel (left) as Garbitsch in *The Great Dictator* (1940).

a yearning to play [the megalomaniac] Napoleon. I've [now] got it out of my system. I've played Napoleon and Hitler and the mad Czar Paul all rolled into one."[20] Though this sounds a bit like Chaplin backpedaling from the *Dictator*-Hitler controversy by noting several frightful despots, the comedian had already spent a great deal of 1930s research time on a script about Napoleon that never got to the big screen. Thus, his composite reference to the French leader was not a random comment. Interestingly enough, during production the film was either referred to as *The Dictator*, or *Dictators*, with the latter moniker presumably because of Jack Oakie's (1903–1978) inspired satirical performance as Benzino Napoloni, a scene-stealing caricature of Benito Mussolini.

Dictator also displays the beginning stages of this craziness being institutionalized. For instance, witness the period interruptions by Field Marshall Herring (Billy Gilbert, a character patterned after fat Nazi leader Herman Goering), to demonstrate new military inventions which always end with the casually dark-comic demise of each inventor. Institutionalized absurdity eventually means man's chaos-making abilities attain irrevocable steamroller proportions, which is the precise point reached by *Dictator* when Chaplin introduces his putting-the-brakes-to-war controversial close.

In another 1940 article Chaplin revealed a provocatively personal view of the dangers of even the most modest example of institutionalization. He found himself acting arrogantly abusive by merely wearing the elaborate but regimental Nazi-like uniform called for by his Hynkel part. And this was off-camera, before any shooting was done. To Chaplin, the "uniform undoubtedly is a great deal to blame [for Nazi superiority]. The wearing of it often creates a false value of being better than one's fellow man, when in most instances the reverse is the case."[21] (Chaplin's inventive satirical take on the Nazi uniform's swastika was to have his cinematic villains wear a "double-cross" logo on their clothing.)

Though a correlation between a uniform and threatening authority might be tied to several nationalities, it is especially pertinent to Germany, a country created by the battlefield "diplomacy" of "Iron Chancellor" Otto von Bismarck (1815–1898). Born in Prussia, a North German country noted for its warlike and militaristic spirit, Bismarck would unite through war what had previously been a loose confederation of German states. For Bismarck the military was the state, and what was good for the military (uniform) was more important than the individual citizen. Needless to say, this view was later greatly admired by Hitler.

Obviously, Chaplin skewers that perspective throughout the *Dictator*.

He constantly comes back to the movie's dark overtones, such as the late film observation of Hynkel's Minister of the Interior (Henry Daniell): "In the future each man will serve the interests of the state with absolute obedience. Let him who refuses beware." Chaplin's ongoing comic undercutting of that view is best captured in naming the character Garbitsch, a punning put-down of Goebbels, Hitler's propaganda minister.

Appropriately, Chaplin manages to include uniform-directed humor throughout the movie. Examples would range from the aforementioned "double-cross" insignia to Hynkel's opening speech warning, "We must sacrifice, tighten der belton." Immediately, the heavy Herring rises to do so, only to have his belt split when he sits down, sending its clanging attachments (such as his dress sword) to the ground. Later in the scene Herring accidentally butts Hynkel down a flight of stairs, and the dictator comically strips the medals off the plump one's uniform.

The uniform-directed humor remains equally broad during the Jewish ghetto sequences. For instance, when a storm trooper paints "Jew" on the barber's window, the altercation that follows finds the Charlie-like barber whitewashing the trooper with the latter's own paint brush. (The scene is reminiscent of a barber whitewashing clown sketch from Chaplin's *The Circus*, 1928.) The *Dictator*'s uniform-focused comedy is even broader during the next trooper invasion of the ghetto — the barber escapes after throwing a bucket of paint on a German soldier.

There are numerous other uniform-directed comedy *Dictator* scenes, such as Hynkel putting on a pompous cape that fittingly acts more like a straitjacket, a near foodfight with Oakie's equally uniform-obsessed Napoloni, and a second Hynkel attack on chubby Herring — including ripping off buttons and medals, tearing his gargantuan pants, snapping his suspenders....

On another comedy level, the use of a uniform acts as the ultimate turning point for the film. On the eve of Tomania's invasion of Austerlich (Austria), Hynkel goes duck hunting and the barber escapes from a concentration camp. The dictator, amusingly dressed in what might be called "the basic Tyrolean short pants, suspenders, and feathered cap duck hunting ensemble," is promptly mistaken as the barber and arrested. The fleeing Tomanian "double-cross" uniformed barber is just as quickly accepted as Hynkel. Indeed, at this point his military uniform has a rather Pied Piper affect, as armed troops methodically fall in around the barber as he walks toward the Tomania-Austerlich border. The uniform, or the absence thereof, has made all the difference.

The power of the uniform might even be used as a provocative explanation for the controversial conclusion, when filmmaker Chaplin seems to speak for the Jewish barber. It could be argued that the coat gave the Tramp-like figure the sudden assertiveness to speak out strongly for peace.

Regardless of one's perspective on this hypothesis, a final note about uniforms merits inclusion. Chaplin and Hitler were both great fans of the 1920s film movement German Expressionism. The most acclaimed movie of this school was *The Last Laugh* (1924), in which a doorman (Emil Jannings) bases his self-respect and importance upon a military-like posh hotel uniform. Only this seems to impress his neighbors, because when he loses the position and uniform due to age, these same people turn on him. Consequently, in the first half of the 20th century, it is hard to over-estimate the significance of the uniform in German society. Or, in Chaplin's case, the importance of derailing military garb in one's satire.

The third theme of black comedy is the omnipresence of death. This component permeates everything about the *Dictator*. This fact escalated further after World War II, when the extent of the Nazi crimes against humanity became known. Chaplin himself later wrote, "Had I known of the actual horrors of the German concentration camps, I could not have made *The Great Dictator*."[22] Thus, when Garbitsch tells Hynkel that the Jewish prisoners are complaining about the quality of the sawdust in their bread, the dictator's indignant reply is that much darker today: "It's from the finest lumber our mills can supply."

The most entertaining *Dictator* examples of black humor death involve the nonchalant attitude toward loss of life in the Hynkel camp itself. Billy Gilbert's amusingly plump Herring often acts as a quasi-master of ceremonies in many of the scenes. For example, Herring interrupts the dictator so that a bulletproof suit can be demonstrated. The inventor steps forward and Hynkel tests it by shooting him. The man drops dead and the dictator nonchalantly remarks, "Far from perfect." On another occasion Herring brings in the inventor of a parachute hat. The patriotic fellow heils and jumps out the window. Hynkel and Herring momentarily lean out, and watch the inventor's off-camera demise. The dictator then asks, "Herring, *why* do you waste my time like this?"

Herring's most enthusiastic interruption, and therefore his most memorable dark comedy moment, occurs when he breathlessly enters Hynkel's chambers and happily announces the invention of a wonderful poison gas: "It will kill *everybody*!" Though intended for enemy soldiers, this macabre anticipation of the concentration camps and Herring's gung-ho eagerness to share a blanket endorsement of death is consistent with dark comedy's shock effect values.

Chaplin's Tramp-like barber and his Jewish ghetto girlfriend (the comedian's then wife, Paulette Goddard) in *The Great Dictator*.

All great art works upon several levels. In *Dictator* there are two particular metaphorical death scenes that are especially striking. The first occurs early while the barber is part of a World War I attack. A fog rolls in and when it leaves the little fellow finds himself still advancing ... but with the enemy! Though the barber has obviously lost his own unit in the fog, it also represents a comically chilling symbol of how his fellow Germans could one day see him as a fellow citizen and the next (as in a fog) be transfixed into his potential killers.

The second metaphorical scene involving death is arguably *Dictator*'s most celebrated segment, in which Hynkel does his ballet of world conquest with a balloon-like world globe. Eventually he squeezes too tightly and the "planet" blows up in his face. The standard textbook interpretation is that his mad plans will not come to pass. But in terms of black comedy, the symbolism should be taken further. This is a genre which often embraces the apocalypse, real or imagined. Consequently, win or lose, Hynkel's (or any other crazed leader's) dance of death is about the ongoing threat to civilization as we know it. Indeed, Hitler's final military orders, thankfully not carried out, were a scorched earth policy to his own defeated country. One has only to note the result of General Jack Ripper's (Sterling Hayden) plan to destroy the Soviet Union in *Dr. Strangelove*—world destruction.

What gives the Hynkel globe sequence an added disturbingly poignant aura, however, is the passionate beauty Chaplin brings to the performance. As the comedian's first great biographer, Theodore Huff, observed, "It is a scene that enthralls one, simultaneously with its wit, its irony, its fantasy, and its ballet grace."[23] Yet, despite this charm, the sequence represents a formula for destruction. And like one of Sam Peckinpah's later elegantly violent montage sequences from *The Wild Bunch* (1969), the viewer's inability to resist the terrible beauty of what unfolds implicates him or her in the scene's implied evil.

Fittingly, as if acting as a pioneering dark humor spokesperson, Chaplin stated at the 1940 release of *Dictator*, "There is a healthy thing in laughing at the grimmest things in life, laughter at death even. *Shoulder Arms* ... had to do with men marching off to war.... Laughter is a tonic, the relief, the surcease from pain."[24] Dark comedy had been liberally sprinkled throughout Chaplin's previous filmography, from his own reference to *Shoulder Arms*, to the catalyst for the comedian's inspired *Gold Rush* (1925) being the ill-fated Donner Party, a group of mid–nineteenth century American pioneers who resorted to cannibalism when snow stranded them in the mountains.

Nothing gave more credence to Chaplin's dark comedy commentary than the *Dictator*'s reception in Great Britain, a country which had been at war with Germany since the previous year (1939). While controversy helped fuel the movie's box office success in the still-at-peace United States, Britain's reception was without reservation. The latter country was in need of comic bolstering. Along parallel lines, the classic musical fantasy *The Wizard of Oz* (1939) was also an even bigger hit in Britain, because this country embraced the underdog story as a metaphor for their war with the terrible Hitler. Indeed, the country's air force often referred to military retaliation against Germany as being "off to see the Wizard."

Regardless, it seems more than fitting that dark comedy absurdist author Franz Kafka's (1893–1924) favorite film comedian, Chaplin, had always represented to him a spokesman for people who "could no longer manage to do what they liked with their lives."[25] Moreover, a Kafka biographer would later observe that the writer's perception of his responsibilities as a black humorist "uncannily anticipated the still-to-come [great] films of Charlie Chaplin," such as *Dictator*.[26] Kafka stories like "The Penal Colony" foreshadow the future Nazi concentration camps ... where the writer's three sisters would one day die.

The major difference between the works of Chaplin and Kafka is that the filmmaker was a mainstream artist in a much more high-visibility medium. However, both men were dark comedy prophets sending out a warning about the precarious plight of modern man. And while Kafka experienced none of the fame and fortune known by Chaplin for most of his adult life, each artist's work has only grown in stature through the years. This is especially true of *Dictator*. The pioneering status of its dark comedy components — the very fact that makes it such a "modern" movie today — did not play as universally in 1940.

The film's original controversial nature helped make it a commercial hit, but as suggested earlier, the initial reviews were mixed. Make no mistake, there were many positive critiques, from the aforementioned notices in *Variety* and the *New York Times*, to the gifted Otis Ferguson's *New Republic* take on the picture, which concludes with a see-this-movie pitch: "And again as always where there is a Chaplin picture, there is laughter here, warmth and grace, too. I think it will do you good, just for what is there, let alone that this is still Chaplin the Great, and growing at his age."[27] But most reviews, even the positives ones, had sort of a split personality nature to them best summarized by a period article in the *Los Angeles Times*: "[Many] critics panned Chaplin's picture for its thematic content, while paying great tribute to the comedian's personal performance."[28]

Knocking the thematic content is best translated as being iffy about using Hitler as a dark comedy target. But this genre was so atypical of the times that John Mosher's positive *New Yorker* review opens with a telling overview of the then shell-shocked viewing public:

> There's a general feeling, I discover, prevalent around the town that "The Great Dictator" is a very curious affair indeed, something distinctly odd, and certainly unique. People aren't sure that they like it, or anyhow they aren't very eloquent about why they do, or ... why they don't.[29]

Mosher goes on to say a great many laudatory things about the movie, such as calling "the dance of the dictator at play with the world ... just about as delightful a bit as Charlie Chaplin has ever given us anywhere." Still, Mosher's opening time capsule take on the state of dark comedy in 1940 remains his most telling contribution to the film's literature. (Interestingly, Chaplin's only artistic rival in silent cinema, Buster Keaton, had suffered a total critical and commercial failure with another darkly comic war picture now considered to be his masterpiece, 1927's *The General*. Consequently, *Dictator*'s sometimes iffy critical reception should not have come as a total surprise.)

Chaplin's anger over the mixed *Dictator* reception by the then pivotal Gothem City critics resulted in his turning down the prestigious New York Film Critics Circle Award for Best Actor. This was an unprecedented action, decades before George C. Scott and Marlon Brando made headlines for refusing Best Actor Oscars for *Patton* (1970), and *The Godfather* (1972). While the decisions of Scott and Brando were also controversial, by the 1970s the public was getting used to actors taking public stands. (Scott turned down the award because he felt the Oscar race had become a "meat parade." Brando's refusal was to recognize the plight of Native Americans.) In contrast, Chaplin's denial of the New York Film Critics' honor, like his use of dark comedy, just was not being done in 1940. Thus, it merely added to the provocative impact of the *Dictator*, though unlike the Scott and Brando cases, Chaplin's anger was more logically tied to his picture. That is, the fact that many New York critics "panned Chaplin's picture for its thematic content" struck at the comedian's central reason for making *Dictator*. As he had explained to Hollywood columnist Louella Parsons the year before (1939), "I am treating a very serious problem from a comedy standpoint. If you can make people laugh even at the things that hurt most, you're doing them a service."[30]

In the long run, Chaplin's passionate feelings, and his groundbreaking use of dark comedy, were totally vindicated. By the time of Kevin Brownlow's watershed documentary, *The Tramp and the Dictator* (2002), the comedian's satiric take-down of Hitler was being universally acclaimed. Even the controversial close, where Chaplin steps out of character and makes a personal plea for peace, was heavily praised. For instance, in the documentary Arthur Schlesinger, Jr., said, "The concluding speech ... might have seemed mawkish at the time, but in the context of the nuclear age I think it has great resonance and great power." Sci fi novelist Ray Bradbury described the close as something "I experienced ... with sheer delight, because I thought it was the top part of the film and the best part of the film." Celebrated director Sidney Lumet added, "I wept at the ending. It was something to me that had to be said. If it was inartistic it was inartistic. I don't care; nothing has to be perfect."

While I agree with this poetic praise of Chaplin's need to close the picture on a personal plea for peace, one is tempted to speculate on whether the artist had ever flirted with a more aesthetically grounded ending that limited the Charlie-like barber to the character's visual shtick. For example, Chaplin could have recycled his brilliant pantomime about a Biblical bully in the Tramp's rendition of David and Goliath from *The Pilgrim* (1923). The metaphorical connection to the little barber vs. Hitler would have been a natural. To push the "What if?" equation further, the close might have been further bolstered by having Hynkel and the barber finally meet. Most comedies of mistaken identity ultimately have the entertainment pay-off occur when the duo eventually cross paths. This tendency would include Chaplin's *The Idle Class* (1921), in which he plays both Charlie and a wealthy society type. Had the Jewish barber maybe bested the dictator in some sort of slapstick closing confrontation, one might again have a variation on the David and Goliath story.

These are, however, modest musings about an extraordinary achievement in film art. And probably the most insightfully positive critical summing up of *Dictator*'s special status came from Kevin Thomas' 1972 *Los Angeles Times* review, after Chaplin's reception of an honorary Oscar had the comedian re-releasing several of his features:

> At the time of the film's [1940] release the "New York Daily News" suggested it smacked of Communist thinking. Today it seems as timeless as it is eloquent and one of the bravest moments of any major artist ever. It's as if Chaplin had waited to use the full potential of sound until he had something really important to say.[31]

2

W. C. FIELDS
The Bank Dick (1940)

"I never smoked a cigarette until I was nine."— *Egbert Sousé (W. C. Fields'* Bank Dick *character)*

While Charlie Chaplin's *The Great Dictator* (1940) broke new dark comedy ground, W. C. Fields' (1880–1946) *The Bank Dick* returned the comedian to a familiar target — a biting satire of small-town life and a brilliant companion piece to his greatest picture, *It's a Gift* (1934). General audiences struggled with Chaplin moving away from his beloved long time persona of Charlie the Tramp. In contrast, Fields had forever fluctuated between two screen characters: a late–nineteenth century huckster, and a contemporary small-town, antiheroic, henpecked husband.[1] Though Fields was excellent as either figure, his browbeaten family man anchored to a dead end, small town American life offered him the most potential for poignancy in his comic art. The quiet desperation which often hides under the surface of a Fields antiheroic classic like *The Bank Dick* was best articulated by *New York Times* critic Andre Sennwald during the comedian's 1930s heyday: "Not to be aware of the tragic overtones in the work of this middle-aged, whiskey-nosed, fumbling and wistfully incompetent gentleman is to be ignorant of the same tragic overtones in the comedy of Don Quixote...."[2]

Despite this homage to Fields' small-time antihero, however, a bit of the huckster occasionally surfaces here, too. For example, early in *The Bank Dick* Fields sees a chance to promote himself as a filmmaker, when a modest on-location picture in his town suddenly needs a new director. Thus, he goes on to claim he once directed Charlie Chaplin, Buster Keaton, Fatty Arbuckle, and a pioneering silent comedy star, John Bunny, who might have been the prototype for Fields' own later antihero. W. C.'s character then tops this whopper off by observing, "I guess that's why I just can't get the celluloid out of my blood."

Given that both the real Fields and his screen personae were associated with drink, such as his *Bank Dick* name being Egbert Souse (though pronounced in the movie as "Sousé—accent grave over the e," which is actually a mispronunciation — more self-deprecating humor at the expense of Field's character), the movie's filmmaking subplot is a further exercise in self-satire by the comedian. As Fields biographer Nicholas Yanni notes, "The very idea that ... Sousé would be called in to 'pinch-hit' as a movie director ... is, in itself, inspired."[3] But the comedy payoff is that the in-film director being replaced, A. Pismo Clam (Jack Norton), has been canned for drinking! Of course, one could also spread Fields' cinematic satire of boozing and filmmaking to *The Bank Dick*'s parent studio, Universal. In giving the alcoholic Fields a great deal of control over the picture, as both the chief screenwriter and star, it is tempting to suggest that the comedian was satirically biting the hand that fed him. Indeed, Fields' next picture, 1941's *Never Give a Sucker an Even Break*, more boldly does just that.

Still, the primary satirical thrust of *The Bank Dick* remains the aforementioned skewering of the moralistic American small town. As comedy historian Gerald Mast has suggested, this film was a "culmination of Fields' studies" of the phenomenon — meaning he was not going to let his antiheroic alter ego go as quietly as normal into the night.[4] Consequently, whereas his underdog figure in *It's a Gift* is a milquetoast grocer beaten down by a domineering wife who only steals a stress-releasing drink whenever he can, Fields' harried *Bank Dick* character is now the town drunk. Sousé has all but dropped any pretense of playing at the middle class game. Plus, this time his loveless marriage is further stacked against him by a live-in mother-in-law. Yet, these two women do not so much nag as provide a darkly comic sort of matrimonial Greek chorus on all the negatives of being one Egbert Sousé. Given this hellish existence, Fields' figure flirts with being more combative then his antiheroic grocer. For instance, Sousé almost throws a potted plant at his nasty nine-year-old daughter (Evelyn Del Rio), after she has beaned him with a catsup bottle. Later, when Sousé assumes the position of a bank detective (dick), another bratty child (shooting a toy pistol) is perceived to be a security risk and the comedian starts to strangle the kid! This is a far cry from his *Gift*'s patience of Job grocer, who even manages to remain comically calm when a curmudgeonly blind customer destroys half his store. *The Bank Dick* implies that Fields' nearly over career had reached the point where he felt it was time for audiences to meet him halfway, instead of the other way around.

Coupled with this satire of small town life and the movies, *The Bank Dick* also does a typical Fields number on the American work ethic. Just how the Sousé family gets by financially is unclear, though there is the suggestion that Fields' character has won the occasional movie bank night prize and is active in entering the random radio and magazine quizzes. Certainly, part of the reason for Sousé eventually receiving his "bank dick" position was not so much for accidentally capturing a crook but rather to give the bank a salary they could tap for delinquent home mortgage payments.

The pièce de résistance, however, for Fields' satire of the American success story comes at *The Bank Dick*'s conclusion, when his thwarting of a second bank robbery wins him a large reward, and some seemingly worthless stocks (for Beefsteak Mines?), which Sousé has been hoodwinked into buying, suddenly turn out to be valuable. Thus, as with the miracle ending suggested by the title of *It's a Gift*, in which Fields' character parleys a bad investment into a priceless California orange grove, Sousé closes *The Bank Dick* as a wealthy man in a beautiful mansion. America's Horatio Alger hard work ethic has been derailed by a crazy touch of absurdity. This darkly comic take on life — that success is completely random — is central to Fields' films. The self-educated but well-read Fields might have borrowed this basic theme about the significance of chance and circumstances from such literary giants of his youth as Charles Dickens and Leo Tolstoy. Along related lines, modern cinema's greatest comedy auteur, Woody Allen, also keys upon the randomness of success in much of his work, including the periodic forays into drama, such as *Match Point* (2005).

As often happens with this great comedian, Fields' satire doubles back on itself. That is, besides undercutting America's hard work formula for success, these fantasy finishes also burlesque Hollywood's then traditional happy endings. Sousé's turnaround is so entertainingly unlikely it rivals director Mike Nichols' brilliant close to *Catch-22* (1970), when Yossarian (Alan Arkin) decides he can escape the war and his conscience by simply rowing a rubber dingy from Sicily to Scandinavia! The only happy endings in dark comedy, as well as the Fieldsian universe, are comically absurd. But whereas the 1970s film renaissance of black humor as a mainstream genre made such outrageous conclusions acceptably trendy, Fields' pioneering dark comedy was not fully appreciated in 1940 — a lesson already learned by Chaplin with *The Great Dictator*. Ironically, period audiences were more taken with Fields' slapstick-orientated automobile chase near the close of *The Bank Dick*, in which the comedian's character is forced at gunpoint to drive a crook's getaway car. While not without some laughs, the obvious rear-screen projection and frequent use of a body-double for Fields in long shots distracts from the fun for modern viewers.

W. C. Fields' ongoing battle of the sexes plays out here with a stranger as he throttles her bratty kid in *The Bank Dick* (1940).

If one did not want to christen *The Bank Dick*'s close with the accolades of seminal early dark comedy, Fields' satirical ending is also a textbook take on the antiheroic male. Comedy theorist Steve Seidman knowingly wrote, "Fear of matriarchal power [á la both a wife and a live-in mother-in-law] is such that it cannot be countered by the strength of the male. Rather it is dissolved by a near-magical occurrence."⁵ With the possible exception of James

Thurber's classic antiheroic short story, "The Unicorn in the Garden" (a rare example of a Thurber male winning the "battle of the sexes"), Seidman's insight about a "near-magical occurrence" and antiheroic males seems tailor-made for Fields' *Bank Dick* conclusion.

Besides Thurber, another of literature's watershed architect's of the antihero was Fields' friend Robert Benchley (1880–1945), who split much of the 1930s between East Coast writing for *The New Yorker*, and West Coast filming in Hollywood. A schoolyard jingle of Benchley's youth was equally appreciated by Fields:

> My Mother-in-law has lately died,
> For her my heart doth yearn.
> I know she's with the angels now
> 'Cause she's too tough to burn.[6]

The top candidate for Fields' toughest mother-in-law would be Jessie Ralph — *The Bank Dick*'s Mrs. Hermosillo Brunch. Moreover, the character is pivotal to the film, because she is on his antiheroic case nearly from film-frame one, even before he makes his initial appearance. This prologue of sorts both builds the viewer's interest in meeting the comedian, and gives us an unofficial tutorial on being an antihero. Consequently, as we first meet this dysfunctional family she complains to her daughter about that Sousé of a husband: "Smoking and drinking and reading those infernal detective stories. The house just smells of liquor and smoke. There he goes again [Fields has just appeared] down to the saloon to read that silly detective magazine." The Fields-authored original script, despite numerous departures from the finished film, is wonderfully consistent and succinct in its description of Mrs. Brunch: "An old nag and a scold."[7]

An indirect put-down of this "old nag" also occurs with *The Bank Dick*'s conclusion, when Sousé's unexpected wealth reveals the hypocrisy of Brunch and her daughter — they suddenly treat Fields' character with respect. Granted, it is not the total antiheroic victory of the aforementioned "Unicorn in the Garden": a husband tells his wife he has seen a unicorn, only to have her attempt to get him committed ... which backfires when the husband denies having seen any mythical animal, and the wife is committed! But like this Thurber fable, the only gender victory for an antiheroic Fields figure requires a touch of fantasy.

Characters like Brunch remove the natural joy of living. In fact, I'm reminded of my favorite Ralph Waldo Emerson quote, from an essay entitled "Circles": "Nothing great was ever achieved without enthusiasm." The

Brunchs of the world *pulverize* enthusiasm. Though we would undoubtedly embrace Sousé because of the inherent humor in any Fields characterization, this figure's ability to simply endure in a household with Brunch and her clone daughter (Cora Witherspoon) draws the viewer all the more to the comedian's antihero. Plus, Sousé not only perseveres, but his occasional acts of comic fifth columnism further enhances his audience appeal, from the aforementioned potted plant incident, to his propensity to mumble such caustic asides as, "I shall repair to the bosom of my family, a dismal place I admit." Moreover, for those period viewers who enjoy dark comedy, Fields' satirical take on the angst behind being a small town drunk was probably more accessible and acceptable than Chaplin's burlesque of Hitler in *The Great Dictator*.

As suggested by the name, Sousé's greatest joy and most rebellious acts are his trips down to his favorite watering hole—the provocatively titled "Black Pussy" Café. In fact, Fields' ability to get that name into a picture brings to mind a comment by period critic James Agee about an amazingly sexy plot twist in director Preston Sturges' *The Miracle of Morgan's Creek* (1944): "...the Hays [censorship] office has been either hypnotized into a liberality for which it should be thanked, or has been raped in its sleep."[8] (Sturges' *Miracle* is another satirical sideswiping of small-town life examined at length later in the text.)

With such an in-your-face title for a "café," Sousé's rebellious drinking is further enhanced—since an establishment called the "Black Pussy" would continue to raise eyebrows today. Though this is an inspired name choice for a wannabe rebel, Fields was also recycling the title as a tribute to his drinking buddy and fellow comic actor Leon Errol (1881–1951), who owned the original Black Pussy bar on Los Angeles' Santa Monica Boulevard.[9] Fittingly, Errol, like Fields, had an antiheroic screen persona often associated with drinking and being a henpecked husband. He appeared with Fields and an all-star cast in both *Alice in Wonderland* (1933) and Fields' follow-up to *The Bank Dick—Never Give a Sucker an Even Break* (1941).

While Fields' use of the bar title Black Pussy somehow got by the censors, the comedian could never have broached some of his private X-rated comments about alcohol or its alternatives in a mainstream movie. For example, he once observed, "I never drink water because fish fuck in it."[10] However, alcohol and water were the catalyst for *The Bank Dick*'s most memorable line, a crack that was widely quoted around the country upon the film's initial release. Fields' mistress at the time, Carlotta Monti, would later describe this wonderful Black Pussy scene in her memoirs:

Standing at the cocktail bar, he ordered scotch and a little water chaser. He put his fingers in the water and wiped them on a paper napkin. Then he said to the bartender, "Make it another one, and another chaser. I don't like to bathe in the same water twice."[11]

Today's film comedy connoisseur gets an added bonus from all the Black Pussy scenes upon recognizing Shemp Howard (1900–1955) as Joe the bartender. In the early 1930s Howard had been part of the act, "Ted Healy and His Stooges." Leaving the team in 1932, Shemp was replaced by his brother Curly. After the remaining Stooges broke with Healy, to become the "Three Stooges," the group became a film hit in short subjects and the occasional feature. Shemp continued as solo comic character actor but achieved his greatest fame upon re-joining the Stooges in 1947, after Curly had suffered a stroke.

While the story does not give Shemp a great deal to do, his bartender does assist Sousé in comically placating another *Bank Dick* supporting player — Franklin Pangborn's (1893–1958) scene-stealing bank inspector, J. Pinkerton Snoopington. As amusing as his character's name, Pangborn is yet another antiheroic type, one who elevated being flustered to an art form. Fields' "bank dick" has encouraged his clerking soon-to-be son-in-law Og Oggilby (Grady Sutton) to "borrow" some money from the vault. Sousé's get-rich-quick plan — buying questionable stock — is to have Og eventually repay the "loan." But naturally, Snoopington appears before that can be done.

Sousé must delay the audit by several days, which is where Howard and the Black Pussy are utilized. Fields' character's initial tactic is to give the inspector a casual tour of the town (Lompoc — somewhere in Kansas). Their walk takes them past the bar, where Sousé convinces Snoopington to stop for a little drink of fruit juice. The inspector reluctantly agrees, but not wanting to be seen in such an establishment, he asks if the blinds can be pulled. Fields replies with my favorite line from the picture: "Oh, sure. You can pull anything you like in here. It's a regular joint."

Fields soon asks Joe the bartender if he has seen Michael Finn, code for a "Mickey Finn" — an appropriately Irish sounding knockout drink. Snoopington is then given *two* of these heavily spiked drinks. As film historian William K. Everson later observed, Pangborn's figure is immediately such a comic "quivering mass of agonized nausea that any thought of work is out of the question, and he asks to be taken to his hotel."[12]

Though Fields was a student of comic realism, and advised artists to simply "exaggerate ... every day incidents," the comedian enjoyed the occasional surrealistic scene.[13] One such example occurs in the hotel. Shortly after Sousé has gotten Snoopington checked in and they disappear upstairs, Fields suddenly shoots back through the lobby like a track star. He quickly returns with a dazed and disheveled Pangborn — the drugged inspector has had an off-camera fall from his second-story room!

When Sousé finally has the sickly and scuffed Snoopington tucked in bed, Fields comically acerbates the situation by suggesting his patient needs some pork chops and onions. After this produces the inspector's exit to upchuck, Sousé's delaying game is further strengthened — the comedian suggests that a doctor is needed. As with Shemp's bartender, the move allows Fields to bring in yet another sneaky sidekick. This ally turns out to be the appropriately named Dr. Stall (Harlan Briggs).

Fields' creation of this character demonstrates both the comedian's generosity in giving minor supporting players funny material and a consistency of tone which reinforces the film's dark comedy base. For instance, when Dr. Stall arrives and makes small talk with Sousé, the subject of business comes up. The good physician (or is that bad sawbones) says things are okay but he misses the profitable days of the last whooping cough epidemic.

Even before Briggs' Dr. Stall arrives at the hotel, Fields' film comically and efficiently demonstrates how the doctor and Sousé could be good friends. The comedian was suspicious of most fads, especially related to health. Plus, as in dark comedy, Fields had little faith in the common man. Consequently, when Sousé calls Stall, the doctor is examining a cadaverously thin patient named Otis, played by burlesque comic Bill Wolfe. Stall's diagnosis is to cut out all health foods, which probably generates more laughter now, in the health-conscious modern setting, than it did in 1940. But the topper to the scene is the doctor's close, "That'll be ten dollars; the nurse will return your clothes with your receipt."

The skeletal Wolfe merits a footnote. The comedian used the character actor in so many movies that biographer James Curtis called Wolfe a "Fieldsian trademark." The writer added:

> Wolfe appealed to Fields' sense of the grotesque in a way that no actor had since the days of the ["believe it or not" nineteenth century] dime museum. He looked like a medical specimen, and injecting this walking sight gag into ... [a movie was one of Fields'] genuine pleasures.[14]

This taste for the grotesque is just one more connection Fields had with Chaplin, and further explains their pioneering propensity for dark comedy. But the bigger picture is that both comedians were a product of the Victorian era's fascination with the macabre. While Fields never wrote an autobiography, Chaplin's memoir is full of grizzly tales: the murder scene of a

Japanese prime minister; an acquaintance who develops leprosy; a clinical examination of what the electric chair does to its victim; often vivid descriptions of the suicides of several friends; a chance meeting with a man condemned to hang; the story of a Buddhist monk who, because he had spent a lifetime floating in oil, had skin so embryonically soft that a finger could be put through it; and on and on.[15]

Fittingly, celebrated Victorian novelist Charles Dickens (1812–1870), who also exhibited an interest in the grotesque, was a writer revered by both Fields and Chaplin. Indeed, Charles Chaplin, Jr., suggested there was a direct link between his father's dark side tendencies and Dickens,' revealing that even the comedian's bedtime stories felt like extracts from the novelist with a "macabre cast to them."[16] Chaplin's oldest son went on to theorize that the reason his father so enjoyed the writing of Dickens and Guy de Maupassant (1850–1893) was "because of the peculiar combination of the humorous and the macabre in their works."[17]

One darkly strange element in the original *Bank Dick* script which did not make it to the screen was a cynical talking raven named Nicodemus. The bird's periodic pronouncements sounded ever so much like a feathered version of the comedian, such as "The suckers must be biting again!"[18] Regardless, the final film is peppered with enough comically bitter confrontations to form a litany of black humor components, starting with a central element of the genre — the dysfunctional family. Besides Sousé's verbal victimization from his wife and mother-in-law, the physical confrontations with his youngest screen daughter, Evelyn Del Rio's Elsie Mae, are just this side of lethal. For example, when Sousé does not give her a part in the film-within-the-film, she conks him from behind with his director's megaphone. Then, attempting to take the high road, he makes the mistake of turning his back on her and she nearly takes Fields' head off with another missile she throws his way. The comedian seems to have grafted a Grimm's Fairy Tales approach to this small town satire, with an accent on "grim."

Of course, one cannot link Fields and Dickens, beyond that touch of the macabre, without noting their mutual love of goofy-sounding names. In a 1935 interview, the comedian revealed that reading Dickens "was my start in collecting [funny] names."[19] For Fields, this merry moniker tendency even applied to his pseudonym for *The Bank Dick*'s script — Mahatma Kane Jeeves. Whether comically stating the obvious, such as calling a drunk Sousé and a bank inspector J. Pinkerton Snoopington, or simply reinforcing an antiheroic mindset by naming an incompetent almost son-in-law — Og Oggilby, Fields' "labels" are just one more way to be amusingly iconoclastic. Appropriately, like most gifted artists, this also includes kidding himself, a real alcoholic playing a Sousé.

Fields' interest in Dickens, however, went beyond character names and the grotesque. The comedian's aforementioned mistress described him as "an avid Dickens buff" and portrayed his bedside as "something this side of a Dickens library." She went on to add that Fields was taken by Dickens' dialogue and "character delineations ... [which] simply walked off the pages into your life, to live on with you until the end of your days."[20]

Fields' view of his childhood as largely outcast in nature, despite later denials by his family, undoubtedly also contributed to his fascination with Dickens. The English author's work frequently focuses on orphaned or outcast children, with *David Copperfield* and *Oliver Twist* merely the most celebrated cases.

A difficult childhood is obviously the reason why Chaplin, the only major comedy contemporary of whom Fields was jealous, was also greatly taken with Dickens. Yet, while Chaplin created the Tramp, who was often lovingly parental toward waif figures, Fields' screen personae were frequently rough on the overprivileged child — a favored status he had never known as a youngster. Consequently, any Fields-equals-child baiter equations do not necessarily apply to Dickens' literary children. Yet, the novelist would sometimes give dialogue to a young charge, like David Copperfield, which displays devastatingly dark overstatement (though offered innocently, in a wise-fool manner) which the cynical Fields no doubt enjoyed. For instance, David described the frequent punishment of schoolmate Tommy Traddles thus: "He was always being caned — I think he was caned every day that half-year, except one holiday Monday when he was only ruled on both hands."[21] Later, David characterized his dear nurse Peggotty's new husband's (Mr. Barkis) attempt at lucidity in the following biting manner: "I might have stood looking in his face for an hour, and most assuredly should have got as much information out of it as out of the face of a clock that had stopped."[22] Appropriately, Fields' greatest joy as a comic actor was to play Dickens' Micawber in MGM's screen adaptation of *David Copperfield* (1935). The comedian confessed over a decade before his death, "All my life 'David Copperfield' has been a favorite book and I've laughed my head off over Micawber many times, never dreaming I'd bring him to life. It is such coincidences that make acting a thrilling game."[23]

Given Fields' love of Micawber, the comedian was obviously a fan of Dickens the wordsmith, where elaborate flowery language could soar to a kind of verbal slapstick. The comedian demonstrates this appreciation of language's comic possibilities throughout his film oeuvre. A good demonstration of this phenomenon from Fields' *Bank Dick* script would be an excerpt from Sousé's pitch to get Og Oggilby to "borrow" money from the bank: "You can pay it back to the bank when your bonus comes up. You're not a jobber-nowl, Oggie! You're not a mooncalf! You're not a luddy duddy."[24]

One might add, that besides Fields' natural affinity for Dickens, there was another key factor in the novelist's favor, with regard to the comedian. During Fields' many years in vaudeville, he often shared a play bill with a popular performer named Owen McGiveney. According to the comedian's first significant biographer, Pulitzer Prize winner Robert Lewis Taylor, McGiveney "specialized in Dickens impersonations ... [and] had a real feeling for Dickens, and Fields always went out front [in the theater] to watch him after his own act was finished."[25] Coincidentally, Micawber was a special favorite of McGiveney's. But before one puts all the credit for Fields' interest in Dickens on McGiveney's shoulders, keep in mind that during the comedian's vaudeville days he traveled with three trunks; one was for clothes and personal items, the other two were crammed with literary classics, especially those of Dickens.

The best examination of Dickens "Professor" Fields comes from Eddie Cantor's memoir, *Take My Life.* Cantor had been in the 1917 Ziegfeld Follies with the comedian, and Fields took it upon himself to tutor the younger man in the finer things of life — meaning literature and liquor. Cantor failed the drinking part — "Fields brought out a couple of glasses and said, 'Here you are, son. Let's drink to your health.' We kept drinking to my health till we damn near ruined it."[26] But the literature part was much more successful. Naturally, it began with a series of Dickens novels. First up was *Oliver Twist.* Each night after the show Fields would quiz Cantor over what he

Fields' comic affinity for puffy language was balanced by the visual treat of his self-importance in a modest position as *The Bank Dick* (more uniform humor).

had read. This would be Cantor's college of one, his unofficial night school. This continued, on and off, for years. Sometimes having little formal education pushes one to become the best of students — such was the case with Fields and Chaplin.

While Fields is famous for his anti-kid axioms, like "Any man who hates children can't be all bad," *The Bank Dick* demonstrates an exception to that rule which is possibly drawn from Dickens, too. As in many of Fields' films, this picture reveals a special connection between his character and an older screen daughter — Myrtle Sousé (Una Merkel), even though she is engaged to the town simpleton — Og Oggilby. The idealized father-daughter tie has a rich tradition in Victorian literature. In Bram Dykstra's watershed work on the subject, *Idols of Perversity*, this romanticized view is often linked to Coventry Patmore's period poem, "The Angel in the House."[27] Not surprisingly, Dickens' own sentimental father-daughter tendency in his art is also an outgrowth of this "Angel" poem phenomenon.

Still, one need not search overly hard to find the father-daughter connection in American huckster literature, another favorite of Fields. For example, P. T. Barnum's devoted attention to his daughters is a given in his high-visibility nineteenth-century autobiography.[28] And in Mark Twain's writing, of which Fields was also particularly fond, there are several examples of this trait, such as Colonel Seller's inclination along these lines with several surrogate daughters in *The Gilded Age*— a pioneering American satire.[29] Along related lines, I am reminded of a comment by *Time* magazine's managing editor, Richard Stengel, on Twain, which is equally appropriate for Fields: "He represents a vital tradition in American ... culture: the comedic commentator on serious matters, the funnyman as our collective conscience who can utter uncomfortable truths that more solemn critics evade."[30] This sentiment might best be summed up in *The Bank Dick* by the bittersweet soundtrack arrangement of "There's No Place Like Home" that plays during the last sequence of this dysfunctional family comedy.

Fields might have taken his dysfunctional digs even further if he had realized a pipe dream idea to cast Mickey Rooney, then America's number one box office star, in *The Bank Dick*.[31] At that time Rooney was most identified with his title role in MGM's popular Andy Hardy film series, about a wholesome small town American family and the trials and tribulations of being the wisecracking son of the local judge. With the sentimental virtues of domestic tranquility associated with Andy Hardy, the comedian would have had a "Fields" day. Though the comedian must have known this was just not going to happen, maybe his near casting as the title character in MGM's *The Wiz-*

ard of Oz (1939) made the Rooney idea seem possible. (Fields had ultimately priced himself out of getting the wizard part.) Still, the idea of the comedian's drunken Sousé character substituting for the wise Judge Hardy father (Lewis Stone) would have been a comedy treat.

Though Fields never had the mainstream appeal of Chaplin's Tramp, no other comedian's persona did, either. When *The Bank Dick* was released it garnered largely positive reviews, with most critics celebrating the fact that Fields was once again the focus of a film. In his two previous pictures, *You Can't Cheat an Honest Man* (1939) and *My Little Chickadee* (1940), he had to share screen time with first Edgar Bergen and Charlie McCarthy, and then Mae West. Thus, *Time* said of *The Bank Dick*, "The reward is the more rewarding because his recent pictures were impeded by the disconcerting presence of irrelevants."[32] The *New York Times* more baldy stated, "Bill [Fields] is at last given his muffin head again and is not compelled to tag along with such excess baggage as Mae West or even Charlie McCarthy."[33] *Daily Variety* more diplomatically seconded these perspectives:

> This is the best of the recent Fields pictures.... [He] dominates, perhaps more than in most of his late pictures. The performance flows from him naturally. It's full of sly and witty pantomime as well as characteristic dialogue drolleries.[34]

These kind comments might have been penned by the army of Fields aficionados that had gotten on the comedian's bandwagon by the time he was rediscovered in the anti-establishment 1960s and early 1970s. For instance, here is a typical excerpt from a *Los Angeles Times* review of a 1971 *Bank Dick* revival:

> Fields, with those squinty eyes and that bulbous nose, is so monumental an archetype, so completely an original, that his sheer presence makes everything work. What counts is not the quality of any specific joke in question but his unswervingly astringent reaction to life's pretenses and nuisances.[35]

As film historian Leonard Maltin would later write, "[Fields'] comedy and his spirit have not only survived ... his nonconformists attitudes have made his films even more popular today than they were when they first came out."[36]

Ironically, despite such critical acclaim, *The Bank Dick*'s initial box office numbers were disappointing. There is seldom an easy explanation for this happening. But one could easily posit the old axiom, "Satire seldom plays on Saturday night." That is, selection of a popular date night movie often involves avoiding the controversial. Granted, *The Great Dictator* was a satirical success at the box office, but it also boasted the tempting spectacle of Chaplin's beloved Tramp doubling as history's most hated figure — Hitler. In contrast, Fields was sideswiping a more mundane subject — small town hypocrisy, which he had already frequently addressed in the past, though never so acidly.

A stronger case for *The Bank Dick*'s modest returns could be attached to what period critics, such as the *Hollywood Reporter* reviewer, called being "somewhat short of good taste."[37] Though the same publication also credited the movie with being "the funniest picture Fields has made in some years," variations of the taste complaint surfaced in several otherwise positive critiques. For example, *The New Yorker*'s John Mosher was a fan of both Fields and the film but wondered in print why *The Bank Dick* had not received the "major event" attention it deserved in New York:

> I suspect that the exhibitors, our hosts at the movie houses ... may consider ... [*The Bank Dick*] not quite as refined as they would like. There may be an uneasy feeling that dear Mr. Fields ... is yet a trifle eccentric. Perhaps he allows himself a certain license not entirely becoming a man of his years. The character he depicts is wholly unregenerate, and perfectly cheerful about it.[38]

Entertainingly, *The New Yorker* critic showed some satirical humor of his own at the end of his review, as well as further celebrating the comedian: "[Fields works in] a ribald style which even people of position may enjoy, and, of course, they don't have to tell the rector they've seen it."[39] A funny crack, but if even Fields' friends among the fourth estate make note of such 1940 conservatism, it was no doubt a box office issue.

One of the more provocative paradoxes of the parallels between Chaplin and Fields, despite their apparent conflicting personae, was the ease with which either comedian set off poor taste sensors. Moreover, the fact that both were still upsetting people at this late date (1940) in their careers is all the more remarkable. Of course, Chaplin was the pioneer in this comic edginess. To illustrate, early in James Agee's autobiographical novel *A Death in the Family* (1957, a posthumous Pulitzer Prize winner), he writes about a favorite activity of his 1915 childhood — seeing Chaplin short subjects with his father. Yet, his mother had a completely different take on the Tramp: "'He's so *nasty*!' she said, as she always did. 'So *vulgar*! With his nasty little cane; hooking up skirts and things, and that nasty little walk!'"[40]

Fields was probably originally drawn to Chaplin by this very fact. But my pet theory on why Fields eventually became so jealous of Chaplin goes beyond the talent factor. I believe that as Chaplin smoothed out the Tramp's rough edges, the later *Great Dictator* notwithstanding, Fields felt betrayed.

Though the Tramp was the eternal underdog during Chaplin's long career, Charlie's "mean streets" toughness was decidedly softened after the 1910s. Regardless, early on Fields not only admired a vulgar Charlie the Tramp, he stole the bad boy shtick. For instance, in one of Fields' copyrighted stage sketches, "The Mountain Sweep Stakes" (March 21, 1919), he borrows a bit from Chaplin's *The Adventurer* (1917).[41] The sequence in question has ice cream being delivered to Charlie and a young lady (Theda Barra), with the Tramp spilling his into his trousers. But in trying to shake it down his pant leg without distracting Barra, the ice cream drops through both his pants and the floor grating underneath, ending up on the back of an older society matron (Marie Dressler), who is seated below them.

Interestingly, in a later interview (1925), before Fields had found success in film, he acknowledged the source of the scene (though not in connection with his copyrighted sketch), as well as the uniqueness of Chaplin:

> Chaplin [is] the greatest of all comedians.... I think the funniest scene I ever saw was in one of Chaplin's old pictures. He is eating some ice-cream and it falls down his trousers. You remember that one [*The Adventurer*].[42]

Indeed, even the title of this Fields interview, "W. C. Fields Pleads for Rough Humor," underlines the comedian's interest in pushing the good taste scenario, though the aforementioned ice cream sketch seems amusingly tame today.

As time went by, however, Fields stopped praising his greatest rival, though he continued to periodically lift Chaplin material. A classic example from *The Bank Dick* would be Fields' physical comedy after uttering his line, "I don't like to bathe in the same water twice." The comedian wads his cocktail napkin into a ball, tosses it in the air, and as it comes down gives it a comic kick — just like Chaplin's Charlie had done in innumerable movies. Not surprisingly, Fields

An informal Fields moment on *The Bank Dick* set.

was sometimes praised by way of Chaplin, which probably further upset the jealous rotund one. Consequently, weekly *Variety*'s *Bank Dick* review noted, "Several times, Fields reaches into satirical pantomime reminiscent of Charlie Chaplin's best efforts in that line during his Mutual and Essanay days [of the 1910s]."[43]

Still, for every Fields fan who saw lines to Chaplin, or for each blue nose viewer upset by the contentious comedy, there was a W. C. cult (grown larger with each passing year) which identified with *New York Herald Tribune* critic Howard Barnes' 1940 assessment of *The Bank Dick*: "It's a rambling show, part cockeyed fable, part incidental comedy and part just plain W. C. Fields. It's by all odds the funniest show in town."[44]

Just to play the devil's advocate, one could also argue that maybe Fields' initial disappointing returns on *The Bank Dick* were a result of 1940 overexposure. Besides the aforementioned *My Little Chickadee*, the comedian had penned a satirical book about running for the White House — *Fields for President*. Playing upon it being a Presidential year (the incumbent Franklin Delano Roosevelt vs. the Republican challenger Wendell Willkie), Fields gave America an antiheroic option on an assortment of topics, such as the chapter entitled, "How to Beat the Federal Income Tax — and What to See and Do at Alcatraz."[45] Though not a bestseller, Fields produced an entertaining book which generated some positive reviews, such as *Newsweek*'s critique:

> W. C. Fields, that droll one, has gone and nominated himself for President of the United States. It's an idea. This dimmest of all dark horses has run up a little book ... [which] is pretty funny in spots.[46]

Regardless, Fields' *Bank Dick* critical hit of 1940 is now a universally acclaimed comedy hit with all serious students of funny. As critic Richard Schickel has suggested, "[The Fields character] never apologized, explained, or played on our sentiments. Above all, he never learned his lesson."[47] Thus, he might have been an antihero but his comically defiant resiliency gave the rest of us antiheroes hope.

3

ABBOTT & COSTELLO
Buck Privates (1941)

At the start of Buck Privates, *Abbott & Costello are illegal sidewalk salesmen who duck into a former film theatre, now an Army induction center, to avoid a cop. Costello asks an officer on guard, "What picture is playing here?"*
  "You're in the Army now," is the reply.
  Costello tells Abbott, "Oh good, I haven't seen that one." Naturally, they will soon be "buck privates."

Whereas Charlie Chaplin and W. C. Fields were "old school" by 1941 (movie icons whose film beginnings began in the silent era), *Buck Privates* was the first starring role for Bud Abbott (1895–1974) and Lou Costello (1906–1959). Randomly teamed in 1929, in a Brooklyn theater where Abbott was a cashier and Costello a comedian whose straight man called in sick, they went on to be one of show business' most successful comedy duos. For most of the not so great "Great Depression" the team toured the country as headliners in vaudeville and burlesque.

Though their polished verbal routines soon showcased an inspired sense of comedy timing, their contrasting appearances were a throwback to silent film comedy's pioneering team of funny physical opposites — rotund John Bunny and skinny Olive Oyl–like Flora Finch. Thus, Abbott was a tall, thin straight man to Costello's short, chubby comic. Regardless, their non-stop stage work during the 1930s put them in a position to capitalize on some later-in-the-decade opportunities.

In 1938 Abbott & Costello started to acquire their first mass audience exposure, via radio, starting with the then struggling CBS's *The Kate Smith Hour.* They were such an immediate ratings hit that the two became regulars on the program, with their popular material including what is now the duo's signature routine about baseball — "Who's on First?" Given that a *burlesque* team could be a breakout success on the squeaky clean Kate Smith program, with minimal altering of material, underlined to their new audience that the team was more comic than off-color.

In 1939 Abbott & Costello were featured in the Broadway revue *Streets of Paris*. This hit production was a zany variation of the madcap Olsen & Johnson Broadway smash *Hellzapoppin* (1938–40), a lunatic revue with no story but a near-surrealistic desire to be funny — a forerunner of television's *Rowan & Martin's Laugh-In* (1968–1973). Abbott & Costello's success here led to a supportive role in Universal's musical comedy, *One Night in the Tropics* (1940). Though the film underperformed at the box office, everyone seemed to enjoy Abbott & Costello as fumbling operatives of comic villain William Frawley. Couple this with the team then successfully acting as a summer substitute for radio's popular *Fred Allen Show*, and the studio decided to feature the new-to-the-screen team in a series of "B" pictures.

With President Franklin D. Roosevelt starting the first peacetime draft in American history on September 14, 1940, a service comedy about induction into the Army was a natural storyline for Abbott & Costello. But besides great historical timing for a movie about *Buck Privates*, the duo received another break by having Universal writer Alex Gottlieb as their producer on this and their next five movies.

When Gottlieb asked Universal why they were giving him his first opportunity as a producer, he was told expectations for the two burlesque comics were not high. But Gottlieb, having seen *Streets of Paris*, was a huge Abbott & Costello fan. He accepted the position and made a prophetic prediction to studio executive Milton Feld:

> They're [the Universal nay-sayers] all wrong.... I saw those two guys perform [in New York] and the way they affected the [multi-faceted] crowds. Those people never stopped laughing. Milton, if I take this job, I promise you — within a year's time Universal will have the number one box office team in the motion picture business.[1]

As if Gottlieb also doubled as a swami, the following year (1942) Abbott & Costello topped Hollywood's favorite list — the annual top ten money makers.[2] The lowly burlesque comics had suddenly gone from being unknown to the majority of film fans before *Buck Privates*, to leapfrogging the following established stars, in order of appearance, *behind* Abbott & Costello: Clark Gable, Gary Cooper, Mickey Rooney, Bob Hope, James Cagney, Gene Autry, Betty Grable, Greer Garson, and Spencer Tracy.

While Gottlieb had great faith in Abbott & Costello's comic talent, he was also impressed with the two men's work ethic — early to the movie set

Bud Abbott (in suspenders) and Lou Costello (third from right) as physical comic contrasts in *Buck Privates* (1941).

and anxious to do whatever it took to succeed. Much of this drive was based in Costello's long-time desire to make it in the film capital. Early in his friendship with Gottlieb, Costello confessed:

> I'VE ONLY GOT one ambition in my life, and I've had it since I was a boy. I want to be a movie star. I came out here [Hollywood] when I was a kid and I tried it. I nearly got myself killed as a [skinny] stunt man and I nearly died of starvation. I went back East with my tail between my legs. Now I got another chance and I gotta make it. I gotta![3]

Besides being ambitious Hollywood newcomers, Abbott & Costello also had another thing working in their favor — the dynamics of the team's comedy was on the cutting edge of a new wrinkle in American film comedy. Starting with Bob Hope's *The Cat and the Canary* (1939), the modern screen now favored a comedy character which could fluctuate between the most cowardly incompetent of comic antiheroes and the cool, egotistical wise guy. This

Given Costellos' (right) fascination with film, it's fitting he and Abbott (center) become stars with *Buck Privates* by trying to sneak into a movie theatre.

breakthrough development in clown comedy soon had several solo screen comedians, such as Danny Kaye and Red Skelton, copying what had quickly become the Hope persona. Moreover, this antihero smart aleck still remains the norm in American cinema today, from Hope disciple Woody Allen to Owen Wilson. But this schizophrenic silliness received a special 1940s twist from Abbott & Costello, since each man could focus on one slant — wise guy straight man Abbott, and perennial antihero Costello.

With all these things going in the team's favor, writer-producer Gottlieb helped create an Abbott & Costello formula which served the comedians well for years. In a nutshell, this simply meant four or five of the team's solid verbal routines would loosely anchor the most nebulous of storylines, which often featured a litany of supporting players. This admittedly thin entertainment equation was bolstered by a period preference in viewing — a war time propensity for a variety show or cinema vaudeville–like format. Thus, *Buck*

Privates also included the popular Andrews Sisters singing three of their celebrated songs: "Apple Blossom Time," "You're a Lucky Fellow, Mr. Smith," and the classic "Boogie-Woogie Bugle Boy of Company B"—an arrangement sound so original that Bette Midler's cover hit of the same number decades later revealed little change. One might just as well have re-issued the Andrews Sisters' original. Other than the trio's Bing Crosby–assisted rendition of "You Don't Have to Know the Language," from *Road to Rio* (1947), one could argue that *Buck Privates* was the Andrews' best feature film showcase in a supporting role.

Despite the verbal comic brilliance of Abbott & Costello, what the provocatively insightful critic David Thomson has likened to "The marital chemistry (or the weird mix of blunt instrument and black hole) in coupling...," the duo were not comedy auteurs along the lines of a Chaplin or a Fields—writing and directing their own films.[4] John Grant authored most Abbot & Costello routines, though he frequently reworked old vaudeville

Abbott & Costello and the Andrews Sisters, Patty (left), LaVerne (center), and Maxene, on the *Buck Privates* set.

and burlesque sketches for them, a common period practice. For example, this was the approach taken by Red Skelton's first wife and chief writer, Edna Stillwell, who penned all of the comedian's signature early sketches.

Grant received a "special material" credit on *Buck Privates*, which was soon elevated to co-scripter title on several of the team's subsequent films. While these sketches were often inspired, the occasional inconsistency with their characters demonstrated that neither Abbott & Costello, nor their keepers (Grant and uncredited writer-producer Gottlieb) kept track of a basic comedy axiom. As comedy legend Frank Capra noted early in his watershed Hollywood memoir, *The Name Above the Title*—"the integrity of characterization" makes a character.[5] Translation: Funny is not enough. The routine has to fit the comic's persona. In most situations *Buck Privates* honored the wise guy—antihero dichotomy for Abbott & Costello. But ironically, the film's first highlighted sketch, a gambling routine on a troop train, accents comedy over consistency.

Costello inadvertently happens on a dice game in a private car. Ringleader Abbott, sensing easy money, gives his fat friend a quick gambling tutorial on the way to an anticipated fleecing. But as Costello unexpectedly wins toss after toss, his shy little boy character periodically lets slip veteran gambling lingo, like "Let it ride," meaning, "I'll bet my original money and what I've just won." Whenever Abbott questions or roughs up Costello over these slips, the normally antiheroic one alibis, such as it was just something he innocently "heard in the clubhouse," or underlining his naiveness, Costello comically confesses, "Starting Tuesday, I'm going out with girls." Yet, at the end of the routine, after this former stunt man has won all the money, he lets out a stream of gambling terms to comically reveal his real knowledge of the game. Grant has constructed a funny sketch, but it is not true to our character expectations for the team.

In Grant's favor, however, almost everything else in *Buck Privates* is consistent for Abbot & Costello's personae. To illustrate, the team's next two verbal routines in the film showcase inventive numerical humor by Abbott which anticipates the later shtick of a comedian known as "Professor Backwards" (James Edmondson, Sr.). That is, Abbott's first bit begins by having the sneaky straight man attempt to borrow fifty dollars from his not overly bright buddy. Costello only has forty dollars, but by the end of Abbott's fast talking scam, he not only has his money—Costello owes him ten dollars!

The follow-up numerical routine is even more entertaining, given its sexual innuendo window into the burlesque roots of the duo. Abbott poses a provocative question to his sidekick. If he were forty and his girlfriend were ten, he would be four times older, and they could not marry. Costello agrees but shyly offers one possible exception — "Not unless I came from the mountains." Ignoring this, Abbott sketches out the following scenario. If one waited five years, when the girl would be fifteen and Costello forty-five, the lumpy "kidult" would only be three times older. Moreover, if Costello waited fifteen more years, when he was sixty, and she was thirty, the goofy antihero would only be two times older. Now, while this made the mathematically challenged Costello fun to watch squirm (as his overtaxed little brain almost gave off smoke), Abbott soon lowered the coup de grace on his teammate — how soon before the girl would pass him in age? As Abbott surmised, this nearly short circuited Costello's ability to function, and the skinny bully had another comic triumph over his antiheroic stuck-on-stupid buddy.

Abbott as bully does bring up a basic weakness for the team. As film historian Leonard Maltin has noted, "Bud Abbott is not a terribly likable character.... [Plus,] Bud's character isn't really a character at all. He is a straight man for dialogue routines and a sober-sided sounding board for Costello's antics."[6] Maltin goes on to suggest that within their films Costello only exists to maintain Bud's "own self-importance." Though the straight man bully is common to comedy, such as Moe Howard of the Three Stooges, this character is usually allowed to be three-dimensionally comic, too.

These Bud-driven bits are often comedy jems, especially in the team's early film years. But as a complement to the hard-hitting verbal velocity of the duo's sketches, which get to the laugh before embellishing Abbott & Costello's screen characters, one wishes for other figures or plot points which could further flesh out the comedy world of Bud and Lou. For instance, W. C. Fields' writing of the *Bank Dick* had seemingly everything in the script blueprinting a humor history of his antiheroic title character, from a henpecking wife and mother-in-law, to bratty kids and his own blowhard huckster tendencies which might have contributed to some comically self-inflicted "white whale" problems, too. But this kind of character integration is a rarity in Abbott & Costello's films. And since Bud is given the least to do comedically, while the high energy source of Lou's every activity almost bludgeons the funny child-like personality into his every movement, Abbott's film figures seem even more one-dimensional.

To Abbott's credit, he is a brilliant straight man and set-up figure for Costello. The significance on that position was highlighted in vaudeville and burlesque by traditionally having the straight man's name come first in the billing, as it does with Abbott & Costello. While one might suggest that this is yet another weakness of the duo not writing their own material and correcting the problem early, the war years helped to mask the problem. With so many men in uniform, service comedies became a cottage industry, with three of Abbott & Costello's first four films centering their antics on different branches of the armed forces. Thus, *Buck Privates* (Army) was soon followed by *In the Navy* (1941) and *Keep 'Em Flying* (1941).

How did service comedies help hide the thinness of Abbott's one-note bully? A basic component of men-in-uniform comedy is predicated upon some mean man outranking the poor draftees. Consequently, the funniest routine in *Buck Privates* has Abbott substituting for the company sergeant (the underrated second banana Nat Pendleton) in drill practice. The classic bit is sandwiched between the two preceding verbal sketches and completely steals the show. But preparing for war softens the harshness of the relentless Abbott teaching Costello his marching fundamentals. The viewer expects this "tough love" slant, given the situation. Though the routine's physical comedy borrows from a similar scene in Charlie Chaplin's World War I comedy *Shoulder Arms* (1918), the sketch allows Costello to effortlessly demonstrate his often neglected talent for visual comedy; keying upon Lou's ever so expressive little boy reactions. But even the team defined themselves as a "talking act," so it was easy to neglect Costello's gift for physical comedy.[7] Along related lines, for all the laugh-out-loud slapstick featured in the drill sequence, the routine is peppered with verbal exchanges, too. To illustrate, Abbott keeps commanding Costello, "Throw your chest out!" Finally, a complaining Costello responds, "I'm not through with it yet!"

Ironically, while the gruff "following orders" nature of service comedies seemingly made Abbott's screen character more palatable to period audience, the mean sergeant stock character also ultimately demonstrated how easy Abbott might have been replaced. For example, Costello and the aforementioned Nat Pendleton have several *Buck Private* confrontations which team writer John Grant could probably have spun into *Pendleton & Costello* gold had Abbott been canned. As it is, the film includes a funny sketch which creatively involves all three comedians. Since the movie was made on the eve of America's involvement in World War II, patriotism runs rampant in the picture, such as the Andrew Sisters' hit song, "You're a Lucky Fellow, Mr. Smith [for being from the United States]." So when Pendleton gives Abbott lights out orders about curfew and no radio playing, Abbott quietly goads his antiheroic sidekick into being rebellious by telling him it is a "free country," and you are an "American citizen."

The comic pay-off is Abbott ultimately getting Costello assigned to "KP" duty, after a final catalyst where Bud the bully even anonymously pretends to be his teammate, and answers a Pendleton threat with the crack, "I'd like to see you do it." Once again the straight man comes off as less than likeable, especially since he is not caught or punished.

Costello's conflict with Pendleton produced, moreover, one of the movie's most memorable comic lines — Lou's fearful wail, "Oh, I'm a very b-a-a-a-a-d boy!" Overnight the comedian had a signature crack, and children across the country were repeating it at recess. Lou's little boy persona might have been influenced by Red Skelton's "Mean Widdle Kid" character during that same period. But the Three Stooges' Moe Howard always felt Costello had stolen the character from Curly Howard, Moe's brother, when Bud and Lou supported the Stooges in 1930s stage work. In Moe's autobiography he said the duo was forever watching them perform, and "I always felt there was much of Curly — his mannerisms and high-pitched voice — in Costello's act in feature films."[8]

Paradoxically, and ironically, given these comments by Moe Howard, Costello's KP duty offers yet another sketch which allows the boyishly round comic to effectively work with Moe's other comic brother and *Buck Private* chef Shemp Howard, of later Three Stooges fame. As with Shemp's aforementioned appearance in Universal's *Bank Dick* (please see previous chapter), he is not given a great deal to do in *Buck Privates*. But Shemp makes the most of his temporary teaming with Costello, and they are charming in a musically comic number entitled "Three Cheers for the Red, White and Captain Brown."

Though Abbott & Costello's writer for twenty-odd years, John Grant, had a great ear for comic dialogue, it bears repeating that the team's material was still often consciously immersed in entertainingly old material, such as the just addressed routine involving Pendleton. Indeed, whenever Abbott was asked about the secret of their audience rapport, he invariably responded, "Corn, pure corn. Every joke [is] guaranteed to be at least five hundred years old."[9]

Not surprisingly, the "corn, pure corn" scenario would lead to the eventual demise of Abbott & Costello by the second half of the 1950s, when the duo was comically passed by the more creatively edgy material of comic competition like Dean Martin and Jerry Lewis. Sadly, Bud and Lou's exit might also have been hastened by Costello's firing of John Grant, when the writer refused to sign a McCarthyist loyalty oath during the decade's early communist witch-hunting years. This axing was later grist for the movie *For the Boys* (1991, starring Bette Midler), where a Bob Hope–like comedian (James Caan) fires his agent friend (George Segal in a poignant performance) over a similar '50s McCarthyist scenario.

Regardless, *Buck Privates'* only remaining pivotal comedy routine involving Abbott & Costello is a boxing sketch which quickly keys upon the slapstick of the chunky, child-like Lou. Though the bit is nowhere close to comic cinema's best ring routines, such as Chaplin in *City Lights* (1931), or Jerry Lewis in *Sailor Beware* (1951), Costello demonstrates a pleasing ability to milk laughs from physical comedy. Had the comic not died prematurely from a later heart attack (1959), shortly after the team's split, he might have anchored a solo career in a more balanced mix of verbal and visual comedy.

For modern audiences, *Buck Privates* only suffers from a soapbox subplot where a rich boy (Lee Bowman) must learn humility (and patriotic teamwork) before he gets the girl (Jane Frazee). The message is all the more obvious given that Bowman's straight arrow valet (Alan Curtis) is inducted at the same time and offers such a stark contrast to his crass former boss. Of course, sappy subplots are frequently a given in comedy team features, including such seminal works as the Marx Brothers' greatest MGM film, *A Night at the Opera* (1935). For the Marxes, this distracting romantic component was only made more palatable in their earlier superior Paramount pictures, where the romance directly involved the brothers, such as Groucho in *Duck Soup* (1933), or Zeppo in *Monkey Business* (1931).

With the ease of 20–20 hindsight, *Buck Privates'* script might have been strengthened by either more directly involving Abbott & Costello in the romance, or by offering up the less-than-likeable Abbott as the Bowman character in need of a persona transplant. A variation of the latter approach was applied to Martin and Lewis' *The Stooge* (1953), where an egocentric straight man (Dean Martin) does not initially appreciate the importance of his stooge (Jerry Lewis). Such a daring decision might have changed the course of Abbott & Costello's career, establishing a radically different template for the all-important *Buck Privates*. But even if the duo had gone there, this more complex team equation would have been difficult to maintain. For example, *The Stooge* was considered controversially dramatic for its time, and the always comically inventive Paramount shelved it for well over a year after the movie's 1951 completion.

These thoughts are not mere random conjecture. In the immediate years after the huge critical and commercial success of *Buck Privates*, Costello was feeling some sort of change was necessary. Hollywood reporter turned biographer Bob Thomas likened this new Costello twist to the actor getting the "Chaplin disease, a complaint that has infected all comedians from Harry Langdon to Jerry Lewis. The major symptom is an irresistible need to play pathos."[10] However one defines it, the inventively different *The Times of Their*

Lives (1946) was the result. In this fantasy film, where Lou returns as a Revolutionary era ghost haunting a country estate where Abbott and friends come to live in current (1946) time, the normal team has few scenes together. There are no classic Abbott & Costello verbal sketches, and Lou plays much of his comic shtick off of fellow ghost Marjorie Reynolds. The film is more of a comic drama, and both Abbott & Costello acquit themselves effectively. Though Lou had pushed for the experiment, to better showcase his multi-faceted comedy and pathos range, Bud also demonstrated an ability to play a three-dimensional figure not married to comic straight man malice. Though the team would revert to their normal screen roles in the pictures that would follow, *The Times of Their Lives* entertainingly demonstrated that had Abbott & Costello wanted to evolve more off-beat, provocatively funny but fleshed out figures, they both had the talent to do it. But once again, the team no doubt suffered from not being their own auteurs.

Naturally, all these things were in the future when *Buck Privates* surprised Universal and Hollywood in general by being such a smash success. This $180,000 "B" movie (Chaplin's *The Great Dictator* had cost nearly $2 million in comparison) would go on to gross nearly ten times that production outlay — though some texts mistakenly suggest *Buck Privates* made $10 million. Ironically, Abbott & Costello's home studio did not maximize their profits, because *Buck Privates*' weekly film theater rental was relatively low, given that the team had never carried a picture before. Universal rates for all subsequent Abbott & Costello films immediately increased dramatically, with the studio rushing them into three more movies that year (1941) alone. The team was soon making $6,000 a week — but then a movie like *Buck Privates* could be completed in twenty-one working days!

The critics were all but unanimous in their praise of both the picture and the team, and the reviewers often added insightful period slants which further explained *Buck Privates*' success. For instance, *Variety* stated:

> "Buck Privates" is the first of an anticipated cycle of pictures predicated on adventures of rookies in the selective service. Geared at a zippy pace and providing lusty and enthusiastic comedy of the broadest slapstick, it's a hilarious laugh concoction that will click solidly in the general runs [theaters] for profitable biz [business].... Picture has a good chance to sky-rocket ... Abbott & Costello into topflight starring ranks a comedy duo — just as "Behind the Front" [1926] served to launch the [temporary] Wallace Beery–Raymond Hatton team....[11]

American Magazine's Don Eddy confessed, after "listening to some glum war news on the radio" with a friend, that they needed to escape to a movie: "Two minutes after they [Abbott & Costello] first appeared on the screen, we had forgotten the bad news. We were howling and thumping each other on the back and laughing 'till the tears rolled down our cheeks."[12]

The *Los Angeles Times* said, "Well, let's face it, boys — there's going to be an army and there are going to be moving pictures about it. And if they are half as funny as the first one — 'Buck Privates' ... we're going to laugh our heads off...."[13] Even the hard-to-please *New York Times* called the picture "an hour and a half of uproarious monkeyshines."[14] But the *Times* started off their positive review with some comedy of its own! "If a pair of mental bindlestiffs like Abbott & Costello can pass muster, where, pray, is our first line of defense?"

In contrast to the *Times*' opening joke, the *Hollywood Reporter*'s rave review — a movie "that is going to have them laughing from coast to coast" — went on to credit *Buck Privates* as a comic work that realistically "captured completely the spirit of the army camps and defense-minded America."[15] Calling Abbott & Costello's drill sequence "close to a classic," the *Reporter* added that the movie was "great entertainment for the masses and the masses are going to eat it up."

The *Los Angeles Examiner*'s praise for the picture also included an endorsement from a film comedy legend. After the newspaper's critique opened with high praise — "preheralded as nothing short of a laugh riot ... it is everything that has been said and more" — the *Examiner* went on to note, "Even that maestro of comedy, Charlie Chaplin, saw the picture at a private showing and did public acclaim to the wistful Costello and the skillful Abbott."[16]

Paradoxically, given all this praise, and a subsequent screen career which would frequently place Abbott & Costello among Hollywood's top ten moneymakers over the next ten years, the team would never quite merit inclusion among screen comedy's front ranks. Film historian Gerald Mast suggests a familiar explanation when he observes, "The less important sound clowns often succeeded at creating comic characters but not at creating unique sound-film structures in which characters could cavort."[17]

Mast's comment is merely another way of saying Abbott & Costello are not screen auteurs; the duo's lack of control over their movies resulted in a very uneven quality to the team's extensive filmography. For every *Buck Privates*, or *Abbott & Costello Meet Frankenstein* (1948), which critic Kathryn Bernheimer has included in her book on *The 50 Funniest Movies of All Time*, the duo has made several forgettable pictures.[18]

Their sketch comedy entry into '40s film, a medium then providentially geared to a variety show format (a fortuitous bit of timing just as important as Abbott & Costello starring in the first American service comedy on the eve of the United States' entry into World War II), anticipated the team's later popular success as the periodic hosts of a pivotal early television showcase for humor — the *Colgate Comedy Hour* (1950–55). Of course, this underlines again the aforementioned comments of film historians Gerald Mast and Leonard Maltin, with regard to Abbott & Costello being simply film comedians and not movie auteurs, à la Chaplin and Fields.

Still, Abbott & Costello represented a wonderful sort of comedy time capsule for 1940s America which enthralled most of the country's humor fans, including President Franklin Roosevelt, who was especially drawn to the duo's "Who's on First?" routine.[19] But the team's fast-paced verbal sketches, so entertainingly peppered with distinctively American slang and idiomatic language did, however, limit their popularity with foreign audiences. Even at the height of Abbot & Costello's fame, British film comedy historian John Montgomery barely mentions them in his influential book, *Comedy Films, 1894–1954*, a study which is generous in its attention to many American comedy contemporaries of the duo.[20] To paraphrase an old axiom, this is yet another example of two countries separated by a common language.

Yet, for any Abbott & Costello limitations suggested or implied, the old-fashioned comedy purist has to admire the amazing polish of this duo's verbal routines. Today's screen comedians too often operate in a world framed neither by taste nor timing. For example, *The New Yorker*'s Anthony Lane brilliantly capsulized this phenomenon in his review of the uneven personality comedy/parody *Tropic Thunder* (2008), "[This film's clowns] come from the post–punch-line generation, sing words not to wrap and polish a sentiment but to file a stream of [comic] reports from the borders of taste; their deepest dread is to stay in their comfort zone."[21]

Ultimately, historian Maltin summed up Abbott & Costello's career best when he said, though they are not in the pantheon of screen comedians,

> [their] steadfast dedication to getting laughs put them in the front ranks of audience popularity for ten years and keeps their best films fresh and funny today, as they continue to deliver those surefire laughs. And that's no small accomplishment.[22]

And *Buck Privates*, their first starring vehicle, remains their most "fresh and funny" film. As the *New York World Telegram* critic William Boehnel described the picture upon its 1941 release: "Bluntly, it is one loud, happy laugh from beginning to end."[23]

4

JACK BENNY
To Be or Not to Be (1942)

"One of the 10 best American sound films."—Jean-Luc Godard[1]

"What he did to Shakespeare, we are doing now to Poland."— Nazi Colonel Ehrhardt (Sig Rumann) describing Joseph Tura's (Jack Benny) Hamlet in To Be or Not To Be.

Today Jack Benny (1894–1974) is primarily remembered as a watershed radio and television comedian, whose finely honed antiheroic persona built endless laughter upon self-deprecating humor (a seemingly successful figure who cannot even get respect from his valet), an everyman vanity (Benny's age remained "39" for decades), a Scrooge McDuck stinginess, and being the master of the long pause. The latter two traits are perfectly exemplified in the signature joke of his career, in which a crook accosts him, "Your money or your life!" After milking the most extended of pauses, which would generate spontaneous laughter of near-record length by studio audiences, the robber would repeat, "Your money or your life!" A second shorter pause would be followed by an exasperated Benny exclaiming, "I'm thinking!"

At the time *To Be or Not to Be* went into production, a dark comedy about a Polish theater troupe using their craft to fight the Nazis early in World War II, America's annual radio polls of broadcast editors had picked Benny as the medium's "favorite comedian" seven out of eight years.[2] But this chronic worrier, who frequently kidded that he lived on a diet of fingernails and black coffee, had also been a hit in the movies for several years. In fact, his first feature film, MGM's *Hollywood Revue of 1929* (1929), predated his radio career. Benny's involvement in that picture had been prompted by playing a house record eight straight weeks at the Orpheum vaudeville theater in Los Angeles.

Yet, the catalyst for Benny's screen stardom paralleled his mid–1930s emergence as radio's perennially favorite comedian. While his breakout film is sometimes footnoted as MGM's *Broadway Melody of 1936* (1935; he is top billed over Eleanor Powell and Robert Taylor), Benny's entertainingly intense Walter Winchell–like columnist is not a good fit with his standard antiheroic persona. A more providential event that same year, with regard to his screen career, was signing with Hollywood's most comedian-friendly studio, Paramount.

Ironically, the string of hit movies which followed did not always mirror Benny's well-established comedy character of the airways. Still, Benny at his Paramount best, such as in *Buck Benny Rides Again* (1940), represented the studio wisely taking advantage of his radio-proven persona. Indeed, this inspired film grew out of a series of Western parody sketches Benny had done on his program with comic character actor Andy Devine, the perennial country bumpkin and sometimes cowboy supporting player. Undoubtedly, Devine's prominent part in Western director John Ford's stagebrush classic, *Stagecoach* (1939), had been a partial catalyst for the popular "Buck Benny" routines and the subsequent film the following year. Flash forward to the 1950s and little had changed. Benny had successfully moved into television, and Devine was the popular small screen sidekick "Jingles" to Guy Madison's title character in *Wild Bill Hickok*.

Fittingly, the director of Benny's pivotal picture, *To Be or Not To Be*, celebrated filmmaker Ernst Lubitsch (1892–1947), had had a long working relationship with Paramount. Part of the studio's sensitivity to laughmakers might best be demonstrated by the fact that Lubitsch even doubled as Paramount's studio production manager in the mid-1930s. The filmmaker's sophisticatedly subtle humor, "the Lubitsch Touch," was often showcased in a film shot or a series of brief scenes that reflected with wit and irony a microcosm of the movie's message. This had given him the freedom to move from studio to studio on his own terms. Such artistic power was then rare in Hollywood, where restrictive iron-clad contracts were the norm.

Lubitsch had begun his entertainment career as a Jewish comedian in his native Berlin, Germany. Eventually switching to directing, iconic silent star Mary Pickford later brought Lubitsch to America, where their movie *Rosita* (1923) was a critical hit. But *the* film that year for Lubitsch was Chaplin's *A Woman of Paris* (1923), a non–Tramp picture whose witty depiction of sex as a casual pastime among wealthy sophisticates was a catalyst for what would become "the Lubitsch Touch." While this theme is present in *To Be*, the movie also shows the influence of a then more recent Chaplin film, the pioneering dark comedy derailing of Hitler, *The Great Dictator* (1940, see chapter one).

Be that as it may, Lubitsch already had megaphoned so many pantheon pictures in America, ranging from *Trouble in Paradise* (1932), to *Ninotchka* (1939) and *The Shop Around the Corner* (1940), that Benny was overjoyed to be working in a loan-out capacity with Lubitsch at United Artists, telling the director, "If you want me for a picture, I want to be in it." Years later the comedian added:

> It was always impossible for comedians like me or [Bob] Hope to get a good director for a movie ... and here was *Ernst Lubitsch* for God's sake, calling to ask if I'd do a picture with the greatest comedy director that ever lived.[3]

Still, the insecure Benny queried Lubitsch during the *To Be* production on why he had hired a comedian (Benny) instead of an actor for the lead. Lubitsch, a former comedian and clown, provocatively answered:

> You think you are a comedian. You are not a comedian. You are not even a clown. You are fooling the public for thirty years. You are fooling even yourself. A clown — he is a performer what is doing funny things. A comedian — he is a performer what is saying funny things. But you, Jack, you are an actor, you are an actor playing the part of a comedian and this you are doing very well. But do not worry, I keep your secret to myself.[4]

This tongue-in-cheek comment was not without some basis in fact. Legendary New York talk show host Joe Franklin has affectionately written of his friend, "Everyone in show business agreed — most of all Jack himself — that without a script prepared by his writers, Jack Benny was not very funny."[5] In fact, the comedian liked to joke that his only great off-the-cuff crack was predicated upon not being a good ad-libber. Occurring during his famous 1930s pretend radio feud with close friend and fellow comedian Fred Allen, Benny responded to the putdown, "You couldn't ad-lib a belch after a Hungarian dinner," with the comic confession, "You wouldn't dare say that if my writers were here!" Of course, one must be quick to add that Benny was adept at helping to mold a unique comedy persona for himself, and wise enough to forever stay in character — a fault to which even notable comedians can succumb. (See the Abbott & Costello chapter).

Insightful author and entertainer Steve Allen probably best summed up Benny's performer status when he wrote in his watershed book *The Funny Men*, "I submit that basically Jack Benny is an *actor* of sheer comic genius rather than a true essential comedian."[6] But the multi-gifted Allen, who was also a musician and composer, went on to artfully embellish the difference between comic actor and comedian by likening Benny to a great conductor of music, rather than a composer. While some do both, such as a Will Rogers, or a Robert Benchley, most funny men are lucky to excel in one or the other camp. Allen's analogy is well taken, and as a musical footnote, more than one critic has suggested the natural connection between comedy and music — the rewards of timing. Many of the most celebrated laugh-makers were also musicians, including Benny, though he made a joke of his violin skills.

Coming back full circle to Lubitsch's suggestion that the comedian was really an actor playing a great part, Benny's persona was miles away from the real man. Instead of the entertainment world's breezy, vain petty cheapskate, the private Benny was both modest and the most financially generous of people, whose lack of ego and vanity was often masked by being the best comedy *audience* for his many funnyman friends, particularly Benny's favorite — comedian George Burns. Even Benny's aforementioned vulnerable "Why me?" questioning of Lubitsch is 180 degrees from the brilliant shallow-minded confidence of Benny's standard comedy persona ... which is so effectively showcased in *To Be*.

After lining up Benny, Lubitsch considered teaming him with Miriam Hopkins, the star of the director's aforementioned *Trouble in Paradise*. But Lubitsch lost interest once the actress began lobbying for her supporting part to be beefed up. And when word filtered out into the Hollywood community that gifted comedienne Carole Lombard, who had been on an acting hiatus, was looking for a funny film, Benny brought the *To Be* script to his friend's attention.

For Lombard, the production had several things in its favor. Besides Benny, Lubitsch was also an old friend from Paramount. While the topical story was controversial, especially since the United States was not yet in the war, Lombard was the most passionate of patriots, and she felt an anti–Hitler picture was her way of contributing to America's fight against what would now be called "global terrorism."

Benny's campaign for Lombard, however, was not purely an act of friendship. Because Benny was still often perceived as more of a radio comedian than a film star, this provocative independent project needed a "name" performer to guarantee its funding. Ultimately, Lubitsch was flattered by Lombard's interest, but he believed that her enthusiasm for the project would wane after reading the script.

To the director's surprise, Lombard was charmed by the dark comedy script, which would have her playing Benny's screen wife and co-star of their Polish Shakespearean theater troupe — which doubled as an anti–Nazi underground group, exercising patriotism in plain sight. Although Lombard's part was secondary to Benny's lead, she correctly saw *To Be* as an ensemble piece, with some of the most seminal scenes given to relatively minor characters. Always the team player, Lombard appreciated the approach.

There were, moreover, other factors pushing her toward joining the cast. First, since Lombard's early days at Paramount she had always wanted to star in a Lubitsch picture. He had supervised her in *Hands Across the Table* (1935, when the director had been Paramount's production manager), but this time Lubitsch would be directing. Second, after a series of forays into serious, even melodramatic movies, the actress whom *Life* magazine had once christened America's "Screwball Girl" (1938) was rededicating her career to comedy.[7] Fittingly, *To Be* also works as a screwball comedy with a message — a genre in which she had previously so excelled that the moniker "screwball" forever became synonymous with Lombard. Third, though she was again embracing comedy, *To Be* was a win-win proposition — return to her Hollywood strong suit and do something patriotic. Fourth, though the script's black comedy foundation was a bit unsetting to Lombard, she felt that with Lubitsch at the helm something memorable would occur.

Jack Benny (center) and Carole Lombard with their in-film playwright in *To Be or Not to Be* (1942).

Both Benny and Lombard would have concurred with the *Hollywood Reporter* critic who later described Lubitsch's mastery of *To Be*: "The directorial hand of a man incapable of indifferent work."[8] Plus, both performers placed Lubitsch and Charlie Chaplin a notch above the rest of Hollywood. And given Chaplin's then recent critical and commercial success with his anti–Nazi black comedy, *The Great Dictator*, it was very easy for Lombard to follow Benny's lead and sign on for this satire.

The shoot, which started in October 1941, proved to be a pleasant experience for all participants. As with *Hands Across the Table*, Lubitsch allowed Lombard to act as an unofficial producer on the film. She had been out of the movie loop nearly a year and was overjoyed to be back. As with her assistance to insecure leading man Fred MacMurray on *Hands*, the actress spent a great deal of time helping Benny through his *To Be* role. He was a superb entertainer but very insecure about being the star of a picture by the great Lubitsch, especially when he learned the director had had the part written "with me in mind."[9]

Benny's insecurity about getting things right was eventually conquered by Lubitsch's demonstrative old-school directing style. Indeed, writer Ben Hecht once described the energized filmmaker as "resembling a kangaroo on a pogo stick."[10] But more to the point, Lubitsch, like the silent director he once was, enjoyed acting out the various parts, especially in the comedy scenes. Though Benny affectionately described the Berlin funnyman as sometimes a rather "corny comedian," he later added, "Lubitsch was about the only director who ever really directed me."[11] Lombard was equally charmed by Lubitsch's throwback style, likening it to her own silent cinema tutelage under Mack Sennett.

As a footnote to that visual comedy tradition, one of Benny's greatest ongoing bits of physical shtick was his signature walk, which is on display in *To Be*. His confidently deliberate yet almost sissified stride, with broadly swinging arms, was later inspiringly described by film historian David Thomson — with an acknowledgement of Benny's tightness: "He walked with the slow-motion splendor of the ghost of Rockefeller, amazed that so many people can abuse their own church."[12] Appropriately, during the *To Be* shoot, chronic kidder Lombard's favorite way to spoof friend Benny was by referencing the comedian's less-than-masculine walk. Her pet name for him was "Auntie." But one assumes the actress probably also physically mimicked it, just as John Wayne's friends sometimes had fun with his effeminate walk.

Lombard, however, was playing nice with Benny. The beautiful actress' salty language and sexually provocative cracks had also earned her the nickname the "Profane Angel." For instance, she had once tried to get Lubitsch to direct her in a movie he did not think was commercial. As a darkly comic compromise, she proposed the following deal for his services: "If it turns out to be a stinker, you can have your way with me." Though this put a smile on the director's face, Lombard then reached over Lubitsch's desk and grabbed the big cigar from his mouth. "And if it's a hit," she said, "I'll shove this black thing up your ass."[13] Lubitsch declined.

To Be was still in production on December 7, 1941, when the Japanese bombing of Pearl Harbor ultimately brought the United States into war against Japan and Germany. Now everyone involved in the production saw the film as an even more patriotic picture. But this meant *To Be*'s black comedy base, a genre then far from mainstream entertainment, would be more of a 1940s "good taste" risk (mixing war and comedy) with that period's more conservative viewers. (See the *Great Dictator* chapter.) The most sensitive *To Be* pronouncement along these lines came from *New York Post* critic Archer Winsten. Suggesting the movie might polarize viewers, he confessed to being caught in the middle, "enjoying the show but not entirely at ease over the transitions from drama to comedy and back again."[14]

Before focusing on the multi-faceted response to the film, which was further complicated by the plane crash death of Lombard shortly before the movie's release, *To Be*'s storyline needs to be fleshed out. With the help of screenwriter Edwin Justus Mayer, Lubitsch took a screwball comedy farce framework, featuring an antiheroic husband (Benny), a beautifully bored, zany wife (Lombard), and a handsome but dull potential lover (Robert Stack), and married it to a dark comedy about the Nazis' "blitzkrieg" (lightening war) takeover (September 1939) of Poland, which initiated World War II in Europe.

Benny and Lombard's Shakespearean theater troop, whose signature production has been *Hamlet*—thus the title for the film—had been considering doing a contemporary satire of Hitler when war breaks out. While the movie's emphasis is on shish kebabing the dictator, the satire's first target is the vanity of most actors, starting with the company's lead ham—Joseph Tura (Benny). In fact, the picture's best on-going joke is a set-up line Benny frequently utters whenever he doubles as the traitorous Professor Siletsky (Stanley Ridges). Even though masquerading as a double agent, Benny's Tura cannot resist asking whomever he is addressing, "[You no doubt have heard of] that great, *great* Polish actor, Joseph Tura." Such vanity is so true to the self-centeredness of Benny's public persona, it is easy to see why Lubitsch was thinking only of him for the part. Moreover, a further demonstration of the director's sensitivity to Benny's comic character is to be found in the only response Tura's self-serving question about "that great, *great* Polish actor...." receives — no one has heard of him! Just like the persona Benny first established on radio, Tura, for all his vanity, is an antihero.

Lubitsch's witty satirical take on the hamminess of actors, especially stage actors (a tradition he was well aware of from his Berlin theater beginnings), receives a further sly twist by casting someone (Benny) whose well-established comedic persona has pre-conditioned the audience to smile or laugh at him on sight. What's the twist? To see Benny playing Hamlet is comic incongruity at its most basic, like Groucho Marx being president of a country in *Duck Soup* (1933). But Lubitsch even tops the brilliance of casting Marx as a national leader, by the implied spoofing of the stereotype which posits that most comedians want to play Hamlet. That is, they feel that only by succeeding in a tragic part can they garner serious acting kudos. Though Benny was never one of those funny fellows reaching for that artistic angst, casting him as a theatrical Hamlet within the film comically pricks the phenomenon.

Using *Hamlet* as a centerpiece was an inspired choice for the film for several other reasons. The play routinely is labeled Western civilization's greatest work of literature in English and part of that significance is anchored in the title character's indecisiveness. Indeed, nothing makes the character more "modern" or contemporary than that trait. Indecisiveness, à la *To Be or Not to Be*, had a period timeliness, too. The title could be seen as a "barb aimed at those artists who were paralyzed by indecision and stood silent in the face of Hitler's totalitarian onslaught."[15] Indecisiveness also complements the antiheroic norm for both the screwball comedy male, and Benny's stock persona. Plus, given that the film doubles as dark comedy, few things define the form more effectively than the suicide-pondering title *To Be or Not to Be*. Taking one's life is often at the heart of dark comedy, as in such classics of the genre as *M*A*S*H* (1970) or *Harold and Maude* (1972). The most poignantly ironic component of black humor is that one of the few things over which human beings have control is ending their own lives.

While Benny's Tura never exactly considers the act, a flirting-with-unfaithfulness Lombard almost has him to that state. The comic triggering device, paradoxically, is tied to each night's performance of *Hamlet*, when Benny's title character starts his "To be..." soliloquy. Knowing her husband will now be occupied on stage, Lombard has instructed her lover, Robert Stack, to exit his theater seat at this point in the performance, and come to her dressing room. Naturally, for the egotistical "great, *great* Polish actor, Joseph Tura," having someone (Stark) very publicly leave the audience each night during *Hamlet*'s pivotal scene is most comically disconcerting. To par-

Benny, as Hamlet, just as audience member Robert Stack begins his exit during the title soliloquy in *To Be or Not to Be*.

aphrase critic Nancy Franklin, Benny's character is as startled as someone waking up in a dark room in a strange house and not being able to find the light switch.[16] Couple this with the beautiful Lombard's openly flirtatious nature in most scenes, and Tura is one ham who has a lot to be insecure about ... as is the case with Benny's already well established comedy persona.

Poland's plight at the hands of the Nazis, however, pushes the film beyond even Lubitsch's high farcical standards into an edgy compound genre picture—the "Lubitsch Touch" meets war setting black humor. Yet the mix need not seem unusual. Sex is central to both farce and dark comedy. In the former, it drives what polite society calls the "bedroom comedy." In black humor, sex is a central component of a key theme of the genre—"man as beast."[17] For example, mankind's shallow-minded self-centeredness is seldom better demonstrated than through a weakness for carnal pleasure. Thus, the comic inventiveness of Lubitsch allows *To Be* to effectively play both sexual cards simultaneously.

First, along farce or screwball narrative lines, Lombard's manipulative sexuality reduces antiheroic hubby Benny to a nervous Nellie state. But in a farce framework one forgives this gorgeous goofy temptress because she simply seems drawn to an Oscar Wilde axiom, which could be used as a title card opening for any screwball comedy: "One should always be in love. That is the reason one should never marry." Second, *To Be*'s dark comedy use of sexuality—Lombard distracting the enemy through sensuality, redeems her character to sexy saboteur level, or a sort of screwball Mata Hari, while still reinforcing black humor's "man as beast" theme—nasty, sex-obsessed Nazis. *To Be*'s mix of screwball and dark comedy also helps boost the significance of Benny's character. He remains an antiheroic male, but the opportunity to lead his theater troupe in a bumbling undercover operation against the invading Germans allows his hammy egotistical Tura to balance a cuckolded comedy victimization with acts of funny but enduring Polish patriotism.

Interestingly, just as Lombard's real life pet nickname for Benny, "Auntie," might have started after the actor played the title role in the popular 1939 film adaptation of Brandon Thomas' *Charley's Aunt*, Lubitsch probably also drew some inspiration from Benny's posing as a maiden aunt. Though there are no darkly comic political overtones to the farcical *Charley's Aunt*, the title character perfectly mirrors the actor's antiheroic comic persona, just as Lubitsch fine-tuned *To Be* for Benny. Since the comedian's talents were not always fully utilized early in his screen career, *Aunt*'s major critical and commercial success possibly opened Lubitsch's eyes to Benny's screen potential.

There are, moreover, specific parallels between these two Benny parts.

For instance, both movies have him masquerading as the most unlikely of figures — an elderly woman in one, and two Nazi villains in the other — a German spy and briefly, a Nazi officer. Fittingly, each of these pictures also has a theatrical foundation for this play acting. *Aunt* has Benny as an over-aged college student preparing to appear in a university stage production as an older lady. *To Be* has the comedian heading a professional theater troupe initially flirting with putting on a satire about Hitler. And both stories comically manage to have the Benny-in-disguise mention and publicly praise his movie alter ego, a bit of vanity shtick consistent with the actor's radio persona.

A plot twist in each movie necessitates that Benny's character apply his in-film thespian talents to a real world situation. In *Aunt*, two college friends need his cross-dressing skills for a strictly farcical situation — to advance their romantic interests. But Benny's acting skills in *To Be* are a matter of life and death. That is, an apparent Polish patriot, Professor Siletsky (Stanley Ridges), is preparing to leave an English safe haven for a secret mission back to his Nazi-occupied native country. Before departing from London the professor briefly meets with some Polish flyers who also escaped the Germans and are now continuing the fight through Britain's RAF (Royal Air Force). These spirited but naïve young pilots, which include Robert Stack's character, foolishly share too much personal information with the professor, by way of letters or messages which they ask him to deliver to Polish loved ones. Naturally, if these names fall into Nazi hands, the Flyers' missions will be compromised, as will the work of the free Poland underground.

After this meeting Stack becomes suspicious, feeling the professor should have recognized the name to whom his message was addressed — the famous Polish actress Maria Tura (Lombard). This revelation then drives the rest of the plot. Stack is air-dropped into Warsaw to warn Tura and the Polish underground, and Benny's stage troupe can now apply the German Gestapo background they learned for their unproduced anti–Nazi play to a real situation.

While comedy is often about exaggeration and incongruity, such as Benny doubling as a traitorous spy, the fact that *To Be*'s premise has these timorous thespian heroes playing off a script within a script gives their unlikely bravery a degree of legitimate direction. One might even add, at times, the superlative "comic realism," such as when Benny or fellow stage company member Rawitch (Lionel Atwill) puts himself at risk by succumbing to his natural vanity and hamming up a scene where this natural human frailty could result in death ... instead of simply a bad review.

Given that this is also a Shakespearean company, Lubitsch was able to give added plausibility to some of the film's most poignant lines. For example, targeting Germany's persecution of the Jews, *To Be* effectively manages to incorporate the "Hath not a Jew eyes?" speech from *The Merchant of Venice*. This moving scene, coming from a minor character (Lubitsch company regular Felix Bressart), could be called a microcosm of the movie — a clever collision, as suggested by Kathryn Bernheimer, of the "reality of politics with the illusion of the theatre."[18]

Whereas Chaplin's *The Great Dictator* was a one-man tour de force against Hitler's Nazism, Lubitsch's variation on the same theme embraced an ensemble attack. Having said that, however, Benny was wonderfully cast as the satire's centerpiece. A crack he makes to Lombard late in the movie represents an excellent capsulization of his evolving character: "I'm going to meet Herr Siletsky at Gestapo headquarters. And after I've killed him, I hope you will be kind enough to tell me what it was all about." Of course, Benny's character neither kills anyone, nor do we ever think he would. But his false bravado here is antiheroically moving on several counts. He is afraid, for good reason, to do the brave thing. But Benny does it anyway. Ironically, as suggested by his request for Lombard to later explain everything to him, Tura comically underlines yet again that he does not have a clue. Moreover, his questioning of Lombard is ambiguous enough to make the viewer wonder if he is referring to the war or being cuckolded. Either way, his missing-in-action mentality further enhances the antiheroic Benny persona.

To Be's funniest line is a darkly comic undercutting of that "great, *great* Polish actor, Joseph Tura." Quoted at the beginning of the chapter, it guarantees that even when Benny is not on screen, his antiheroic figure will entertainingly dominate the proceedings. Sig Rumann's Nazi Colonel observes, "What he did to Shakespeare, we are now doing to Poland." Paradoxically, when *To Be* was released, this was also the picture's most controversial line. Black humor was then such an extreme comedy gear change that such material was offensive to some. *New York Times* critic Bosley Crowther seemed to take it upon himself to represent those people. He was scathing in his attack on the picture: "To say it is callous and macabre is understating the case."[19] He cited the Nazi Colonel's description of Tura's acting as prime evidence of this offensive new genre.

Despite such reservations by the influential Crowther, one should quickly add that with a few exceptions, the movie was a critical success. But before addressing those prophetic pundits, another Crowther piece questioning both *To Be* and the dark comedy genre represented by the crack about Tura's acting merits noting. The extended quote which follows, about a now uni-

Benny's look of cluelessness could be used as the universal mug shot for antiheroes, with Lombard (seated) and her maid (Maude Ebarne) in *To Be or Not to Be*.

versally acclaimed classic, more fully details just how popular tastes have changed:

> What is the element of mirth in the remark which a German colonel makes regarding Mr. Benny's acting...? Even if one were able to forget the present horror [World War II] which this implies ... [this] would hardly be a matter for jest. Yet all the way through this picture runs a strange imperception of feeling. You might almost think Mr. Lubitsch had the attitude of "anything for a laugh."[20]

Flash forward to today, and "anything for a laugh" is an accepted integral component of black humor. The comedy catharsis to be gained through this laughter from the edge is to better cope with the absurd twists of the *real* world. Lubitsch was addressing this very subject when he penned a *New York Times* rebuttal to Crowther, and other critics offended by dark satire, shortly after *To Be* opened:

> I was tired of the two established, recognized [film] recipes: drama with comedy relief and comedy with dramatic relief. I had made up my mind to make a picture with no attempt to relieve anybody from anything at any time; dramatic when the situation demands it, and satire and comedy whenever it is called for. One might call it a tragical farce or a farcical tragedy — I do not care and neither do the audiences.[21]

Despite Lubitsch's eloquent forward thinking slant on a yet to be burgeoning black comedy genre, many period critics did appreciate this rendition. For instance, the *New York Journal-American*'s Rose Pelswick stated Lubitsch had directed in his "most subtly ironic manner," adding, "Benny ... does his best screen work to date, and the production emerges as one of the most entertaining comedies of the season."[22] The *New York Mirror*'s Lee Mortimer said, "Lubitsch's deft direction and production contribute to make this one of the outstanding comedies of the year. Jack Benny is amazing, the skillful way he plays a straight comedy role, handling satire as if he had been born to it."[23] And the *Hollywood Reporter* added, *To Be* is "a farce of far deeper significance than ordinary, daring to ridicule the practice of Nazism as only Chaplin ... [can, with Jack Benny being] enormously funny as the conceited stage star who puts the ham in 'Hamlet.'"[24]

Some contemporary reviewers attempted to bypass the dark comedy controversy with what would now be called "genre mixing" explanations. For example, *Time* magazine called *To Be* "a very funny comedy, salted to taste with melodrama and satire."[25] *Variety*, in a rave notice which anticipates Lubitsch's aforementioned description of the picture as a "farcical tragedy," christened *To Be* an "absorbing drama with farcical trimmings."[26] *Variety*'s critique is dead-on throughout, including the observation, "Benny, in portraying a straight role, displays top abilities as a farceur, and catches major attention along with Miss Lombard."[27]

Variety's only misfire was a prediction that *To Be* would be a box office hit. Revenues were undoubtedly hurt by the movie's dark comedy component, because even while most reviews were positive, Crowther notwithstanding, many critics were like the *New York Post*'s aforementioned Archer Winsten, who liked the movie but was uneasy about the juxtapositioning of farce and tragedy. The *New York World-Telegram*'s George Ross embraced the same conflicted philosophy, celebrating the "considerable humor that Lubitsch conjures out of this straight mixture," yet confessing "it is difficult to laugh with more than subdued hilarity."[28] But even these iffy critiques found Benny fun, with Ross adding, "Those ardent fans of Jack Benny — and they are legion — will find him in more versatile circumstances than he has been accustomed to, as he runs the comic gamut of impersonations in his war of wits with the Nazis."²⁹

While the artistic tragedy of *To Be* was that the pioneering showcase of dark comedy was not fully appreciated at the time, the picture's period tragedy was the death of Lombard shortly before the opening. The actress and her mother died in a fiery plane crash on their way home from America's first bond rally of World War II. Benny, Lubitsch, and a shocked nation mourned the passing of the country's beloved screwball. President Franklin D. Roosevelt's telegram of condolence to her husband, Clark Gable, summarized a nation's pain: "She is and always will be a star, one we shall never forget, nor cease to be grateful to."

Roosevelt's metaphorical "reading" of the term "star," for both patriot and movie personality, gave greater war-related credence to *To Be*'s anti–Nazi message. But with the controversial dark comedy, Lombard's death, and the limited theater access of the movie's distributor (United Artists), the film's box office returns were disappointing. Of course, this was of no concern to Benny, who was so distraught over his friend's death that he could not do the next installment of his phenomenally popular radio show ... substituting an all-musical broadcast.

One unexpected bit of Benny personal comedy connected to the picture, however, involved an early screening attended by the comedian's dad and sister. The father had a meltdown at seeing his son in a Nazi uniform, a situation no doubt exasperated by the family's Jewish heritage; he stormed out of the theater. Florence had her brother call their father:

> Finally when Jack got a word in edgewise, he managed to convey the *whole* plot of the picture to Dad. When he found out that Jack was only *pretending* to be a Nazi, he calmed down ... [and saw the movie repeatedly] for the rest of its engagement....³⁰

Though *To Be* was easily misunderstood at the time, even by Benny's father, the picture has since achieved universal acclaim, with the American Film Institute closing the twentieth century by selecting it as one of the hundred funniest movies ever made. Critic Kathryn Bernheimer did AFI one better by including *To Be* in her book, *The 50 Funniest Movies of All Time* (1999). Mel Brooks' 1983 remake of *To Be*, though better than the reviews, only underscored the uniqueness of the original. Even as I write this chapter (fall 2008), a stage production of the picture is being prepared for Broadway. This brilliantly conceived Lubitsch story, with a perfectly cast Benny, is now an effective argument for how dark comedy — far from being insensitive — can give the horror of war a human face. To paraphrase critic Terrence Rafferty, this provocative genre, as demonstrated by *To Be*, better demonstrates how men will do extraordinary things to preserve their ordinary pleasures.[31] And by using Benny's seemingly ordinary antihero persona in the central role, the movie allowed the actor-comedian to better demonstrate the range of his alter ego character.

In today's dark comedy as status quo world, Benny's tour de force performance is deservedly celebrated. Of course, black humor is now so ingrained in modern society that one can randomly read a *New Yorker* "casual," such as "Nazis Say the Darnedest Things," and find Hitler plotting his revenge on Chaplin's *The Great Dictator*. Hitler decided to hire Leni Riefenstahl to direct his satire. What follows is an excerpt from their first story conference: "I'll [Hitler] be dressed in a tramp costume, just like Chaplin, and we'll do the scene in 'The Gold Rush' where he cooks his shoe and eats it." Riefenstahl looked confused. "What's the twist?" she asked. Barely containing his giggles, Hitler said, "This time, he'll choke on the shoelaces and die."[32]

Thus, maybe the greatest tragedy of the picture was neither an initially underappreciated genre nor the death of a lovely co-star, but rather an amazing Benny performance which was obscured by these period distractions. Regardless, as with AFI's belated recognition of the picture, Benny's seminal silliness in a watershed film is now front and center. Yes, in answer to the comedian's early fears about playing the part—Lubitsch knew exactly what he was doing. The director's filmmaking friend, Leo McCarey, always felt eighty percent of a movie's success was simply in the casting. Maybe the true "Lubitsch Touch" for *To Be* was not in a particular scene but rather simply having Benny play that "great, *great* Polish actor...."

5

EDDIE BRACKEN
The Miracle of Morgan's Creek (1944)

"[You] Can't expect a girl to see much in a civilian these [war] days, even an unwilling civilian [whose health issues keep him from being able to enlist]. If they had uniforms for them, it might be a little different."
— Norval Jones (Eddie Bracken) in
The Miracle of Morgan's Creek

Eddie Bracken's (1920–2002) movie heyday came during World War II, when his shy and befuddled man-child persona, sort of a young Robert Benchley, struck a responsive chord with a patriotic public. His wannabe soldier in the critical and commercial hits *The Miracle of Morgan's Creek* and *Hail the Conquering Hero* (both 1944), was perfect casting for a sympathetic, antiheroic, "4F" character—an individual whose health keeps him out of uniform. Of course, as with Jack Benny's performance in Ernst Lubitsch's *To Be or Not to Be* (1942, see previous chapter), the magic of *Miracle* and *Hail* is anchored in another gifted writer and director, Preston Sturges (1898–1959).

A Sturges picture often falls under the label screwball comedy, such as his satirical farces *The Lady Eve* (1941) and *The Palm Beach Story* (1942). But just as screwball films parody romantic comedy while jabbing at a litany of other social subjects, Sturges' pictures also frequently satirize feel-good populism, a genre often associated with director Frank Capra, à la *Mr. Smith Goes to Washington* (1939) and *It's a Wonderful Life* (1946). As *New Yorker* critic Anthony Lane later noted:

> Capra comedies dwell on the gentle irony that the perfection you seek may have been sitting in your own home all along—and *that*, Sturges would contend, is the problem with perfection.... [Sturges'] movies remain a bracing tonic against the sentimental ... [and a comic red flag] to caution us against the [populist] perils of overestimating human nature....[1]

Fittingly, in terms of an artist (Sturges) predisposed to skewer populism, casting the squeaky clean Bracken as a film's male lead enhances one's satirical possibilities. Sturges, arguably Hollywood's greatest author of witty dialogue (which helped him win a screenplay Oscar for *The Great McGinty*, 1940, and writing nominations for both *Miracle* and *Hail*), was also an enthusiastic fan of the slapstick go-getter, populist-like *silent* film comedian Harold Lloyd. In fact, Sturges would later affectionately spoof the comedian's persona (with Lloyd coming out of retirement to star) in *The Sin of Harold Diddlebock*, 1947, later re-edited and re-released as *Mad Wednesday*, 1950). Interestingly, the year before making *The Miracle of Morgan's Creek*, Bracken confessed in an interview:

> I do best as the serious guy—like Harold Lloyd used to portray, for instance, who is constantly involved in comic situations—and that's the kind of part I'm always striving for.[2]

After *Miracle* and *Hail the Conquering Hero* but before *Diddlebock*, Sturges and Bracken had even flirted with doing satirical remakes of Lloyd's *Grandma's Boy* (1922) and *The Freshman* (1925), where the silent comedian begins as the mousy small-town type who eventually gets a backbone. This capsulization almost describes Bracken's *Miracle* character, too. But instead of a populist Lloyd figure, with an *individual can make a difference* conclusion to *Miracle*, Sturges makes the picture's numerically frantic happy ending as surrealistically unbelievable as suddenly revealing that each of his romantic leads has a twin at the conclusion of *The Palm Beach Story*. Yet, Sturges' tongue-in-cheek explanation for this modernly absurdist Norval Jones *Miracle* transformation is inventingly borrowed from old, Shakespeare's: "Some are born great, some achieve greatness, and some have greatness thrust upon them." But this is getting ahead of the story.

Miracle came at the close of Sturges' tenure at that most comedy friendly of studios—Paramount. Though friction with the songwriter and producer Buddy DeSylva would eventually derail Sturges' relationship with the studio, DeSylva was the first to suggest Bracken and Betty Hutton for the series of comedy misunderstandings that became *Miracle*. The story involves four main characters: a curmudgeon of a father (Sturges regular William Demarest), his two teenage daughters (Hutton and Diana Lynn), and a sweet, bumbling small-town schnook (Bracken) who has always had a crush on Hutton's character.

The still provocative plot twist early in Sturges' story is that the patriotically promiscuous Trudy Kockenlocker (Hutton) gets pregnant after a night of community-sponsored parties for young military men going to war. To Trudy's credit (and Hollywood's censorship office demands), the girl thinks she got married first. But between too much alcohol-spiked punch and bumping her head during a night of revelry, Trudy can neither remember what this alleged husband looks like, or even his name. But after thinking hard, an often painful task for her, Trudy guesses the mystery man might be named Private Ratziwatzi. (Sturges, like W. C. Fields, enjoyed embellishing comedy with funny names; from a focus family named Kockenlocker, to Ratziwatzi, or Bracken's Norval, this writer-director always keeps it verbally lively.)

As noted in an earlier chapter, the *Nation*'s watershed period critic James Agee was entertainingly impressed by Sturges' ability to simply slip this farce by Will "Hollywood Hitler" Hays and his censorship staff: "...the Hays office has been either hypnotized into a liberality for which it should be thanked, or has been raped in its sleep."[3] But Sturges performs instant damage control on Trudy's shaky morals by doing what he does best—penning a script so fast-forward in its action that the viewer is soon more concerned with how to solve Trudy's problem, rather than belaboring why it happened.

A greater example of Sturges' gift for pricking a subject while simultaneously softening the satire comes from the writer-director's ability to use Norval as a potential patsy fix for Trudy's dilemma (as the substitute father and husband), without making the audience think even worse of Hutton's character. That is, while the aforementioned comments of *New Yorker* critic Anthony Lane are equally applicable here (*Miracle* spoofs Capraesque populism), Sturges so enthusiastically sells the upbeat turnaround ending—predicated upon Trudy's sweet but *so* unlikely sudden appreciation of nerdy Norval—that the film ultimately feels like a celebration of this feel-good genre, too.

Trudy's angelic transformation is made more comically palatable by contrasting it with her sister Emmy's (Diana Lynn) Machiavellian ideas about using poor Norval: "He was made ... [to play the patsy] like the ox was made to eat and the grape was made to drink...." Thus, the attitude of Trudy's beautiful but wickedly wise younger sister brings out a defensive mothering instinct in Hutton's character toward poor Norval. In the speed-of-light pace of a Sturges film, this soon passes as love for Trudy.

Lynn's precocious youngster, who steals every scene she is in, had also "essayed" a similar part in Billy Wilder's directing debut, *The Major and the Minor* (1942). The fourteen-year-old Emmy, played by an eighteen-year-old Lynn and with more sex appeal than Hutton's Trudy, represents a more subtle form of home front satire. Whereas Trudy's loose morals are a direct derailing of populism's virginal small-town mythologized maiden, Emmy's attempt to orchestrate a comic travesty on Norval is even more damning of Middle America. Sturges entertainingly suggests the heartland, like every other place, is without innocence.

If normally virginal Main Street young women are manipulative and naughty, the populist stereotype can be further satirized by showcasing the strong male as clinically weak. Bracken's Norval more than fills that bill. His character anticipates a later celebrated screen antihero:

> [Bracken/Norval is a] precursor of the Jerry Lewis characterizations of the '50s and '60s. He is a complete failure — physically handicapped with high blood pressure, rather confused mentally, and cursed with a pusillanimous character.... He represents to us the weakest and, therefore, most disturbing side of our personality.... (This ... may explain why many reject characters like the ones played by Bracken and Lewis so violently. It is a side of us we do not readily like to admit to.)[4]

Diana Lynn (right) and Betty Hutton on either side of Eddie Bracken (center), with William Demarest in the suspenders in *The Miracle of Morgan's Creek* (1944).

This analogy between Bracken and Lewis is further strengthened by noting that Lewis later even loosely remade *Miracle* as *Rock-a-Bye Baby* (1958), directed by another brilliant satirist — Frank Tashlin. One could also draw a further parallel; just as Bracken did his best screen work with Sturges, Lewis was never better than when collaborating with writer-director Tashlin. And while I would argue that Bracken's antiheroic persona plays more realistically funny than Lewis' inventingly cartoon-like character, both clowns definitely tap into that weak "most disturbing side of ... [the American male] personality." (This comically "ugly American" sometimes even plays more effectively abroad, especially in France, where the Bracken-Lewis type is seen as offering a unique insight into the shallowness of our culture.)

Sturges does, however, soften the viewer's acceptability of bumbling Bracken in two ways. First, by anchoring the story in a screwball comedy framework, where males are traditionally manipulated by women, weak Norval simply seems like business as usual for this genre. And keep in mind, calling Bracken's figure a foreshadowing of Jerry Lewis does not negate the aforementioned link to Harold Lloyd. There is a fine line between Lloyd's nerdy go-getter and Bracken's conscientious antihero. Both of these comedians spend most of their screen time struggling. Indeed, Sturges' screwball comedy satirical take on Lloyd's persona in *The Sin of Harold Diddlebock* underlines that point. Harold Lloyd's similarly named title character, Harold Diddlebock, has been stuck in a dead-end accounting clerk job for twenty-plus years, a fate one might predict for Bracken's bank clerk at the outset of *Miracle*.

A second way Sturges makes nondescript Norval more tolerable to the audience is that the movie's only other pivotal male, Demarest's put-upon papa, is a comic antihero, too. Though perennially exasperated, like so many of Laurel & Hardy's nemeses (in movies dearly loved by Sturges), Demarest's inspired bluster still makes him no more successful than the milquetoast manner of Bracken's Norval. Demarest spoofs the big mouth, take-charge male who is always willing to get physical; his Constable Kockenlocker is forever trying to give people the boot ... which results in some amazing pratfalls. Though he plays a small-town cop, he acts more like a comic gangster. Whether coincidently cleaning his gun on the porch when Norval comes to visit for some potential son-in-law advice, or offering darkly comic axioms on the nature of women, Kockenlocker is an Army veteran whose forcefulness has forever failed him in civilian life. (Here is his take on a daughter telling him she does not want to talk: "A woman doesn't care to talk? The only time a woman doesn't care to talk is when she's dead!")

Constable Kockenlocker's (Demarest) gun cleaning coincides with a visit from his daughter Trudy's (Hutton's) suitor (Bracken) in *The Miracle of Morgan's Creek*.

In contrast, nerdy Norval's loving willingness to marry the pregnant-by-someone-else Trudy, after she finally finds affection for the young man, could also be seen as more savior than sap. But before one calls the Sturges satire police for offering up this positive spin on Bracken's antiheroic character, keep in mind the comments by *Miracle*'s lawyer Alan Bridge (Sturges regular E. L. Johnson), about the typical male response to marriage and children: "No man is going to jeopardize his present or poison his future with a lot of little brats hollering around the house, unless he's forced to." Based upon this criterion, Bracken's character sounds downright noble and romantic. The brilliance of Sturges is that he can offer this point as more evidence of Norval's less than manly ways and yet make a potential positive from it. This writer-director both affectionately mocks populism while embracing it in small doses.

Given all these crazy dynamics, *Miracle*'s helter-skelter script pinballs towards a resolution in a manner reminiscent of Robert Benchley's observation, "Insanity runs in my family. In fact, it practically gallops." Speed is of the essence, because as Lynn's Emmy tells Trudy, "Nobody believes good unless they have to, if they've got a chance to believe something bad." But before Bracken's character can rescue Trudy by way of marriage, they have to address her undocumented first union to phantom hubby Private Ratziwatzi.

Up until this point, Norval's antiheroic status might have been described as anticipatory of Charlie Brown, where the world is forever pulling away that metaphorical football just before the big kick. Unlike the dust cloud that hovers around his playmate Pigpen, Charlie has an invisible black cloud over his head. Yet, this antiheroic fate is not just about life's random actions. The comic poignancy escalates when the underdog attempts to assert himself. For example, when Charlie Brown pitches in the big game, he not only suffers a line drive hit right back at him, the power of the batted ball further humiliates him by comically stripping him of his clothes. Likewise, when Bracken's Norval attempts to assert himself, his comic problems are compounded.

The comic dangers inherent to Norval's plan to solve the Ratziwatzi dilemma are amusingly obvious even *before* he spills the specifics to Trudy: "This [idea] is airtight and watertight. It's foolproof, and almost legal." The Bracken scheme involved marrying Hutton under an assumed name (so Trudy's undocumented ephemeral first marriage could be legally ended by divorce), before they married again using their real names. Unfortunately, Norval the romantic forgot to sign his phony moniker on the first marriage certificate, and the comic fuss, budget justice of the peace (Porter Hall) gets the couple arrested. Norval is soon also charged with impersonating a serviceman (he has donned an amusingly distinctive World War I uniform during World War II — Private Ratziwatzi had been an Army man), and attempting to corrupt a minor.

Norval's arrest is also a catalyst for *Miracle*'s comic pace to further escalate, fueled, in part, by an increase in the physical comedy, such as Constable Kockenlocker orchestrating a jail break for Norval. But Bracken's character is so straight arrow naïve that Demarest's law officer practically has to shoo the young man off the premises. Between the constable falling out of a jailhouse tree, and a brief stop at Norval's place of business that naturally turns into a bank robbery, fast-forward zaniness abounds.

There is, however, a brief lull just before the big finish. But this is not predicated by that old school comedy theory about viewers needing periodic breaks from funny — sort of an aesthetic breathing space. No, Sturges' motives are entertainingly plot driven. Getting Norval out-of-town for several months after the jail break allows the story to flash-forward to Trudy's due date, minimizing what was almost a 1940s movie verboten — showcasing a woman near term.

More importantly for the iconoclastic Sturges, the calendar movement now makes it Christmas time—*the* season for populism. That is, the genre that Sturges satirizes in *Miracle* is anchored in the belief that people inherently do the right thing. But to further hedge that bet, populism often gerrymanders its story around this sacred holiday — knowing audiences will be more likely to accept such feel-good behavior at this time of the year. For instance, Capra uses a Christmas Eve backdrop for the conclusion of both *Meet John Doe* (1941) and *It's a Wonderful Life* (1946).

Along related lines, Capra scripts also frequently draw verbal parallels between their protagonists and Christ, from the metaphorical "crucifying" of Jimmy Stewart's title character in *Mr. Smith Goes to Washington* (1939), to references in *Doe* to "Pontius Pilate" and the original Doe who "died 2000 years ago." Capra addressed the Christianity factor directly when he stated:

> I think that the gospels are a comedy — good news. I think that the greatest comedy of all is the Divine Comedy — the Resurrection, victory over death. Every Sunday the Catholics celebrate the mass, celebrate a victory over death. That's what comedy means to me.... Sure, the good people — good hasn't taken over the earth. But neither has evil taken over the earth. And you shouldn't let it.[5]

Why belabor Sturges' use of this populist Christmas component? It is important to underline his satirical audacity — comic blasphemy, if you will, at least for the 1940s. Trudy is pregnant and without a documented husband, despite Norval's flawed best efforts, and it will take the "miracle" of the title to save her from disgrace. Undoubtedly, the satirical Sturges is flirting with a comparison to the back-story of the Virgin Mary — another hard to explain pregnancy, and a soon-to-be husband struggling with these developments ... until a "miracle" is explained to him in a dream. Consequently, with regard to Bracken, instead of Sturges spoofing Capra's tendency to use a male lead as a Christ-like figure, *Miracle* has Norval more in the Joseph mold — after getting an explanation from a "dream" girl, he is also a *bystander* to an amazing event which will make everything all right.

Sturges' *deus ex machina* "miracle" involves Trudy giving birth to sextuplets — a brilliant defusing of his having fun with the Christmas story, though the satire now takes several new twists. Since Betty Hutton has been, to borrow a crack from film critic Eric Jonsson, "thoughtful enough to transcend her disgrace with sextuplets," Sturges will soon demonstrate how hypocrisy is often pronounced "hurrah," if the transgression catches the public's fancy.[6] Moreover, having six babies (all boys) was also grist for pop culture satire, since the total topped the era's ongoing fascination with the Dionne Quintuplets (all girls)—born to a Canadian couple in 1934, a decade prior to the film. Playing upon the Depression America's obsession with the Dionne Quintuplets, a war period's need for boys, and Capra's filmmaking fondness for newspaper headline montages, Sturges scores more satirical points with a *Miracle* montage of his own: "Canada Protests," "Mussolini Resigns," and "Hitler Demands a Recount."

The multiple births at the small-town hospital are a surprise. When the maternity ward nurse announces a boy has been born, Grandpa Kockenlocker merely says, "So what?" But then she dashes for additional blankets — a process Sturges milks for bigger laughs each of the five times it occurs, as the nurse makes like a track star through the waiting room, forever upping the baby count with a show of her fingers. This animated physical shtick is a good example of what auteur critic Andrew Sarris once generalized about the writer-director: "What distinguishes Sturges from his contemporaries is the frantic congestion of his comedies."[7] Sarris' description nicely covers both the visual as well as the verbal comedy. But *the* visual topper to these hospital antics occurs when Emmy and Norval, *behind protective glass*, are looking into the baby nursery and facing the viewer. When he asks which one is Trudy's, and Emmy responds all of them, Bracken's character is suddenly the most amusingly demonstrative of silent clowns, like Harold Lloyd during his floor-to-floor panics up a skyscraper in *Safety Last* (1923).

If anyone plays God in *Miracle*, besides Sturges, it is Governor McGinty (Brian Donlevy) of Norval and Trudy's unnamed state. (This casting offers the film fan added laughs, since Donlevy starred as the likeable crooked politician in the movie that put Sturges on the Hollywood map — *The Great McGinty*, 1940). Years before, the Sturges-written film *The Power and the Glory* (1933) had helped break ground for the creative use of the flashback. In *Miracle* the viewer first meets Donlevy just prior to the extended flashback which represents most of the movie. The picture opens with the local newspaper editor (Vic Potel) calling the governor about an amazing event which has just occurred in Morgan's Creek. This then segues into the telling of the Trudy-Norval story.

Once the secret is finally out (sextuplets), the viewer is returned to the framing device with the governor. Donlevy's character then proceeds to fix everything. Here is a snippet of his conversation with the journalist:

McGINTY: "You mean he's [Norval] still in jail, you dumb blockhead." [Bracken's character has been arrested again after returning from his fruitless search for Private Ratziwatzi.]
EDITOR: "Yes."
McGINTY: "Well, get him out."
EDITOR: "But how can I, Mr. Governor, with all those charges against him."
McGINTY: "By dropping the charges, you dumb cluck. [Later in the conversation the governor decrees:] As a matter of fact, he's a colonel in ... [the state guard]. I'm bringing him [Norval] his commission tomorrow."

Most importantly, McGinty as God eventually decrees to the editor and all the world—"She's [Trudy] married to Norval Jones. She always has been."

Despite Sturges' gentle spoofing of populism, this satirist ultimately gives the viewer what the genre's greatest auteur (Capra) always delivered — a happy ending. Only Sturges tweaks things with a worldly "wink wink," as if to say, "Only in the movies ... or a Biblical manger." This is not unlike W. C. Fields' wonderfully unbelievable close to *The Bank Dick* (1940, see earlier chapter). But in contrast to Fields' biting satire of most small-town stereotypes, such as the gossipy neighbor or the coldly clammy banker, Sturges manages to invest most of Morgan Creek's citizens with some redeeming qualities, even if they are often nearly as antiheroic as Bracken's Norval.

Fittingly, Sturges frequently showed his left-handed affection for these struggling small-town *Miracle* folks by gifting them with comic lines as memorable as the leads. For example, when Trudy and Emmy go to local lawyer Bridge (the aforementioned E. L. Johnson) for help in tracking down the mysterious Private Ratziwatzi, Bridge responds, "I practice the law. I'm not only willing, but anxious, to sue anyone anytime for anything, but they got to be real people with names and corpuses and meat on their bones. I can't work with spooks." Ironically, this democratic distribution of the verbal gems among the supporting players (sort of a populist production ethic) is a trait Sturges does share with Capra.

In the spirit of this "spread the wealth" philosophy, Sturges was often open-minded about actors wanting to join in the creative collaboration. In an interview Bracken did decades later with cable television's Turner Classic Movies (TCM), the actor said Sturges was generous about letting him improvise.[8] And there was more possibility for improvising on this picture, because Sturges' script was still a work in progress when the production began! Thus, among other things, Bracken helped create his high-strung bumbling character. Of course, the actor had an added incentive for increased involvement;

he felt Paramount was throwing the movie to his friend and *Miracle* love interest, Betty Hutton. Based upon their previous co-starring outings for the studio, he had every right to be concerned. In James Curtis' biography of Sturges, Bracken confessed:

> Because of the way I was deceived [by Paramount], I decided I was going to work every magical trick I ever learned in my life, including upstaging, downstaging ... I came up with stuttering, and the spots before my eyes, and the nervous twitch ... it wasn't a fight with Betty, it was a fight with the studio.[9]

Years later, during Bracken's national tour with the stage production of *Sugar Babies*, I was able to ask the actor if there were any other wrinkles to Sturges' willingness to improvise. Surprisingly, Bracken revealed that the free-spirited writer had allowed him and Hutton to megaphone themselves in an all-important *Miracle* scene — Trudy's return from her mysterious partying marriage.[10] Given that the multi-talented Sturges juggled writing and directing with both running a Hollywood nightclub (The Players) and a machinist factory (the filmmaker was also an inventor), he was sometimes missing in other creative action.

The scene had Trudy driving to the local movie theater, where she had stranded Norval all night. That is, when her father had refused to let her attend a series of dances for departing soldiers, the teenager had cooked up an alleged film date with Bracken, only to then borrow his car and party anyway. But instead of returning for Norval that night after the movie double-bill ended, Hutton's involvement with "Ratziwatzi" kept her away until eight A.M. Drunk, oblivious of the time, and having apparently had an accident with Norval's old Ford, Trudy finally drives up irritatingly chipper. But the conversation which follows, including her admonition of Bracken for keeping her out so late, comically demonstrates the extreme romantic spell she has over him. One might describe the phenomenon by paraphrasing that age-old cracker-barrel axiom, "Whoever loves the least in an relationship has the most control." This truism is all the more pertinent here, given that Trudy had yet to express *any* romantic awareness of Norval. Of course, a crass take on Hutton's magic can be found by recycling a Sturges line from another film, *The Palm Beach Story* (1942): "Sex [appeal] always has something to do with it, dear."

Sturges does, however, reconfigure his sex appeal formula for *Miracle*. Granted, men are never a match for women in this satirist's cinema. As Claudette Colbert tells husband Joel McCrea in the aforementioned *Palm Beach Story*, "...men don't get smarter as they grow older, they just lose their

A publicity still of Preston Sturges (circa 1944) accenting the sexual innuendo often associated with his films.

hair." Still prior to *Miracle*, Sturges' male leads were Hollywood handsome and at or near success, such as Henry Fonda's millionaire in *The Lady Eve* (1941), or Joel McCrea's star film director in *Sullivan's Travels* (1941). In contrast, *Miracle*'s Bracken is a pleasantly goofy-looking child-like man stuck in a dead-end job. Being such a romantic lost cause is another, sadder explanation as to why Bracken would allow Betty Hutton to treat him like such a doormat.

Now, while Hutton's attractiveness is more in line with prior Sturges beauties, she is hardly the sharpest tool in the shed, either. This blunting of the traditional sophisticated sexy Sturges female lead, coupled with Bracken's sweet goober, is undoubtedly part of the writer-director's further satire of small-town life, à la a dumbing down factor. Only Trudy's beautiful smart aleck of a younger sister (Diana Lynn) is reminiscent of the previous sexy cynic norm.

That being said, the supporting players are variations of earlier Sturges figures — none more than the simply recycled "Great McGinty," who in fixing everything finally and legally puts Bracken's Norval in uniform. But even with that "miracle" of an ending, the viewer half expects satirical Sturges to repeat a trick with which he opens *Palm Beach Story*, where a couple is getting married and the title appears: "And They Lived Happily Ever After." But then the playing of the "Wedding March" hits a sour note and the camera tracks back to another questioning title: "Or Did They?"

Sturges might have offered up what many *Miracle* viewers were thinking — how long would the Norval-Trudy-babies scenario work? For instance, one might go the *Rock-a-Bye Baby* remake route, where the Bracken-Lewis character becomes a full-time baby-sitter for updated Trudy (Marilyn Maxwell), a movie sex symbol who does not want her fans to know she has had triplets. Thus, Bracken's Norval is probably looking at a future best summarized with another Lewis title — *Cinderfella* (1960).

Be that as it may, *Miracle* went on to huge box office returns, no small accomplishment in a year (1944) which produced a number of American comedic classics, including Vincente Minnelli's musical comedy *Meet Me in St. Louis*, Leo McCarey's populist *Going My Way*, and Frank Capra's detour into dark comedy, *Arsenic and Old Lace*. The *Miracle* critics were equally kind. *The New York Times* observed, "For a more audacious picture — a more delightfully irreverent one ... has never come slithering madly down the path."[11] *Variety* predicted, *Miracle* ... [will do] good business in all situations ... [and Bracken's] a comedian who is coming along rapidly and should attain major stature ere long."[12] The *Nation*'s aforementioned James Agee, who could be hard on Sturges, given the higher standard to which he held the director, stated the Bracken-starring *Miracle* "seems to me funnier, more adventurous, more abundant, more intelligent, and more encouraging than anything that has been made in Hollywood for years."[13] *PM* said, "[While] the Legion of Decency doesn't like it ... almost everyone else will find something to his taste in it ... [such as] the endearing frustration of Eddie Bracken...."[14] The *New York World Telegram* warned, "If Preston Sturges doesn't watch himself in his writing and directing he is going to have the responsibility for a whole nation laughing itself sick."[15] *New York Journal American* critic G. E. Blackford was so entertainingly positive about the picture and Bracken that the opening to his review would not have been out of place in a Sturges sketch:

> You want to laugh? Go to the N.Y. Paramount [theater] and see the new picture there.... Even if you don't want to laugh and you do go there, you will laugh. If you don't, it can only be because you're both deaf and blind."[16]

Though the post–World War II Bracken was not able to sustain his antiheroic persona at a high profile level for anything approaching the longevity of the classic clowns, he represents an important transition from the ripe-for-satire yet populist-orientated Harold Lloyd, to the ultimately demented oeuvre of Jerry Lewis and his contemporary copycats, such as Jim Carrey. But with Bracken there was an inherent likeableness to the man and his vulnerable comic persona that made him easy to root for and secretly identify with, even in such minor late roles as the Walt Disney–like "Wally World" creator in *National Lampoon's Vacation* (1983). As with Sturges, Bracken burned brightest for only a short time in the 1940s, yet it is a comic light we still remember and honor.

6

BOB HOPE & BING CROSBY
The *Road to Utopia* (1946)

The handsome Hope did have one comic feature — a ski-nose, which was often the target of his co-stars. But the self-deprecating entertainer kidded about his proboscis, too: "It was my mother who [first] discovered my nose. 'Call back the doctor,' she cried. 'He's taken the baby and left the stork.'"[1]

While it is safe to say Charlie Chaplin is the greatest of all screen comedians, one might also suggest that Bob Hope (1903–2003) is *the* performer most likened to an American ambassador of goodwill. For 60-plus years he entertained the nation via vaudeville, radio, television, the movies, and books. But the topper was both his tireless entertaining of troops abroad and countless domestic benefit appearances for every conceivable cause. Hope's unique position was acknowledged as early as the mid–1940s: "The gap left by the [1935] death of [revered comedian and humanitarian] Will Rogers, as a comedian whose barbs at politics and politicians were particularly appreciated in Washington, has been filled. Bob Hope has stepped into the shoes of Will Rogers...."[2]

As with many personality comedians, Hope's movies often have a parody foundation — the antihero as fool when trying to copy a real hero. His talents in this genre were best showcased in seven Paramount *Road* films with Bing Crosby: *Road to Singapore* (1940), *Road to Zanzibar* (1941), *Road to Morocco* (1942), *Road to Utopia* (1946), *Road to Rio* (1947), *Road to Bali* (1952), and *Road to Hong Kong* (1962). Besides spoofing the action adventure genre, the *Road* pictures are a parody of Hollywood itself. As one might assume, given the celebrated nature of the series, the magic of this parody pairing was immediately recognized. The 1940 *Hollywood Reporter* was probably, however, the most perceptive in its praise of the first *Road* movie: "In pairing Bing Crosby and Bob Hope, Paramount has created one of the greatest comedy teams in

The ongoing "Road" trio of Bob Hope (right), Dorothy Lamour, and Bing Crosby on the *Road to Utopia* (1946).

film history ... a demand for more of the same is an unqualified certainty."³ The immediate critical and commercial success of the *Road* pictures was not lost on Hope, who used them as one more topic in his stand-up patter on stage and for radio. The subject also surfaced in the first of his numerous comic autobiographies, *They Got Me Covered*. "I don't know what will happen in our next picture ... *The Road to Morocco*, but anyway, Dorothy, Bing, and I are having a lot of fun ... besides I'm getting a salary for my performances in these 'Road pictures' ... which, as one critic pointed out, is a perfect example of highway robbery."⁴

Each successive *Road* outing was stronger, with the team peaking on the *Road to Utopia*. It was originally to be the *Road to Moscow*, but because two then-recent Hollywood films on Russia, *Mission to Moscow* and *North Star* (both 1943), had not been commercial hits, production company Paramount decided it needed a new title. It was also a providential change, since the paranoia about communism that followed World War II resulted in the Hollywood blacklisting of many talented artists, all because they might have "red" interests. Even some people involved in the production of *Mission to Moscow* and *North Star* were later hassled by communist witch-hunters — and this was during a time when the Soviet Union was a U.S. ally (1941–45).

The change from a Moscow destination was especially fortuitous, given that the *Utopia* production was actually finished by early 1944, though it did not go into general release until 1946. This fact is indirectly footnoted during Hope and Crosby's most entertaining *Utopia* duet, "Put it There, Pal," where the two plug their then most recent films — Crosby's *Dixie* (1943, with Dorothy Lamour) and Hope's *Let's Face It* (1943, with Betty Hutton). The reason behind the delayed *Utopia* release was movie box office numbers during World War II were so great that studios resorted to stockpiling pictures, with Paramount even selling releasing rights of some films to United Artists. Still, when the Moscow destination was scrapped, Paramount was stuck with winter sets and the need for an appropriate story.

But like most comedies, the *Road* pictures are not married to a script. As the reviewer for *The New Yorker* wrote: "The plot, if you care, has the boys whooping around Alaska in search of a gold mine, and Miss Lamour [the ongoing *Road* show romantic interest] is present as the owner of the property."[5] It is the late 1890s, and gold in the Klondike makes *Utopia* the only period *Road* picture, which might contribute to the film's unique status. And given Hope's great future success with Western parodies, it is also fitting that the best of the team's pairings has a frontier setting. As if to be on the safe side, with this period departure, *Utopia* has a contemporary framing device. Hope and love interest Dorothy Lamour are thus well into their white-haired senior years at the film's opening, with an elderly Crosby joining them here and at the close, after the story has unfolded in an extended flashback.

All the *Road* pictures spoof the movies, but none as effectively as *Utopia*. And it all begins before the story proper. That is, as *Esquire's* critic noted, humorist "Robert Benchley 'supplies' another element of [parody] importance; [he's] a prologue without portfolio."[6] Prior to the opening titles, one sees Benchley standing behind the desk he normally used in his award-winning short film subjects. Appropriately, these shorts at their best, such as the Oscar-winning *How to Sleep* (1935), spoof professorial figure presentations. Most acclaimed for his inspired and often spoofing essays, which helped bring the figure of the comic antihero to a broader audience (starting in the 1920s), Benchley had also found major antiheroic success in film and radio. Regardless, with tongue firmly in cheek, Benchley introduces *Utopia*:

> The motion picture you are about to see is not very clear in spots. As a matter of fact it was made to demonstrate how not to make a motion picture and at the same time win an Academy Award. Now someone in

what is known as the front office has thought an occasional word from me might help clarify the plot and other vague portions of the film. [chuckling] Personally, I doubt it.

Periodically, Benchley reappears in the corner of the screen and shares bits of comic wisdom, such as, "This is a device known as a flashback," or, "Did you ever stop to think of one of those dog teams? The lead dog is the only one that ever gets a change of scenery." Appropriately enough, the *New York Herald Tribune*'s critic used Benchley as a symbol of the film's parody: "He kids the film as much as it kids itself. His ironic explanations of the screen's flashback or calling attention to a group of people as obvious 'extras' underline the superb humor of the show."[7] *Esquire* said, "His cheerfully inane ad libs do more than merely compound the confusion. They give the idiotic events on the screen a certain related reality."[8] Years later when Hope was asked about the Benchley comments, as well as other examples of spoofing the movies, he said, "They [audience] love anything that gives them a little mental jerk and they want to be 'with it.'"[9] Neither before *Utopia* nor after would the *Road* pictures have such a supporting comedian as gifted as Benchley. Sadly, Benchley died of a cerebral hemorrhage shortly before the release of *Utopia*. Fellow humor great James Thurber would later say of his friend, the witty master of wee hour revelry, "They're going to have to stay up late in heaven now."[10]

In addition to Benchley's screen corner appearances, numerous scenes detail what plot exists and shout "movie spoof." For instance, the picture includes a talking fish and a talking bear who feels underappreciated. ("A fine thing. A fish they let talk. Me, they won't give one stinking line.") This is a perfect commentary on the saturation comedy of the *Road* pictures, or parody in general — anything for a laugh. And although there is a loose plot reason for the fish and bear to be there, the comments are hardly expected.

Master antihero Robert Benchley (circa 1945), the spoofing guide to this "Road" exercise in personality comedy parody.

Hope does his own animal sound (wolf) when he has a big kissing scene with Dorothy Lamour's character (Sal), adding in direct address to the viewer, "As far as I'm concerned this picture is over right now."

Duke Johnson (Bing Crosby) and Chester Hooten (Bob Hope) even discuss being off on another *Road* picture as they dogsled across the Klondike. Chester then looks off into the distance and observes, "Get a load of that bread and butter." While Duke is mystified, the camera cuts to a snow-covered mountain with stars around it — the logo for Paramount, the studio producing the film. At another point a character dressed like a magician strolls through their scene. When asked if he is in the movie, he answers, "No, I'm taking a shortcut to Stage 10."

The biggest spoof, of course, is having Hope and Crosby posing as two murderers who have stolen a gold mine map belonging to Dorothy Lamour's character. It is a funny premise that plays even funnier when the film's other figures accept the trick for a while. Chester and Duke, hardly two tough guys, have difficulty staying in character. The funniest recovery finds Hope's Chester ordering lemonade in a bar. Immediately recognizing his mistake, he quickly growls to put it "in a dirty glass."

Bing Crosby has said, "The basic ingredient of any *Road* picture is a Rover Boys–type plot, plus music. The plot takes two fellows, throws them into as many jams as possible, then lets them clown their way out."[11] The *Road* pictures use travel to get Hope and Crosby into as many comic "jams" as possible.

Crosby, however, has left one ingredient out of his *Road* formula. He does not examine the difference between these "two fellows." Though they are both women-chasing con artists (in *Utopia* they have a huckster game called Ghost-O that involves a magic box which increases, if they choose, however much money is placed inside), Crosby's Duke is in charge of all the team's misadventures, as is the case in all the *Road* pictures. For example, in *The Road to Morocco* (1942) Crosby's character goes so far as to sell Hope's into slavery!

And the romantic Crosby normally gets the girl — Dorothy Lamour — except in *Utopia*. But this lone Hope victory must be qualified. When the film closes with a return to its contemporary framing device, an elderly Duke drops in on longtime marrieds Chester and Sal, taking the couple by surprise. Duke had seemed to be a goner at the end of *Utopia*'s flashback. An earthquake had suddenly opened an abyss separating Duke from Chester and Sal, and Crosby's character was last seen with an angry mob bearing down upon him. Still the skirt chaser, Duke arrives at Chester and Sal's with two beautiful young "nieces." The topper to this action has Chester and Sal's only child coming into the scene — he is the spitting image of Duke, and is naturally played by Crosby. Hope's one "success" with Dorothy Lamour finds him to have been cuckolded despite help from an earthquake.

Hope's favorite description of his *Road* character came from a 1953 *Saturday Evening Post* article: "Fate is determined to make [him] a jerk. He brags and blusters, but there isn't a child over five who can't outwit him, disarm him or steal his pants."[12] Hope's *Road* character could still be the wise guy, as in his bragging situations. But as Hope observed of these pictures, "We put more emphasis on the 'boob' aspect of his 'Road' character."[13] As a reviewer noted, "Theatre ushers report that spectators all laugh at Hope and identify themselves with Crosby."[14] But Crosby's *Zanzibar* character is most succinct: "Stick with me and if you live, we're going to do all right." In Crosby's taking-advantage-of-Hope defense, the ski-nose's character is ripe for the plucking. Here is a typical *Utopia* bit of verbal slapstick between the sometimes team:

> HOPE: "I was Shangri-la'd."
> CROSBY: "Shanghaied."
> HOPE: "Well, one of them towns in Egypt."

As one *New York Times* review of *Utopia* stated: "Bob [Hope] is the natural-born fall-guy...."[15]

Part of the inspired saturation comedy effect of *Utopia* could be attributed to the fact that it was scripted by two of Hope's former radio gag writers, Norman Panama and Melvin Frank. This talented duo's first screen credit was the story idea for Hope's *My Favorite Blonde* (1942). They would later script his *Monsieur Beaucaire* (1946) and the *Road to Hong Kong* (with Frank producing and Panama directing this final Hope and Crosby teaming).

Hope and Crosby did not write and direct their films, but they peppered their scripts with much additional gag material, from themselves and from their radio gag men. (During the 1940s Hope and Crosby had competing radio programs.) Thus, many names might have appeared under script credit. Moreover, like other independent personality comedians mentioned earlier in the text, Hope (the team's designated comedian) was directed *if* he wanted to be. For instance, probably the best director Hope worked with was Frank Tashlin, who co-scripted and directed *Son of Paleface*. Tashlin comically described how Hope would get his way: "His narrowed eyes squinting [anticipating the future look of an angry Clint Eastwood?] at you down the maligned nose, is a withering experience. Your puttees curl and your megaphone sags [Tashlin spoofs what was once standard fare for a director]."[16]

In *Road to Utopia*, Hope and Crosby had an especially casual approach to filmmaking, though the production of all the *Road* pictures had an easygoing strategy. Crosby observed, "We had a ball [on the *Road*] pictures. We had directors who let us suit our own schedules."[17] World War II "Pin-up favorite" Dorothy Lamour seconded her co-star's comments about the *Road* pictures, adding a comic confession about her only difficulty in making *Utopia*:

> You can often see me laughing in places I'm not supposed to even in the final version. You just can't help yourself; you just never know what to expect with those two wild men [Hope and Crosby] around.[18]

Although the *Road* films are famous for the comic asides of Hope and Crosby (*Utopia* included), American humor has always placed a high premium on visual/slapstick comedy, whether in the movies or on the printed page. For instance, the beloved James Thurber's greatest book is *My Life and Hard Times* (1933), which is so full of visual comedy (not to mention his delightful drawings) that even his episode titles create cartoon pictures: "The Night the Bed Fell," "The Day the Dam Broke," and "The Dog that Bit People." And film's greatest comedy period has long been considered the silent days of Chaplin, Buster Keaton, Harold Lloyd, Harry Langdon and Laurel & Hardy.

With this in mind, it is interesting to note that the *New York Herald Tribune*'s critic went so far as to credit the visual side of *Utopia* as the key to its success: "Much of the show is premised on the violently witty asides of Crosby and Hope, but it is not the dialogue which sustains the production. It is at its best when pantomime is the springboard for crazy characterizations and ludicrous scenes."[19] Examples include the pickpocket scenes with Hope and Crosby (stealing a billfold-laden nest egg, back and forth, from *each other*), their reduction to crying babies when they find out what they lost by not believing in Santa (Claus, in a cameo appearance, had intended to give these womanizing wannabes two beautiful girls), and Hope's accidental romancing of a bear.

The latter scene finds Hope thinking Lamour, in a fur coat, has cuddled up next to him one cold northern night ... but it turns out to be a real bear. Plus, the animal not only gets the best of Hope visually, the bear exits the scene with that inspired verbal crack — complaining that the picture has a talking fish but she doesn't get a line. (The previous *Road* picture, *Morocco*, had comically scored with a brief aside from a camel.) Hope mistakenly wrestling with a bear he thinks is a fur coat attired person also brings to mind Chaplin (Hope's idol) doing the same thing in another frozen north comedy picture, *The Gold Rush* (1925).

Minnie, the *Utopia* brown bear dyed black by Paramount, roughed up Hope in one of their unused "romantic" close-ups. This was grist for a series of comic ad-libs by Hope which were later played up in the newspapers. The most entertaining documentation of these quips surfaced in an early 1944 *Hollywood Citizen News* article entitled "Hope Fades for Hope as He Sees Bear."[20] Dangerous Minnie had the comedian riffing: "What a way to weed out the stock players.... Have we got a direct wire to Utter-McKinley [an undertaking establishment]? ... You see what that bear did? She sniffed me. That's a good sign. I guess she doesn't like ham."

Minnie was not the only *Utopia* animal-related problem. The brief Santa bit required getting seven reindeer for his sleigh. Producer Paul Jones told the head of Paramount's prop department, E. C. Stratton, to find the reindeer: "Jones thought no more about it. Stratton did. He thought plenty. He's still thinking."[21] Finding reindeer, especially trained ones, was very difficult and expensive in early 1940s Hollywood. Stratton eventually found three acceptable reindeer in a Milwaukee zoo. But he had to negotiate with a hard bargaining Shuster's Department Store, which used the animals in its annual Christmas parade. Four more reindeer were eventually brought in from Canada. Yet, special shipping permits were then required by Washington; reindeer moss for eating was difficult to find; the prop department had to build antlers for the animals.... Maybe Hope and Crosby were crying in the Santa scene at all the time and expense involved for roughly a one minute routine.

While no reindeer actually attacked anyone, like Minnie giving Hope a split lip, Crosby briefly developed snow blindness from "long hours of work in artificial snow under 10,000 watt studio lamps."[22] And when the comedy team was not fighting the fake snowstorms produced by bleached cornflakes thrown in front of giant wind machines, the duo logged time in a refrigerated set. So while Hope and Crosby always relished their various *Road* teamings, making *Utopia* sometimes belied its name.

The most interesting item to be weeded out of the pre–*Utopia* release press material, however, had nothing to do with either Hope and Crosby's encounter with Santa's reindeer or Minnie the bear. The forgotten fun fact addressed the unique period popularity of the *Road* series, with Paramount suggesting *Utopia* would be the final installment. For example, in late 1943 the *Los Angeles Daily News* reported:

> The decision to make this the final "Road" picture was not prompted by downhill profits. Paramount has made a neat little fortune out of ... [the series]. If it seems incongruous that a studio should call a halt when it's making money, consider how much bigger the profits could be if those three stars concentrated on separate pictures.²³

Indeed, Paramount's original press kit material (April 28, 1944) for *Utopia* revealed that a similar end the series decision had been attempted after the previous hit *Road* picture (1942's *Morocco*): "[such] a deluge of letters flooded the [studio] mail department ... [that] the head man decided they would be without places to hang their hats if they didn't give the public what it wanted."²⁴

Still, one can understand Paramount's money position, with regard to maximizing the box office potential of Hope and Crosby in solo productions. For instance, in 1944, the year *Utopia* was originally slated to be released, Crosby was America's number one box office star, with Hope a close third; little had changed when the film opened two years later — Crosby continued as the revenue champion, and Hope came in at number five.²⁵ In fact, Crosby ruled the box office roost for five consecutive years (1944–1948), only to slide to second in 1949 ... behind Hope. Moreover, Crosby's value to Paramount during this period was further increased by the Best Actor Oscar he received for the populist *Going My Way* (1944), made just prior to joining Hope on *Utopia*. (That same year Hope would be recognized with a "Special" Academy Award, an honor he would receive five times, for humanitarian and unique contributions to the film industry, over the course of his career.)

Despite such pop culture acclaim, one cannot help briefly addressing the "arty" notion of giving this *Road* picture an idealized metaphorical destination (utopia), the only movie in the series without a specific geographical location in the title. For Hope and Crosby, their "garden of eden" always involved the pursuit of girls and gold. But given that womanizing and get rich schemes (read scams) often produced irritated lovers and losers, it was often hard to tell whether the catalyst for the duo's ongoing travel was a sense of adventure ... or comic escape.

While *Utopia* is yet another variation on the team's lust for girls and gold, the movie's opening framing device briefly suggests that the now elderly Hope has long achieved the ideal of that title. He is married to his dream girl (Lamour), a woman he normally *never* wins in the *Road* pictures. The couple are Bond villain rich, and most importantly for Hope's character, his friend and nemesis Crosby seems to have been vanquished. So in a comic reversal of *Paradise Lost*, ski-nose had attained his Eden or utopia.

Yet, once an antihero always an antihero, and paradise is soon found to be flawed. The *Wall Street Journal* Hope is reading by the fire is merely a cover for his girlie magazine. His nearby now octogenarian wife is scolding him about cleaning his teeth, and next they hear Crosby singing outside. Hope quips, "And I thought this was going to be an 'A' picture." The crooner's entrance further sours the comedian's evening, given that Crosby is apparently wealthy, too, and has successfully continued his womanizing ways, given that he is accompanied by two beautiful young "nieces." But the coup de grace to this "paradise lost" occurs at the comic conclusion of the movie. After the extended flashback that comprises the bulk of the film, the ending returns to the senior-aged framework, with the aforementioned comic surprise that Hope's romantic triumph (getting Lamour) was a lie — given that she was already pregnant with Bing's baby.

Granted, Hope does get the closing comic line, alibing that Crosby, Jr., was adopted. *But* it is just the audience that is finally finding out about this cuckolding. Comedy or not, it dawns on the viewer that ski-nose has seemingly had to deal with this humiliation for half a lifetime. A "paradise lost" indeed. Of course, one could argue that Hope's adopting comment is yet another example of his "boob" mentality on the *Road*. Yet, he delivers the line with more of the knowingly smart aleck aplomb of his dual focus solo comedy character (part antihero, part wise guy). Consequently, his breezy casualness in seemingly masking what in therapy would certainly be a "paging Dr. Freud emergency" merely heightens the comic poignancy of the moment.

If one puts this close in comic life lesson terms, one might suggest that while most of us traffic in small self-deceptions to help us survive, Hope's *Utopia* persona needed an industrial-strength variety to soldier his way through his nonstop *Road* misadventures. And it is this sort of comic resiliency which draws viewers to gifted clowns like Hope. If truth be told, we all live a comic way ... in a darkly comic world. As the old joke goes, "He was a self-made man ... who was not as well-made as he might have been." Who does not like to credit himself with a "self-made" moniker, yet secretly cries to himself that the less than well-made confession is closer to truth? There is a universality here in the comic particular.

Though comic brilliance does not guarantee initial critical success (note the disappointing receptions first received by such classic pictures as Buster Keaton's *The General*, 1927, and the Marx Brothers' *Duck Soup*, 1933), *Utopia* was a box office hit and a critical favorite. The *New York Times* stated, "Not since Charlie Chaplin was prospecting ... [in *The Gold Rush*, 1925] in a Hollywood-made Alaska many long years ago has so much howling humor been swirled with so much artificial snow as it is in 'Road to Utopia'...."[26] The *Los*

The concluding return to the framing device, and a comically surprising revelation: Crosby (left), Lamour, and Hope in *Road to Utopia*.

Angeles Examiner baldly observed, "THERE ARE NO PICTURES being made that surpass the 'Road' pictures in wacky, wonderful fun — or any that even approximate them in their lighthearted, nonsensical gaiety.... The [*Utopia*] amusement never lets down long enough for you to catch your breath."[27] Like the *Examiner*, the *Hollywood Reporter* was equally ga-ga over *Utopia* and *Road* pictures in general: "They are made to see, enjoy and then pass the word on to friends."[28]

The always entertainment business-orientated *Variety* sang *Utopia*'s praise in dollar signs:

> Box office receipts should do a double take with "Road to Utopia." The names of Bing Crosby, Bob Hope and Dorothy Lamour ... guarantee heavy initial pull and the show is plenty good to keep the customers coming thereafter.[29]

In contrast, several other publications keyed upon simply documenting screen audiences' responses to *Utopia*. The *Hollywood Citizen-News* reported, "The peals of laughter and the tidal wave of chuckles emanating from ... [Los Angeles theater] houses indicate that Bob Hope and Bing Crosby ... are scoring another hit.[30] From the opposite coast *Cue* added:

> To the accompaniment of gales of laughter that roll like summer thunder through the Catskills canyons of the Paramount [theater in New York], the delicious trio [Hope, Crosby, and Lamour] are pitching gags ... at the howling audience — kidding the Klondike gold rush, Paramount Pictures, movies in general, and themselves in particular. It's lots of fun.[31]

Hope and Crosby would become the prototype of future comedy "teams"— solo stars occasionally joining forces for a film. But no casual comedy duo was ever so successful. And with the passage of time, Hope's contribution seems ever more significant. But by having him forever victimized by Crosby, the *Road* pictures gave Hope a greater sympathy than many of ski-nose's solo outings. Either way, however, his screen persona relied more heavily on verbal jokes than most comedians. But these are not random cracks. Woody Allen explains:

Woody Allen, heavily influenced by Bob Hope, on location for one of the younger comedian's greatest homages to his idol, *Sleeper* (1973, with Diane Keaton).

Jokes became a vehicle for the person to display a personality or attitude. Just like Bob Hope. You're not laughing at [just] the jokes but at a guy who's vain and cowardly and says to some guy who is menacing, "you're looking good — what do you hear from your embalmer?" You're laughing at the character all the time.[32]

And Hope was the best of comedy editors in protecting the integrity of that character, fluctuating between antihero and wise guy. Or, as entertainer author Steve Allen more succinctly observed, "Hope is funny by nature, but he also understands his nature."[33]

7

DANNY KAYE
The Kid from Brooklyn (1946)

Danny Kaye (1913–1987), a "kid" actually from Brooklyn, could relate to the shy antiheroes he often played on the screen. Even prior to his feature film success, Kaye described himself as, "the kind of guy who stood behind the guy who whistled at the girls."[1]

After struggling for years to find high profile success as an entertainer, Danny Kaye had his breakout opportunity on Broadway with the late 1939 hit the *Straw Hat Revue*. Coupled with "Great White Way" follow-up smashes, the *Lady in the Dark* (1940) and *Let's Face It* (1941), Hollywood soon came calling. While Kaye had already appeared in some late 1930s short subjects, his feature film career was launched by famed producer Samuel Goldwyn (1882–1974). A former glove cutter and salesman, Goldwyn was a 1910s film pioneer at a time when Hollywood was emerging as the movie capital of the world. Though never David Selznick–like brilliant as a producer, Goldwyn had a sixth sense about putting together creative teams. Thus, the opening screen title "Samuel Goldwyn Presents" usually meant solid entertainment, in a variety of genres. Prior to *The Kid from Brooklyn*, this list would include: *The Kid from Spain* (1932, an Eddie Cantor comedy), *Dead End* (1937, gangster film), *Stella Dallas* (1937, melodrama), *Wuthering Heights* (1939, tragic love story), *Ball of Fire* (1941, screwball comedy), *The Pride of the Yankees* (1942, biography), and *The Princess and the Pirate* (1944, Bob Hope comedy).

In 1943 Goldwyn signed Kaye to a long-term contract based upon catching the comedian's nightclub act. So the same year that Paramount brought the former Kaye stage vehicle *Let's Face It* to the screen with Bob Hope, Goldwyn took a cinematic chance with Kaye. *The Kid from Brooklyn* was preceded by two Goldwyn-Kaye productions, *Up in Arms* (1944) and *Wonder Man* (1945). Both features were critical and commercial hits. But even including their entertaining later collaborations, *The Secret Life of Walter Mitty* (1947),

A Song Is Born (1948), and *Hans Christian Andersen* (1952, all released through RKO studio), *Brooklyn* is arguably the best of the Goldwyn-Kaye teamings. The movie showcases Kaye as a struggling early morning milkman thrust into the limelight when it appears he has knocked out the middleweight boxing champion (Steve Cochran).

Kaye's screen persona is a marriage of several factors. First, during an extended performing tour of the Orient (1934–36), he adapted to frequently non–English speaking audiences:

> [Kaye] developed his face-making techniques, pantomiming, and "scat" singing — the expressive presentation of gibberish with an occasional recognizable [English] word to emphasize a point.[2]

The unpredictability of the constantly changing backstage production crews, in an ever increasing number of Eastern theaters, also further honed Kaye's ability to improvise without props or technical assistance.

Second, during summer 1939 rehearsals for what became the all-important *Straw Hat Revue*, Kaye met pianist and comic composer Sylvia Fine. Her sophisticatedly satirical novelty numbers found the perfect creative mouthpiece in Kaye, whose delivery and scat singing tendencies were already predisposed for Fine's work. This first creative teaming produced what became such signature Kaye numbers as "Anatole of Paris," Stanislavsky," and "Pavlova," with the last novelty piece being featured in *Brooklyn*. Kaye and Fine married early the following year (1940), and her compositions and managerial influence would strongly influence the rest of his career.

Third, Kaye's characters for the Goldwyn films of the 1940s were, ironically given the comedian's verbal skills, patterned after silent funnyman Harold Lloyd's antiheroic persona, the shy schnook who makes good in the final reel. In fact, as movie historian Leonard Maltin has noted, "Goldwyn purchased Lloyd's talkie film *The Milky Way* [1936] in order to reshape it for Kaye as *The Kid from Brooklyn*."[3]

There are two reasons, however, to not belabor the paradox. First Goldwyn's Lloyd emphasis was a key model for *so many* screen comedians of both the silent and sound eras — a vulnerable underdog winning against all odds. Besides, given the physical comedy legacy of Kaye's Eastern work, his putty-faced, rubber jointed antics would have been successful in any period, with or without English. Second, like many other movie comedians, especially ones later influenced by Kaye such as Jerry Lewis and Jim Carrey, there is a comic Jekyll and Hyde component to his often split personality persona. But unlike the groundbreaking antihero, wise guy duality of Bob Hope's screen character, addressed in the previous chapter, Kaye's antics can have a merry madness to them. For example, during his *Brooklyn* musical rendition of "Pavlova" he sings, "Everybody's in great confusion." Then, stopping his double-talk scat with a direct address look at the camera, he adds, "But not me. I am unconscious." Kaye then punctuates this unhinged comic confession with a crazy giggle and proceeds with his number.

What makes the comedian's manic transformations more disjointed than any other 1940s norm is that Kaye's movie characters border on being multiple personalities — a comic male "Sybil." Thus, while it is not unrealistic for an antiheroic figure (in or out of film) to occasionally have a smart mouth, albeit in an aside, à la Hope (with both types, underdog and wise guy, being likable), Kaye's entertaining transitions are often neither natural nor characters one would want to know. Period critics, like *The New Yorker*'s John McCarten, would sometimes address this provocative development. In his otherwise rave review of *Brooklyn*, he writes:

> It is perhaps hardly credible that anyone as simple-minded as ... [milkman] Kaye is supposed to be at the outset ... could become the sophisticated braggart [boxer] that he develops into later, but if the transition is jarring, it does bring its rewards, since it enables Mr. Kaye ... to burst into his old rapid-fire ["Pavlova"] ditty about the ballet.[4]

This "jarring" less-than-likable yet still mesmerizing metamorphosis brings to mind Dennis Lim's more recent *New York Times* piece on Jim Carrey succinctly summarized by its title, "Unsettling Goofiness of the Divided Mind."[5] But one could just as likely note Jerry Lewis' greatest solo film (after his breakup with comedy partner Dean Martin), *The Nutty Professor* (1963). The film has Lewis playing both the sweetly sappy title character as well as a satirical take on Martin — Buddy Love.

While the oversexed Love is not someone parents would want their daughter to bring home for a special "family visit," Lewis' "nutty [science] professor" did have a narrative catalyst for changing into the Martin caricature. Romance inspires him to be a better lover by inventing "the greatest new drink since Dracula discovered bloody marys."[6] Though there is nothing that clear-cut about Kaye's character change in *Brooklyn*, I would argue that what makes this film his best from the 1940s is that, aforementioned critic McCarten notwithstanding, the film does provide a plausible point for the milkman briefly becoming a "braggart."

After Kaye's "fighting milkman" is conned into believing that he has real boxing skills by the most amusingly sneaky of ring managers (Walter Abel), the rookie pugilist "wins" a series of fixed fights prior to a set-up championship. Consequently, Kaye's normally "milquetoast" figure returns from these orchestrated victories with an egotistical big head. This is a logical explanation for why Kaye's antihero briefly dovetails into the brash extrovert of the "Pavlova" routine. The legitimacy of this "reading" is reinforced within the movie narrative when Kaye's screen fiancée (Virginia Mayo) takes him to task for changing: "You're a Dr. Jekyll and Mr. Hyde." In contrast, the norm for this type of Kaye cinema situation is for everyone within the movie to metaphorically look the other way when he assumes another comic identity.

Whether one accepts this explanation or not, Kaye's mousey milkman was also praised at the time for not repeatedly morphing into something or someone else, as was often expected of him. For instance, the *Motion Picture Herald* critic said:

The kid's (Danny Kaye) training to be a boxer parallels the comedian's engagement to his frequent screen love interest (Virginia Mayo) in *The Kid from Brooklyn* (1946).

> "The Kid From Brooklyn" ... is different from its [Kaye] predecessors in that it relies far less on its star's unique style of [scat] song delivery [with its accompanying change into an aggressive persona] and almost completely [focuses] on him as a [vulnerable] comedian ... the "Pavlova" number is Kaye's single specialty.[7]

Kaye's comic antihero is also wonderfully assisted by a strong supporting cast who reinforce his underdog status by peppering him with controlling cracks. The chief source of this material is the aforementioned Walter Abel. When his manager senses reluctance on Kaye's part to become a fighter, the boxing veteran simply scares the milkman into acceptance: "Would you like to be drowned in a bathtub?"

When Abel's huckster lives up to his "Gabby" Sloan nickname, he often further reveals the comic simplicity of Kaye's character. For example, Gabby attempts to entice him by playing the fame card associated with being a boxing champion: "[The crowds will yell,] 'There he goes!'" Instead, the inspiringly childlike milkman enthusiastically asks, "Who?" Like all pivotal Simple Simons of the cinema, from Buster Keaton's sacrificial attempt to please a girl in *Cops* (1922), to Will Ferrell's delightful title character in *Elf* (2003), Kaye sells his character with kindergarten innocence.

When Gabby attempts to use the milkman's relationship with the gorgeous Mayo (Kaye's perennial girlfriend in the Goldwyn films), he manages to set up a Kaye love statement that applies to most of cinema's sappy clowns. That is, Abel's ring manager tells Kaye he will make a great deal of money in the ring, and women like money. The milkman answers, "Polly [Mayo] wouldn't take it [money]. She's a nice girl." And true to form, the sexy Mayo is a "nice girl" to Kaye. Of course, Gabby gets the last laugh here, with a punning dose of real world cynicism he adds, "The 'nicer' they are, the more money they take." (Maybe Mayo's sweetness to Kaye is even more surreal, despite the genre norm of dorky comedians invariably having lovely, loyal leading ladies, because this actress also excelled at playing sexy gold diggers, including her later sultry two-timer in the nourish gangster classic, *White Heat*, 1949.)

Those scoring highly on the *Brooklyn* supporting cast smart aleck meter, besides Abel's Gabby, would include the manager's girlfriend Eve Arden, trainer Spider Schultz (Lionel Stander, reprising his role from the *Milky Way* original production), and middleweight champion Speed McFariane (Steve Cochran). When Arden's character assists the unathletic milkman's timing by humming a Viennese waltz as he tries to box, Speed deadpans, "Who's his first bout with, Fred Astaire?"

Arden, who made a career of playing the caustic comedienne sidekick, always had a *Brooklyn* barb when there was a threat of dead air time. Her crooked lover of a manager attempted to alibi how the champ could have been knocked out late one night by a then unknown stranger, complaining that the assailant had "hands as big as watermelons." Arden cracked, "How does he wind his watch?" When Gabby was waxing poetic about "nice" women and money, he started to make a reference to Arden, who self-deprecatingly cut him off, "Oh, I'm president of the [gold digging] union." Arden is the movie's great leveler, democratically undercutting everyone, including herself. She's Kaye's only semi-ally in Gabby's crooked clan.

Lionel Stander's gravel-voiced Spider is an entertaining supporting player to Kaye, too. The script gifts him with some inventive lines, such as his dim-witted explanation on how Cochran's Speed could have been KO'd by a milkman outside a nightclub, "I don't know. It's puzzling ain't it?" But Stander's greatest comic complement to Kaye comes in the area of visual comedy. For instance, when the two are preparing to spar, Spider patiently helps the milkman on with his boxing gloves. Then, in the best tradition of Laurel and Hardy (where one has "two minds without a single thought"[8]), as Stander struggles to get his gloves on, Kaye removes his in order to assist Spider ... and then they start the process once again.

The comic physical shtick continues once this dumb duo gets inside the ring. When Kaye's character attempts to mimic Stander's traditionally methodical defensive directed boxing movements, the milkman acts more like a kangaroo on steroids. Eventually giving up on teaching the finer footwork points of the sport, Spider concentrates on the milkman's punch. Sadly for the trainer but comically for the viewer, this ends up with Kaye on his knees patting Stander's shoes with the inside of his gloves, which Jerry Lewis uses verbatim against his own boxing opponent in the ring scene from *Sailor Beware* (1951). At this point Spider gives up, and Arden comes to the rescue with her Viennese waltz approach to pugilism.

As one watches the comic ring movements of Kaye drive Stander to distraction, one glimpses three generations of celebrated cinema clowns. That is, the only talent the milkman brings to the fight game is a little skip hop that helps him avoid haymaker punches. This Kaye step is borrowed from Harold Lloyd's *Milky Way*, which is a fun variation of something the silent comedian had created much earlier in *The Freshman* (1925). Lloyd is the personality comedian foundation here. Kaye then further fleshes out the comic possibilities of the ring scenes, such as his kangaroo action. Flash forward to Lewis' *Sailor Beware* boxing sequences, and one simply sees a great deal of recycled Kaye, with additional homage to the fight scenes in Charlie Chaplin's *City Lights* (1931).

Of course, Lewis' appreciation of this footnote to Chaplin might also be credited to the original *Milky Way*. The real auteur of that picture was not Lloyd but the great film director Leo McCarey.[9] This still neglected comedy master had always been fascinated by Chaplin and *City Lights*, with the boxing bout the movie's signature comic routine. Add to this the fact that McCarey's father was a legendary longtime fight promoter in the Los Angeles area, and one has a natural basis for both an entertaining film about boxing, and a strong model from which future comedians could draw. This range of borrowing varied from literally remaking the picture, à la Goldwyn and Kaye, to Lewis' apparently being more a specific student of the ring material itself, and Kaye in general. Indeed, critic David Thomson's sound bite on Kaye's screen persona, focusing on the comedian's nearly "inhuman energy"—

Director Leo McCarey (left) and Harold Lloyd during their collaboration on the *Milky Way* (1936) ... remade as ***The Kid from Brooklyn***.

likening him to being "somewhere between child, machine, and rogue cuckoo clock"—is also true of the young Lewis.[10]

The challenge for McCarey, however, in doing the boxing movie with Lloyd, which also had later repercussions for both Kaye and Lewis, involved the conflict of same subject (boxing) and different comedians. For example, Chaplin's Tramp boxer used conning to survive in the ring. In contrast, McCarey's reinvention of the Lloyd persona as a pugilist necessitated tapping into the silent comedian's go-getter tendencies, such as the aforementioned hip-hop move—originally created to help his screen character be popular his "freshman" year of college. Moving on to Kaye's "fighting milkman," the figure still exhibits much of the innocently conscientious Lloyd. For instance, Kaye's first response to the standard opening fight mantra from the ring referee about "a good clean fight" has the innocently diligent request, "Could I write all that down?" Yet, Kaye's underdog persona also has the potential to suddenly flirt with the comic dementia now associated with Lewis. In fact, *Sailor Beware*'s boxing sequence even accents this cartoon-like phenomenon by briefly speeding up Lewis' action as he literally runs "rings" around his boxing opponent.

Comedy historian Alan Dale has written, "Slapstick may always mean the same thing—a response to the frustration of physical existence—but it has been blended with other tones in ... American movies."[11] Beginning with Kaye, and escalating for Lewis and the much later Jim Carrey, slapstick seems a window into their characters' split personalities. Oh, the "frustration of physical existence" message still applies, but the "other tones" revealed by Kaye and company are that, like much of the unraveling human world around them, we *all* seem on the road to crazy town.

The safety valve significance of these "other tones" gifts the viewer with laughter *and* the acknowledgement that most people are just hanging on ... in every possible way. I am reminded of Jim Knipfel's darkly comic memoir *Quitting the Nairobi Trio*. The title is a reference to comedian Ernie Kovacs' surreal slapstick sketch involving three violent characters in ape masks, trench coats, and bowler hats. The once suicidal Knipfel, who has struggled through the most literal of personal challenges, now sees life metaphorically as an ongoing series of self-destructive slapstick sketches, à la the *Nairobi Trio*. The secret for survival is to recognize this fact, and then "figure out who—or what—[is putting you at risk]."[12] Consequently, safety is made possible by "*Quitting* the Nairobi Trio." The suicidal Knipfel's greatest enemy was himself. The multiple personality comedy of Kaye, Lewis, and Carrey provide that same *Nairobi Trio* warning light—do not take anything too seriously, existence is simply a variation of the same pattern, and one's own dark side is frequently the source of what ails you. Seeing the connection and being able to laugh at it does not eliminate the problem ... but a slapstick epiphany can make it more palatable.

The student of Kaye knows that the private life of this comedian was often anything but comic or consistent. This might best be described by the subtitle of Martin Gottfried's darkly definitive biography: *Nobody's Fool: The Lives of Danny Kaye* (1994).[13] One reviewer was so surprised by the contrast between the public persona and the private person he paraphrased Neil Simon, "He was an actor you couldn't touch and a person you didn't want to touch."[14] In fairness to Kaye, most of the many comedians I have profiled were less than happy campers in private. Moreover, as Steve Allen has amusingly noted in his seminal book on humor, *The Funny Men* (1956), "I have never known a successful comedian who was not somewhat neurotic. The unsuccessful ones must be in even worse condition."[15]

I only note this Jekyll and Hyde component because it seems relevant to a Kaye persona often described in the same manner. While this is neither an attempt to rent a couch and announce over the intercom, "Paging Dr. Freud," nor the beginning of a manifesto on "Method Comedy," Kaye's late 1940s screen stardom did parallel a time in the arts when the boundaries between real and make-believe were blurring. Indeed, my favorite broadly generic definition of the "memory-mining" technique drawn from Russian director Konstantin Stanislavsky and bottled at the time as the "Method" sounds a great deal like Kaye in *Brooklyn*: a "mix of casualness and intensity, technique and spontaneity."[16]

The egotistical milkman spouting Sylvia Fine's satirical "Pavlova" seems all "intensity" and "technique." And the goofy sweet antihero who falls in love with a beautiful customer, or struggles to be a "fighting milkman," appears the picture of "casualness" and "spontaneity." But maybe this is fitting, given that the aforementioned description, from critic Jeremy McCarter, is meant to blanket a diverse collection of Kaye's ground-breaking creative contemporaries, including Jackson Pollock, Charlie Parker, and Marlon Brando.

At the time of *Brooklyn*'s release, however, this would have all sounded like deep-dish analysis. In 1946 the movie simply represented an anxiously awaited comedy from arguably America's then hottest funny man. This is broadly evident in the reviews, which were not just generally glowing but often euphoric. For example, the opening of the *New York Times*' critique anticipates the sort of pop culture hysteria one might associate with the young Sinatra, or the Beatles:

> The widely expanding popularity of the incredible Danny Kaye will reach the flood level, no fooling, when the comic's new Samuel Goldwyn film ... gets out on the nation's theatre screens. So let this be an unsolemn warning: look out for the inundating wave. For whatever cause the gent has given for delight in his two previous films is repeated with drums....[17]

Along similar lines, *The New Yorker* said, "[Danny Kaye] is rapidly reaching that happy point where he can do no wrong. His face aglow with innocent madness, Mr. Kaye dashes excitedly through the picture...."[18]

Variety credited the Goldwyn-Kaye team with having "outdone itself in 'The Kid from Brooklyn,' topping ... [their] two highly successful previous efforts in almost every phase.... Looks certain to ring in top grosses wherever played."[19] As so often happens with the predictions of the knowledgeable entertainment Bible *Variety*, *Brooklyn* went on to become one of the top moneymaking films of 1945–46.[20]

Fittingly, for such a "high flying" picture, a special promotion for *Brooklyn* even had the *Los Angeles Examiner*'s Dorothy Manners chronicling Kaye's comedy as the "first movie preview ever 9000 feet in the air, and while the [Douglas Skymaster plane's] sound was not always perfect ... it could have gone off completely and this would still rate as one of the funniest comedies ever made."[21] Manners, putting the visual Kaye on par with the comedian as scat man, added, "If you have to see any actor in near-pantomime, Danny's your boy ... to watch him [comically] wave his beautiful hands is a pleasure."[22] And just as Manner's favorite Kaye material involves him as a boxer, the *Motion Picture Herald* seconded that perspective:

> The routines in the fight ring are inevitably heading for audience howls. This goes for the opening and closing [non-boxing] milkman sequences and it also goes for practically all of the footage in between.[23]

The only rare period critical knock against the movie was a storyline that the *Hollywood Reporter* described as old-fashioned "corn." Yet, the same publication was bowled over by the Goldwyn production values of a Technicolor comedy epic "which reportedly cost $2,000,000 or more to put on film"— an amazing sticker price for any 1940s film production.[24] *Time* magazine also felt the script did some "creaking" but then the review went out of its way to document the comic scenes which really delivered:

> [Kaye's] first setup, portraying pure terror's [boxing] victory over a brutish pushover, good & funny; funnier still, his buttery effort to put on boxing gloves. Funniest: Kaye, in arduous training for his first fight, kneels lovingly in the grass, pulls, tugs, yanks, heaves, ultimately uproots a daisy.[25]

These celebrations of the less wild, vulnerable side of the Kaye persona imply, as suggested earlier, that part of *Brooklyn*'s great critical and commercial success is in presenting an antiheroic figure to which a larger audience can relate. That is, while his split personality shtick (from mousey milkman to egotistical boxing challenger) can be cathartic for some viewers, too much strangeness (at least for 1940s fans) might have been off-putting. Put another way, mass audiences often want a goofy fun favorite to simply fit into society. Comedy historian Henry Jenkins further articulates this phenomenon in his clown text with the inspired title, *What Made Pistachio Nuts?* (1992). The following Jenkins quote, though initially directed at a Joe E. Brown character, applies equally to Kaye's *Brooklyn* milkman:

> The normalization of Brown's performance becomes a measure of his character's social integration; earlier moments of stylization and expressive incoherence are read as signs of the comic protagonist's social immaturity rather than as moments where the performer's [alternate] personality surfaces.[26]

This return to a "normalization" is especially obvious in *Brooklyn*'s framing device. The film begins with Kaye as a screw-up milkman at a Sunflower Dairy sales promotion meeting. First, he gets the hiccups during his boss' long-winded presentation. Then Kaye's co-workers lace his paper cup drink with ink ... and so begins our initial look at the life and hard times of an antihero. The movie's conclusion comes full circle back to another Sunflower promotional meeting with a now retired "fighting milkman." Granted, Kaye has become part of management and is giving the sales pitch. But the dangers of professional boxing (physical violence and ego-producing personality change) have been put safely behind him. Or, have they? Ironically, there is a comic edginess — a potential for pomposity in Kaye's speaker — which suggests another "normalization" exorcism will probably be necessary in the near future.

As a footnote to this framing device, both the opening and closing sequences also trick the viewer with an in-film joke. The movie's first images are of the beautiful "Goldwyn Girls," as central to the producer's films as Flo Ziegfeld's lovely "showgirls" were to his Broadway "Follies." *Brooklyn*'s sexy start has these long-legged dancers as farm girls in a dairy barn beginning the milking, with the prettiest of the crew providing a deadpan job description appropriate for all of Ziegfeld and Goldwyn's statuesque temptresses: "I don't do anything. I simply let them look at me." But just when the more strait-laced viewer might wonder how all this voluptuousness connects with a comic story about a Danny Kaye underdog, the segment concludes and one realizes

Though Mayo (right) provided the romantic sparks for Kaye, a brief comedy sketch with Fay Bainter was a *Kid from Brooklyn* highlight.

it was simply a Sunflower Dairy promotional film being shown to an audience of milkmen.

Conversely, the in-film concluding joke is more of a sudden bang. As *Brooklyn* appears to end, after the "fighting milkman" has become the most unlikely of champions, the whole movie is revealed to have been yet another PR movie for the dairy! But the trick seems somehow appropriate for a picture which frequently uses its high roller, good time characters (the Gabby Sloan boxing entourage) to feature beautiful Virginia Mayo or Vera-Ellen in a nightclub number. With each of the *Brooklyn* characters pre-established as professional entertainers, the story occasionally dovetails into variety show mode — a "something for everyone" tradition very popular with period audiences. This always close-to-show-business narrative helped simplify the inclusion of Kaye doing his "Pavlova" number at a pre-championship gala party.

Either to mask the sexiness of the subplots, or anticipate the "creaking" labeling some still affectionate reviewers would paste upon this feel-good remake of a Harold Lloyd film, one marketing ploy for this Kaye classic was to describe the setting as "the small town [Brooklyn] where the laughs come from."[27] Yet, "Big Apple" critics were full of kudos. The *New York World Telegram* advised, "Wear a hat when you go to see Danny and the rest of them [the cast]. You'll want it for tossing into the air when you come out of the Astor [Theater]."[28] New York's *PM* was almost poetic in the opening of their review: "Samuel Goldwyn's artistic chefs have whipped up Harold Lloyd's old *Milky Way* into a rather spectacular soufflé for the unique talents of Danny Kaye."[29] The *New York Journal American* said "Danny Kaye's new picture is his best yet, a buoyant comedy that's loaded with laughs."[30]

All in all, one might best summarize this Goldwyn dream factory attraction with another *New York Times* critical endorsement which appeared shortly after the newspaper's initial rave review: "...the incredible Danny Kaye gives a wildly hilarious performance amid surroundings that are easy on the eyes."[31] As the song lyric asks, "Who could ask for anything more?"

8

THE MARX BROTHERS
A Night in Casablanca (1946)

There is an apocryphal story that has British Prime Minister Winston Churchill watching a Marx Brothers movie when Hitler's Nazi sidekick Rudolph Hess parachuted into Great Britain (1940) during the early days of World War II. Even though a misguided Hess felt he could orchestrate an early peace, Churchill would not exit said film until its completion: "I wouldn't leave if Goebbels, Hitler, Goering and Hess all landed by parachute; they couldn't possibly be as funny as this."[1]

When the Marx Brothers as a team first retired from film (1941), predating America's entry into World War II, it appeared that the natural satirical mix of Groucho, Harpo, Chico, and Nazis would never happen. But fortuitously, shortly after the war, the team decided to cinematically reunite for a film about stolen Nazi loot and the surviving Hitler henchmen out to retrieve it. Set in the world's then favorite espionage capital, Casablanca (thanks to the Humphrey Bogart and Ingrid Bergman memorable movie of the same name, 1942), the Marx Brothers had a typical target for their saturation comedy. The same year (1946) that the Marxes' timely *Night* came out, several other post-war Nazi-related movies were released, including Orson Welles' *The Stranger* and Alfred Hitchcock's *Notorious*.

Before examining the Brothers' often inspired comeback picture, one should first address the catalyst for the comeback. One most often reads that Groucho and Harpo made the film to financially rescue a perennially broke Chico, whose gambling addiction debts to gangster types sometimes also put his life at risk. Probably a more balanced take on the subject came from Arthur Marx's entertainingly affectionate biography, *Life with Groucho: A Son's-Eye View* (1954): "[*Night* was made] mainly to keep himself [Groucho] from disappearing completely from the public eye [his solo career had yet to jell], but also because Chico was running out of money again..."[2]

Still, there were undoubtedly other factors pulling the Marxes back to the movies, starting with a loyal fan base. Even by the mid–1940s students of classic pictures were most taken with "one series of films to which a ... circle of devotees throughout the world return again and again: [Marx Brothers movies]."³ But the general rank and file fans wanted to see the Marxes reunited, too. Groucho, after entertaining at military bases throughout World War II, would reveal in an unpublished 1945 letter:

> The first thing I'm asked when I play service camps is, "When are you fellows going to make another picture?" As a matter of fact, this was one of the reasons for my return to the screen [*Night* was in pre-production] ... I don't care for movie acting and I'm not particularly eager about any other kind (other than radio and service camps) so I am doing this partly for my bank roll and partly for the boys—and when I say "the boys," I'm not referring to Harpo, Chico and Gummo [the one Marx Brother never to appear in the movies].⁴

Ironically, *A Night in Casablanca* is probably best known today for a whole series of published letters Groucho purportedly wrote to the Warner Brothers legal department concerning the studio's supposed contesting of the title use of Casablanca. The issue was whether Warners, because of its earlier celebrated film *Casablanca*, had exclusive rights to titular use of the city. The question generated a great deal of comic interest in 1945 and 1967, the latter date being when some of Groucho's correspondence was published in book form.⁵

Groucho's Warner letters are indeed humorous, fluctuating from comic outrage to outrageous comedy. For example, he asserts that if Warner Brothers has exclusive rights to Casablanca, then the Marxes have a similar claim to Brothers, because "Professionally, we were brothers long before you were."⁶ But in an obviously unpublished 1945 letter to longtime Midwestern friend Samuel Salinger, Groucho confessed:

> We spread the story that Warners objected to this title purely for publicity reasons. They may eventually actually object to it, although I don't think so.... At any rate, the publicity has been wonderful on it and it was a happy idea. I wish they would sue, but, as it is, we've had reams in the papers.⁷

Groucho nearly received his wish. Warners eventually lodged a formal complaint, but it was ironed out quickly in arbitration.⁸ Appropriately, one of the picture's premier con artists had applied this approach to real life. (Interestingly, Chico apparently had a legitimate gripe with Warners at this time, or maybe he was just playing huckster like his brother. Regardless, Chico briefly attempted to sue the studio over unauthorized use of his name in *Rhapsody in Blue*, 1945.)

A more basic non-controversial Marx Brothers tie to Warners' *Casablanca* had to do with the comedy team's natural affinity for mixing film parody with their satire. For instance, the team's seminal film *Duck Soup* (1933) spoofs the early sound era's fascination with the musical, besides doing a darkly comic number on war and politics. And the Marxes' tour de silly *Monkey Business* (1931) is even more pointed in its affectionate dismantling of the then emerging modern gangster genre. Thus, in *A Night in Casablanca* the team has a chance to spoof both that era's attraction to the aforementioned espionage movie thriller, and the period's newest cinema genre — film noir, or what "pulp fiction" writers referred to as "tough guy detective stories." But these pictures need not have a professional private eye. Often the protagonist is simply an amateur in the most dangerous of urban mysteries.

During the 1940s, moreover, the espionage thriller and film noir sometimes combined. Bogart's *Casablanca* would be an early prototype, though noir was still years from being labeled as such. One might add that the decade's closing classic example of this genre mix would be director's Carol Reed's *The Third Man* (1949, with an uncredited assist from Orson Welles, who so-starred). But that was in the film future for the Marxes; their mid–1940s target was *Casablanca*. In fact, the initial *A Night in Casablanca* script was meant to be a fairly specific spoof of the Bogart movie, including names like "Humphrey Bogus" and "Lowan Behold" (Lauren Bacall, Bogart's real life wife and sometimes film noir co-star, though not in *Casablanca*).[9] Thankfully, wiser heads prevailed, and the parody quotient was toned down to being more tastefully generic, with *Night* limiting most of its spoofing fun to simply unleashing the Marxes on noir and espionage.

The Marxes are arguably sound cinema's greatest team (my compromise to dissenters would be to credit Laurel & Hardy with a comparable silent film status), and the Brothers' theater of the absurd team needs no introduction.[10] But given *Night*'s comeback status, one should note a few basic dynamics of the team. The Marxes are the Cliffs Notes for early twentieth century American humor. The children of Jewish German immigrants to New York, the Marxes applied the hard knock experiences of their youth to comedy. That is, Groucho, Chico, and Harpo embraced variations of the con artist.

Con artist, confidence man, grifter, huckster, diddler ... whatever the name, the type has been around as long as there have been people. But this character has some special ties to American pop culture. In Edgar Allan Poe's 1844 comic essay on the confidence man, "Diddling: Considered as One of

Humphrey Bogart (center) and old flame Ingrid Bergman, with Dooley Wilson, in the film which launched countless parodies, *Casablanca* (1942).

the Exact Sciences," the watershed writer observed, "To diddle is his [Man's] destiny.... This is his aim — his object — his end. Perhaps the first diddler was Adam."[11] Although most associated with the horror genre, Poe was both a student of the diddle and an active practitioner. For example, his essay "The Balloon Hoax," about a fictitious three-day crossing of the Atlantic, was originally published as fact in the *New York Sun* newspaper. But Poe was just as apt to play diddler detective. In "Maelzel's Chess-Player," he offers a huckster's explanation as to how this "mechanical" figure seated in a box (a popular period attraction) could play chess: by hiding a small chess player inside!

Poe's work appears early in what might be called *the* huckster time and place: nineteenth-century America. Literary historian Susan Kuhlmann nicely describes the era's con artist as the "individualization of [America's] manifest destiny ... the belief that a free man may be whatever he claims he is, may have whatever his skills can win."[12] Kuhlmann goes on to suggest that the

Three variations on the confidence man, "top to bottom": Chico, Groucho, and Harpo in *A Night in Casablanca* (1946).

characteristics of those who "opened" our country — resourcefulness, adaptability, nomadic tendencies, and a desire to get ahead — also describe the con man. While most cultures, past and present, have no doubt had confidence men, there is recognition even outside this country of nineteenth-century America's special affinity for the genre.

Indeed, as early as 1855, French cultural commentator Charles Baudelaire linked this country's fascination with and fondness for the con man with the fact that "Americans love so much to be fooled."[13] That might seem like a strange claim to the contemporary reader, but literary historian Stephen Matterson bolsters the position by citing the great period success and popularity of America's greatest real-life huckster — P. T. Barnum.[14] Barnum's autobiography, *Struggles and Triumphs*, which also appeared in 1855 and was revised and updated throughout the showman's long life, is generally considered the most widely read book in America (after the Bible) during the second half of the nineteenth century. His biography represents a blueprint for success based on an affectionate kidding of the public. One could easily tie Groucho into this "affectionate kidding" category on appearance alone. Here is a diddler so false that even his big mustache and bushy hydraulic eyebrows are painted on. Throw in Groucho's bent-over, dirty old man loping gait and one has a character worthy of distrust even before he opens his mouth.

For shell-game purists, however, there is an occasional distinction that herein merits noting because of its unique applicability to the difference between the manipulative screen personas of Groucho and Chico: "A huckster gets out of town as quickly as he can. A con man doesn't have to leave until he wants." Based on this criterion, Groucho best qualifies as a "con man." His film persona's slickness is often anchored in a permanent position, which early in Groucho's screen career (at Paramount) was also assisted by power and prestige, such as being president of a college, *Horse Feathers* (1932) or of a country, *Duck Soup*. Thus, in the latter picture he sings:

> I'm strictly on the up and up,
> So everyone beware.
> If anyone's caught taking graft,
> And I don't get my share,
> We stand 'em up against the wall...
> And pop goes the weasel!

While Groucho's *Night in Casablanca* role is merely that of a hotel manager, he is still in charge and is entertainingly controlling towards his guests. When he receives a complaint by phone at the front desk, Groucho replies, "You've been up in your room three-and-a-half hours and your trunks haven't arrived? Well, put your pants on; nobody will know the difference." The mustached one's eternal con artist is defined by his machine gun-paced patter, like the German army's strategy for World War II — a "blitzkrieg" (lightening war). Like a cross between a general and a bribe-master, Groucho's hotel manager bluntly tells the staff:

> Never mind the staff! Assemble the guests. I'll tell them what I expect of them ... courtesy towards the employees. They must learn that a kind word will get them further with a bellboy or chambermaid than a couple of drinks. Of course, a kind word *and* a couple of drinks will get them still further....

A modern variation of this warp-speed comedy, which often eliminates the need for comic segues, can be seen in some of Robin Williams' later signature characters, such as the inspiredly manic radio monologues of his army DJ in *Good Morning, Vietnam* (1987). But whereas Williams' accelerated verbal slapstick seems to be merely a safety valve verbiage release for someone densely populated by multiple personalities, Groucho's tidal wave of talk is invariably a constant controlling con, often after sex or money. (In fact, his various film figures are sometimes given added cinematic powers, too. Groucho's "control" is periodically allowed to break the fourth wall, via direct address — the only Marx Brother seemingly aware of the viewer.)

A good example of Groucho's direct address con man, boldly honest about his sneakiness, is the first time he flirts with *Night*'s sexy femme fatale, Lisette Verea. After telling her, "I think you're the most beautiful woman in the whole world," Verea's character asks him if he really believes that. Staring into the camera, Groucho admits, "No, but I don't mind lying if it will get me somewheres."

If Groucho aspires to be a big-time "con man," Chico is a small-time "huckster," often facing a need to get "out of town as quickly as he can." Fittingly, Chico frequently plays street peddler types, whose exact whereabouts are in a constant state of flux. Consistent with this "road" scholar focus, which allows both easy access to an endless supply of suckers, and unlimited getaway options, Chico is the operator of Casablanca's Yellow Camel Taxi service.

Chico's slick patter often also spews out rather quickly. But because of his cute theatrical dialect, sometimes referred to as "ice cream Italian," there is not the hard sell huckster approach associated with Groucho. Moreover, due to comic stupidity, or American humor's "wise fool" mentality, Chico's verbal slapstick is not as polished as Groucho's. While the mustached one dazzles the viewer with provocative use of the language, such as his *Night* line,

"It's a funny thing. I've met a lot of pin-up girls but I've never been able to pin one down," Chico's misadventures in language often simply depend upon bad puns and malapropisms. Consequently, one is more susceptible to Chico's confidence man shtick, because this Marx Brother doesn't seem that bright. Appropriately, sometimes Chico wins by virtue of stupid persistence. For example, back in the Marxes' first film, *The Cocoanuts* (1929), in which Groucho was also a hotel manager, Chico's inability to differentiate between a "viaduct" and "Why-d-duck?" so wears down Groucho that he eventually concedes everything to his seemingly daff brothers. This is reminiscent of an old insult routine from vaudeville, "He was an idiot — all that was missing was a little hat with a propeller on it." Of course, one should keep in mind that the signature article of Chico's comedy costume is his almost pointed hat ... a variation on the dunce cap, from an earlier elementary school age.

Probably Chico's greatest bit of denseness occurs near the close of *Animal Crackers* (1930), when he shares his thoughts on what happened to a stolen painting. After much rambling he hypothesizes the work of art was eaten by "left-handed moths." Groucho's Captain Spaulding is at first speechless, eventually requesting that his brother, "Go away. I'll be all right in a moment." Recovering, he tells Chico, "I'd buy you a parachute if I thought it wouldn't open." But Chico immediately disables him with another stupid bad pun: "I got a pair of shoes [parachute]." This reduces Groucho to jumping up and down while holding his head and moaning.

One gets a semblance of Chico's mind-numbing persistence in *Night* by way of his lobbying Groucho over his need for a bodyguard. But once Chico is on the job, the disruptions to the mustached one's life only escalate. For instance, Chico brings in perennial assistant Harpo to test the food. Besides providing the perfect segue for the mad mute to perform his standard human billy goat eating of everything in sight (from a candle to a phone), Harpo destroys any chance of Groucho having supper. Thus, while a defensive Chico observes, "[You don't] want to get poisoned," an exhausted Groucho confesses, "I'm not sure that I'd mind anymore."

Ironically, while Groucho is the funny yet frightening, big-time future of the shakedown artist, Chico's throwback to the nineteenth-century huckster and humor's eternal wise fool invariably gets the best of his brother. This is consistent with that hoary maxim of humor being leery of authority. Yes, we enjoy Groucho because he often pricks the high and the mighty, but when he battles Chico it is the mustached one who invariably occupies the vulnerable authority position. As French film critic Louis Chavance wrote in 1932, "[Chico] is the smiling accomplice of the public."[15] His is the everyman prom-

As this picture from *A Night in Casablanca* demonstrates, while Groucho (center) often controlled others, his brothers Chico (left) and Harpo usually controlled him.

ise of the early small-change scam artist out to transfer "Manifest Destiny" into the individual profit column.

Surprisingly, *Night* even documents Chico's seemingly simple-minded huckster besting Groucho at his favorite activity — chasing women. The sexy aforementioned Lisette Verea, whose character lives at the hotel and is the mistress of Sig Rumann's in-hiding Nazi, constantly attempts to lure Groucho into a trap. Rumann's band wants to kill the hotel manager in order to better facilitate access to a walled-off room of stolen Nazi loot in the building. Their plan is to have Rumann, who is also in residence there under the alias Count Pfefferman, catch Groucho in a compromising position with his betrothed, and shoot Groucho — protected by an old school code of honor.

Chico, as his brother's bodyguard, constantly breaks up these trysts, necessitating that Groucho and Verea forever bounce back and forth between his room and hers. This then becomes the catalyst for the movie's most entertaining series of scenes, beginning with Chico's warning, after Verea has provocatively sauntered across the lobby, "But boss, I'm tryin' to keep you alive."

Groucho responds, "If I go that way [nodding towards the curvaceous retreating form of Verea], that's the way I want to go." The movie then cuts to later that evening, with Groucho arriving outside her room, loaded down with a large floral display, champagne in an ice bucket with retractable legs, and a huge food platter. With each Chico interruption, part of the comedy simply involves Groucho trying to repack things ... with additions, such as Verea's record player. The next time Groucho resorts to being a packhorse in front of her, she asks if he has everything. Groucho answers, "Well, I got enough to begin with." But the following romantic packing situation prompts a Groucho comment without a question. He observes, "If we're going to go steady, we'll have to get a small truck."

Chico's standard to-the-rescue interruption — a knock at the door, and some variation of "Do you have a woman in there?" — constantly has creatively comic twists. Initially, the viewer simply gives him bodyguard points for the dense persistence chronicled earlier. But in the final analysis of these almost sex scenes, he is more the *wise* fool. For example, gauge this brotherly exchange, spoken through a hotel door:

> CHICO: "Remember, I'm your bodyguard."
> GROUCHO: "I'm too old to have a bodyguard."
> CHICO: "Then you're too old to be in there."
> GROUCHO: (In direct address to the camera) "Well, it's pretty logical at that."

Still, the final comic twist on these attempted trysts favoring Chico is a surprise. Assuming the pattern will simply remain entertaining variations upon his aforementioned interruptions, the last time the viewer sees Groucho again weighed down by all his romantic baggage, he is the one in the hall knocking on Verea's door:

> CHICO: (From inside the door) "Hey Boss, you got a woman out there?" [Groucho's negative response produces the Chico bombshell:] Well, go away, I've got one in here." As Groucho leaves, Chico opens the door and grabs the champagne from his brother's assorted items.
> GROUCHO: "Save me the cork; I'm going fishing," which is spoken casually as he retreats down the hall.

This extended sexy series of *Night* scenes involving lovely Verea and the two contrasting Marx "diddlers," also represents Groucho simply being witty and wise towards the temptress. For instance, just after Verea has written a note to Rumann's wannabe assassin, revealing where her and Groucho's "movable feast" would next be, she flirtatiously turns to the mustached one and purrs, "You men are all alike."

In direct address to the camera, Groucho states, "Yeah, and don't let anyone tell you any different." This laugh-producing line is comic as yet another Groucho acknowledgement of his character's dirty-old-man mentality. But when one remembers that his character knows he is in danger, thanks to Chico's non-stop warnings and interruptions about Verea, the line has a funny fatalism concerning the extremes of his, or all men's, sexual obsessions. Pushing this dark envelope a step further, one could also credit Groucho's agreement that "men are all alike" as including Rumann's murder plot. That is, both the Nazi and this Marx Brother are using Verea. Groucho is quite content to have sex with someone, regardless of why she is making herself available, and Rumann coldly assigns his lover the task of being sexual bait.

Though such musings might seem rather deep dish for a Marx Brothers movie, they do address world weary issues consistent with the noir thriller genre *Night* is spoofing. For instance, the aforementioned Hitchcock movie *Notorious* has secret agent Cary Grant falling for party girl Ingrid Bergman, who consents to help break a post–World War II Nazi ring in South America. But what she does out of love for Grant (winning the heart of Claude Rains' likeable villain), all but destroys Grant emotionally. Now, while no one is putting *Night* on the analytical level of a pivotal Hitchcock vehicle, the Marxes' parody offers a multi-faceted look at their noir thriller target, for anyone willing to read between the lines.

If Groucho and Chico are two extremes of the American diddler, the modern "con man" versus the old-fashioned huckster, Harpo's take on the subject is other worldy, which is reinforced by his silence. An arty "reading" of Harpo the diddler might be to call him surrealistic, a runaway id on holiday. But in many ways he is simply an amoral little child out to be entertained. His tricks are not so much cons as they are inventive pranks or acts of self-defense. This persona mix of instant gratification and protection was born during Harpo's childhood. Chico's real life addiction to gambling had surfaced early, which resulted in him pawning everything that was not nailed down in the Marx Brothers' various childhood homes. From this "gone in 60 seconds" scenario, young Harpo developed a "one day at a time" philosophy, especially in terms of not building up any stockpile of boyhood treasures. Harpo's change went for readily disposable things, from food to film tickets.

The threat of Chico's five-finger removal service eventually inspired the surreal in Harpo, anticipating his comedy character by years. To safeguard a

Harpo (right) and Groucho as children (circa 1905).

cherished pocket watch, Harpo removed its hands. No matter that it no longer told the time: it was now "Chico-proof."[16] Thus, unlike the nightmare symbolism of a handless clock of death in Ingmar Bergman's art house *Wild Strawberries* (1957), Harpo's action was an off-beat comic victory of life — perfectly in keeping with the reasons his later screen character became so celebrated.

Harpo's delightfully eccentric joys could also be a pathos-tinted window to childhood poverty. For instance, though the Marx family had only one left-footed ice skate, Harpo managed to be entertained at length haphazardly making his way along the border of the frozen pond in New York's Central Park, one shoed foot on the bank, one skated foot on the ice.

There seems a direct link between Harpo's early reframing of real world negatives, to the comedian's duel scene in *Night*. As Rumann's valet, he is physically mistreated, not unlike Harpo's situation in *A Night at the Opera* (1935). When Rumann's assistant (Frederick Glerman) continues this abuse by drawing a sword, the mad mute suddenly surfaces in the protective gear of a baseball catcher. Eventually, a sword duel evolves, which showcases a Harpo parrying style that might have drawn from his combination shoe and skate misadventure in Central park. That is, he fluctuates between the graceful movement of a swashbuckling Errol Flynn, and a funny little two-step movement jump (an exaggeration of his opponent), where one foot comes down hard in a stomp, like someone trying to cover loose change. Naturally, just like his childhood "duels" with Chico, Harpo prevails against Glerman, eventually reducing this assistant villain to exhaustion, while the comically bored silent Marx Brother yawns and begins munching an apple.

Just as Harpo wins his one-on-one challenge, the Marx Brothers team slowly wears down the Nazi gang, whose inherent dummkopf tendencies (the lovely Lisette Verea notwithstanding), are immeasurably enhanced by Sig Rumann's Nazi count. This gifted character actor (1884–1967) was actually born in Germany, though stage work brought him permanently to the United States during the 1920s. He specialized in caricatures of Prussian pomposity, though the Prussian part was optional, such as his often flustered Soviet emissary in the watershed Ernst Lubitsch picture *Ninotchka* (1939, with Greta Garbo). Rumann's standard pompous shtick was a great addition to the Marxes' best MGM pictures, *A Night at the Opera* and *A Day at the Races* (1937). And his mere presence enhances *A Night in Casablanca*, though he has no lines as memorable as his movie-defining dark comedy analogy between Nazi Germany and Jack Benny's acting in Lubitsch's *To Be or Not To Be* (1942, see earlier chapter): "What he did to Shakespeare, we are now doing to Poland."

As with Margaret Dumont, who graced so many Marx Brothers pictures, Rumann upped the comedy quotient of any movie in which he was cast. But unlike Dumont, whose gift was always playing this entirely humorless grande dame of society (which made her actually very humorous), Rumann's large bulging eyes, lumpy body, and bald dome (*Night*'s script utilized some toupee gags) made him visually cartoon funny even without lines.

Still, it would have been fun for Rumann's irate Nazi to catch Groucho in bed with Verea. But then all those brilliant Chico interruptions would have been unnecessary. Maybe a compromise topper to even best the surprise of Chico seemingly bedding Verea, would have been a later non sequitur scene where Rumann comes back to his own Casablanca hotel room, disgusted at the murder plot's failure, only to catch *Harpo* in a compromising situation with Verea.

Unlike Rumann, someone new to the Marxes also provided a visual boost to *Night*—writer Frank Tashlin (1913–1972). His background as a former cartoonist was just starting to be utilized in live action personality comedies during the latter half of the 1940s. Though he only received an "Additional Material" credit on this Marx Brothers picture, he provided Harpo with one of his greatest ever sight gags. *Night*'s introduction to the silent one has him casually leaning against a building. Yet another Casablanca Hotel manager has been murdered (the position soon to be Groucho's), and all "the regular suspects" (a footnote to a line from Bogart's *Casablanca*) are being rounded up. The comic implication is that Harpo is a perennial police suspect, with a dragnet cop sarcastically asking him, "What do you think you're doing? Holding up the building?" Harpo gives the policeman a goofy affirmative nod, and then to demonstrate his slapstick power, he takes his extended hand from said building. The place collapses into a pile of rubble.

Tashlin was also responsible for a visually creative later *Night* scene, in which the Marxes are searching the assorted trunks in the living room of Sig Rumann's hotel suite, unaware he is in the adjoining boudoir. Startled that the Nazi will discover them, Chico hides in a huge upright steamer trunk, Harpo occupies a more traditional treasure chest-type trunk, and Groucho slips into a closet. (This is a comically logical move for the sex-obsessed Groucho, because as he later explains to a nervous Chico, "Take it easy, this isn't the first time I've hid in a closet.")

What follows is an effectively choreographed series of movements, as Rumann attempts to pack and the ever elusive Marxes undo everything, as well as play "musical chairs" with their assorted hiding places. For example, Rumann takes a full (with Groucho) top coat from the closet and hangs it up in the steamer trunk. But as the densely populated coat is being so placed, Chico is able to briefly slip outside the trunk. As Rumann then turns his back to retrieve more clothing, Groucho manages to rehang himself in the closet, and Chico once again re-enters the large trunk.

This comic "dance" continues with several entertaining variations, periodically topped off with Rumann's growing panic that he is losing his mind—since packed things are suddenly unpacked, followed by simply disappearing — the Marxes like to give some variety to their chaos. Thus, Rumann starts to mix packing with drinking. But just as the sketch seems to have exhausted every possibility, all three Marxes end up in the closet, with the still unsuspecting Nazi dummkopf trying to get in. Yet, each innocent movement of a sliding door by Rumann produces a matching motion of an opposite end sliding door by the hidden Marxes — which keeps them hidden. While not as inspired as the team's acclaimed mirror sequence from *Duck Soup*, in which a Groucho-like Harpo plays his brother's reflection, the magic of Tashlin's routine is also sold by its perfectly synchronized movements. Fittingly, the cartoonish Tashlin would soon go on to write and direct several great comedians in such signature comedies as Bob Hope's *The Paleface* (1948, co-script), Red Skelton's *The Fuller Brush Man* (1948, co-script), and Martin and Lewis' *Artists and Models* (1955, script and direction).

The reviews for *A Night in Casablanca* were invariably full of praise, such as the *Hollywood Reporter*'s nonstop rave: "It has been five years since they appeared in a picture, and it is a joy to herald the return of Harpo, Groucho and Chico in as hilarious an entertainment as" this film.[17] But an early review in *Variety* possibly helped establish a sort of left-handed compliment to the praise: "A Marx Bros. picture is ripe for public consumption, and while this isn't the best they've made it's a pretty funny farce."[18] Indeed, the notable pioneering film critic James Agee stated a close variation of this sentiment in his *Nation* critique. Yet Agee, the sometimes poet, gave an added eloquence to his critique comments about the Marxes:

> ... it is unnecessary to urge anyone who has ever enjoyed them to see "A Night at Casablanca." It is also beside the main point to add that it isn't one of their best movies ... [but] the worst they might ever make would be better worth seeing than most other things I can think of.[19]

Agee's review went on to suggest that because no audience could fully appreciate the "sophisticated wit" of the team's mustached leader, "I suspect that we lose, in Groucho, the funniest satirist of the century."[20]

Time magazine was simply happy to open their notice by stating: "*A Night in Casablanca* restores the Marx Brothers to the screen, which has been deprived of their irreplaceable weirdness for five years."[21] And among the critic's balanced praise for each of the Marxes, he revealed an entertainment insider's knowledge of comedy by quoting humorist-actor Robert Benchley's obscure take on Chico's "shooting the keys" piano technique: "Chico, whom Bob Benchley called 'the Annie Oakley of the piano,' obliges on that instrument as pleasantly as ever [in *Night*]."[22]

The *Canadian Forum*'s D. Mosdell brings the viewer back full circle to the original parody catalyst for the Marxes, and pronounces it a success:

> Mix all ... [the noirish basics of *Casablanca*] with Ingrid Bergman and Humphrey Bogart and you get heavy romance; mix it with the Marx Brothers, and a more sanguine observer might imagine that you get a Casablanca picture to end all Casablanca pictures, since nothing with the slightest claim to high seriousness will ever be able to happen there again.[23]

What makes Mosdell's review most interesting, however, is its sometimes satirical jabs at period critics hedging their praise by claiming the Marxes sometimes return to variations on old material, or that Groucho is too deep dish for viewers to appreciate. For example, Mosdell addresses both these complaints in the following tweaking of the aforementioned Agee:

> At the risk of identifying myself with Agee's bucolic audience, I should say flatly that Groucho is an excellent clown who ... makes some of the oldest and worst lines in the world sound funny. "Marriage is impossible," says the nominal [romantic subplot] hero of the picture. "Not until after you're married," replies Groucho with a roll of his enormous eyes. It is his wittiest, though not his funniest line, and as far as I could judge the audience had no trouble getting it.[24]

The only mean-spirited review reference to the Marxes' material sometimes seeming dated was a *New York Times* crack by Thomas M. Pryor, "They still are wonderfully funny when hitting on all six but too often ... the gags sound as wheezy as an old Model T Ford...."[25] Of course, this was tempered by a quick follow-up *New York Times* profile of the team and their new movie written by the newspaper's top film critic, Bosley Crowther. Entitled "Those Marx Men," it minimizes any problems about "old stuff," and ultimately gives them the pantheon treatment: "They are in a class with Charlie Chaplin and the best that the Keystone age produced."[26]

The paradox in any critical complaint about the Marxes and dated gags is that the subject has been part of the team's baggage from the beginning of their screen career. For example, in gifted critic and later filmmaker Pare Lorentz's review of the Marxes' *Horse Feathers* (1932), he baldly states: "It is accurate enough to say they do nothing new in this one but if they did anything novel they wouldn't be the Marx Brothers. You either like them or you don't. I like them...."[27] And this was the film that put the team on the cover of *Time* magazine (August 15, 1932).

What Lorentz was really suggesting is that the Marxes had honed their unique surreal slapstick through years of vaudeville. Moreover, even their first

Paradoxically, while the Marxes normally get away with murder, *A Night in Casablanca* finds Chico (left), Groucho (center), and Harpo briefly jailed for doing the right thing.

two films, *The Cocoanuts* (1929) and *Animal Crackers* (1930), were screen adaptations of the team's Broadway hits. A Marx Brothers aficionado, like any fan of a given personality comedian, simply expected and savored a certain comfortingly familiar shtick (with modest variations) from their film favorites. As *New York Sun* critic Eileen Creelman observed, "The Marx Brothers are back and ... 'A Night in Casablanca' is good news for the people who liked the comics in their youth, both vaudeville and stage."[28]

A Night in Casablanca, with a script polished and reworked by the Marxes in a series of pre-production live shows at various military bases, gives fans of the team a quality final film creatively anchored in what the team does best. Plus, as movie historian Leonard Maltin notes, "[*Night* also restored] some of the spirit lost in the last M-G-M films and ... provided some honestly amusing moments."[29] Chico and Harpo would cinematically join forces one more time in the disappointing *Love Happy* (1949, with essentially a cameo by Groucho) but *Night* better represents a quality close to the team's screen career.

Regardless, a tongue-in-cheek explanation Groucho had made for what was to have been the team's original retirement film, *The Big Store* (1941), has never remotely come to pass: "...the people are about to get sick of us. By getting out now we're just anticipating the inevitable public demand...."[30] Instead, with more than a little irony, the iconoclastic Marxes have become icons of comedy. But do not try to make sense of that. Instead, follow Groucho's hotel manager's lead in *Night*; after creating chaos by suggesting all the room numbers be randomly scrambled (with someone complaining, "Think of the confusion"), the mustached one opines, "But think of the fun."

9

HAROLD LLOYD
The Sin of Harold Diddlebock (1947) (a.k.a. *Mad Wednesday*)

> *Silent comedy great Harold Lloyd was also adept at the verbal quip. When writer and director Preston Sturges first introduced him to his* Sin *co-star, the beautiful but tall model actress Frances Ramsden, Lloyd said, "You know, Preston, she can eat beans off the top of my head."*

By the mid–1940s, celebrated silent comedian Harold Lloyd (1893–1971) had been in screen acting retirement since the indifferent critical and commercial response to *Professor Beware* (1938). The clown that critic James Agee would later (1949) lionize (with Charlie Chaplin, Buster Keaton, and Harry Langdon) in the famous *Life* magazine essay, "Comedy's Greatest Era," had had less success during the sound era.[1] This was in marked contrast to the silent 1920s, when Lloyd's industrious optimistic "squared" boy-next-door persona eventually made him the highest paid performer in filmland.

Lloyd's signature movie, *Safety Last* (1923), with the comedian's defining thrill-comedy skyscraper-climbing extended sequence, is the perfect metaphor for the actor's perennial story: "climbing" to success. Lloyd himself was without the physical grace and skills of Chaplin and Keaton, but he compensated for this with a nonstop manner married to a Puritan work ethic; he was a latter-day Horatio Alger on speed. Still, the Lloyd silents are also funny because they merge ageless gags, such as the basted-together suit that begins to come undone in *The Freshman* (1925), and a zanily upbeat young man whose ambitious innocence is still winsome, though without the emotional complexities that make Chaplin's Tramp so fascinating.

What hurt Lloyd in the 1930s, besides the public's new fascination with dialogue-emphasized comedy (over slapstick), was the onset of the Depression. Cynical sorts with worldly wise cracks were suddenly the screen clowns

The iconic image from Haroly Lloyd's thrill-comedy defining film, *Safety Last* (1923).

with which to be reckoned, such as Groucho Marx, Mae West, and W. C. Fields. And at a time when even the most hard working of Americans were struggling to keep their jobs, the young "can do" spirit of Lloyd's persona suddenly seemed passé. Ironically, a final liability for Lloyd was that even his sure thing component, thrill comedy, was hurt by sound. That is, no matter how wonderfully edgy the comic stunts (and Lloyd's minimal use of doubles enhanced the action), without sound there was almost a surreal one-step-removed-from-reality base. Thus, as in a Road Runner cartoon, one could be comically thrilled without being concerned for the safety of Wile E. Coyote and his inevitable over-the-cliff scene. In contrast, when Lloyd is actually yelling for help in his first sound picture, *Welcome Danger* (1929, which reworks material from *Safety Last*), much of the humor slips away — too real.

All this, however, is not to say that his sporadic sound films were not without interest. Indeed, his collaboration with gifted film comedy auteur Leo McCarey on *Milky Way* (1936, about a milkman turned boxer) found almost universal critical acclaim. In fact, the *Chicago Tribune* reviewer observed, "When it really gets under way it has the Chaplin movie [*Modern Times* had opened earlier that year] beat by a mile."[2] Though one would be hard pressed to find that assessment today, *The Milky Way* remains a wonderfully inventive picture that briefly encouraged viewers, like the *New York Herald Tribune* critic, to rediscover Lloyd:

> "The Milky Way" proves to be an exceptionally diverting cinema farce. I do not recall all of Mr. Lloyd's silent films well enough to make any comparisons but I can assure you that the new photoplay at the Paramount Theater represents by far the best work the Lloyd workshop has accomplished since the screen began to talk.[3]

Though this film did not catapult Lloyd to new sound era heights, a curious phenomenon was underway by the mid–1940s — a Hollywood revival of interest in the comedian and his persona had occurred. As examined in an earlier chapter, one of the decade's most talented writer-directors (Preston Sturges) had affectionately satirized a Lloyd-like character and small-town setting in the box office smash — *The Miracle of Morgan's Creek* (1944). Moreover, the picture's male lead (Eddie Bracken, whom servicemen frequently voted their favorite comic actor during World War II), defined his antiheroic persona in Lloyd terms.

At approximately the same time, power producer Samuel Goldwyn signed the then Broadway comedy sensation Danny Kaye and orchestrated a multi-picture deal which would turn his protégé into a sound era Lloyd. Goldwyn even went so far as to remake Lloyd's best sound film, *The Milky Way*, as a vehicle for Kaye — *The Kid From Brooklyn* (1946, see previous chapter).

Lloyd's on-screen hibernation from the movies did not blind him from this renewal of interest in his work. In early 1946 the comedian won a $50,000 damages suit against Universal on film plagiarism charges, successfully claiming that *So's Your Uncle* was patterned after his early sound picture *Movie Crazy* (1932). And in March of the same year (1946) Lloyd filed a similar "double-barreled [federal court] action against Columbia ... [asking] in separate suits ... $250,000 each for plagiarism."[4] Lloyd claimed Universal's two-reeler, *Three Wise Fools*, plagiarized his *The Freshman*, and that the comedian's aforementioned *Movie Crazy* was the basis for another Universal short subject, *Local Boy Makes Good*.

Fittingly, these multiple court cases were hitting the papers at a time Preston Sturges' collaboration with Lloyd, *The Sin of Harold Diddlebock*, was nearing completion. A partial catalyst for the picture was Sturges' success with *The Miracle of Morgan's Creek*, and a follow-up Lloyd-related gentle satire, *Hail the Conquering Hero* (1944, also co-starring Eddie Bracken). Sturges and Bracken next flirted with doing a sound remake of a Lloyd silent, like *Grandma's*

Boy (1922), or *The Freshman*. However, Sturges decided, "Why not get Lloyd himself?" Accomplish this casting coup and he had a creative chance at an inspired mix of new and old — another satirical tweaking of the Lloyd persona ... *but with Lloyd himself.* Plus, instead of a remake, use the climatic comic conclusion of *The Freshman*, in which Lloyd's college football sub somehow manages to win the big game, as the opening for a new film about the comedian's go-getter persona twenty-two years later. Sturges had concocted a brilliant comic plan, given that Lloyd's involvement would give the picture an added legitimacy, sort of an "authorized satire" status. Add to this some comically cynical introspection by the former "what cheer" character, and the viewer also has a potential invitation to some bittersweet poignancy. Lloyd might have sued Sturges ... had he *not* come up with this scenario.

Of course, a Lloyd–Sturges collaboration had a built-in capacity for dissent, too. That is, one artist's affectionate satire can also ultimately be offensive to the target (Lloyd). Sadly, a variation of this phenomenon occurred in the latter half of the *Sin* production. Lloyd had been fine with Sturges' idea for a sort of darkly comic *Freshman* sequel, what film critic and biographer Richard Schickel later described as a potentially "touching examination of what might have happened to Lloyd's football hero ... after he entered the adult world."[5] But while both Sturges and the comedian wanted to cut from Lloyd's young man-on-the-make screen alter ego to a middle-aged failure surrounded by now ironic signs — such as "Success is just around the corner" — the two artists differed on just how the title character should address being laid off. Total cynic Sturges wanted to again play the comic randomness of life card he had so effectively used to close *The Miracle of Morgan Creek*. Conversely, Lloyd wanted to revert to his figure's traditional values:

> In order to get himself out of this trouble [being fired and a drunken lost Wednesday], he [Harold Diddlebock] has to start thinking again. And when he begins thinking, he returns to his original [successful] character.[6]

Adding to the Lloyd–Sturges differences was the comedian's perception that the film's conclusion, as the production started, was still open-ended — his go-getter persona could resurface triumphant. Yet, as film historian John Belton has suggested, Sturges' merry milieu, especially in *Sin*, merely embraces a darkly comic given of the post–Great Depression world:

> Lloyd still participates in the middle-class American success myth but both Lloyd and the myth have lost their ideals. No longer are industry, energy, and ingenuity necessarily rewarded. Lloyd and his success myth have fallen victim to experience.[7]

The unlikely football star (Lloyd) in the close of *The Freshman* (1925), which opens *The Sin of Harold Diddlebock* (1947).

Lloyd's "success myth" is still a valuable part of the "American dream." Yet, it is handicapped here by not only 1940s reality, but by conflicting comedy genres — Lloyd's "anything is possible" populism versus Sturges' darkly comic world view. One is always free to embrace any -ism, comic or otherwise. But Lloyd signing on with Sturges always had the potential for creative sparks.

The good news is that *Sin* is an excellent picture, if one embraces the Sturges perspective. While the writer-director often shot two versions of each scene (Sturges versus Lloyd) — which is one of the reasons the film went way over budget — Sturges usually went with his own take. Their differences were undoubtedly heightened by the fact both of these comedy artists could have doubled as humor scholars. For example, Lloyd's earlier memoir, *An American Comedy* (1928, written with Wesley W. Stout), is essentially a dissertation on laughter filtered through an autobiography, with chapters like "Recipe for a Laugh."[8] And while Sturges' own insightful on humor memoir would not surface for decades (posthumously published in 1990, thirty-one years after his death[9]), the writer-director was entertainingly articulate about comedy whenever journalists cornered him, such as film critic and scriptwriter Frank Nugent's early 1945 *Variety* essay, "Genius with a Slapstick." Nugent shared Sturges' own laws of what govern film box office, a list composed during the director's early Hollywood days (1934):

1. A pretty girl is better than an ugly one.
2. A leg is better than an arm.
3. A bedroom is better than a living room.
4. An arrival is better than a departure.
5. A birth is better than a death.
6. A chase is better than a chat.
7. A dog is better than a land-scape.
8. A kitten is better than a dog.
9. A baby is better than a kitten.
10. A kiss is better than a baby.
11. A pratfall is better than anything.[10]

An added paradox to these jousting artists was that both were fans of physical comedy. Though this is hardly news when applied to a silent comedian like Lloyd, Sturges' well-deserved reputation as arguably Hollywood's greatest writer of witty dialogue also came with a healthy regard for visual shtick, as underlined in the aforementioned law number eleven of Sturges' guide to box office success: "A pratfall is better than anything." Essay profiles of the director often even heralded his unexpected sound era celebration of physical comedy in their titles, such as the *New York Times'* Bosley Crowther's 1944 article, "When Satire and Slapstick Meet,"[11] or Nugent's "Genius with a Slapstick." Maybe this was stated most poetically when playwright Alexander King aptly called Sturges, in yet another period profile of the writer-director: "The Toscanini of the pratfall."[12]

Sturges' dialogue, which he once defined as "the bright things you would like to have said except that you didn't think of them in time," is, however, more apt to operate independently of the visual than in the work of his similar film comedy contemporary, director Howard Hawks.[13] That is, Hawks once observed, "I don't use funny lines. They're not funny unless you see them."[14] For instance, in Hawks' screwball comedy classic, *Bringing Up Baby*, Cary Grant's absentminded professor type (modeled upon Lloyd's persona) finds himself all but kidnapped to a Connecticut estate by a society madcap played by Katharine Hepburn. Once there his clothes are removed and he is forced to explore the setting in a lacy nightgown. Cornered for an explanation by another guest, the frustrated and feminine-attired Grant suddenly leaps into the air, explaining, "I went gay all of a sudden." Grant's observation is not intrinsically funny, but coupled with his jumping visual the line is hilarious.

In contrast, Sturges' first cousin to Oscar Wilde dialogue is funny, with or without a visual. To illustrate, as Lloyd's *Sin* character exits his accounting office after being fired, he stops at the work area of a young woman with whom he has fallen in love, beautiful Miss Otis (Frances Ramsden). He confesses that he had also wanted to marry each of her lovely six older sisters, all of whom had previously worked, one after another, in the same department. But financial problems and personal travail had kept even any engagements from happening — something of which Miss Otis is sympathetically aware. As Harold chronicles his background with these seven "Miss Americas," Sturges manages to both weave sexual innuendo in his stand alone comic dialogue, and still be true to Lloyd's practical axiom-spouting character. The following abbreviated excerpt demonstrates the witty power of Sturges' dialogue even on the printed page:

> HAROLD: "Your mother seemed to be making them [daughters] nicer each year...."
> MISS OTIS: "[By the fourth one] Mother had more practice."
> HAROLD: "Practice makes perfect."

Of course, if Sturges' dialogue acted more independently of the visual than a comparable Hawks scene, one could argue, as did famed critic Manny

Farber, that the pace of Sturges' verbal exchanges metaphorically linked his work to the fast forward physical action of silent comedy. In an essay co-authored with W. S. Porter, Farber noted:

> Sturges perversely thought up a new type of dialogue by which the audience is fairly showered with words. The result was paradoxically to speed up his movies rather than slow them down, because he concocted a special, jerky, spluttering form of talk that is the analogue of the old, silent-picture firecracker tempo.[15]

This analogy is brilliant, and perfectly consistent with how a young silent era Sturges, who idolized Lloyd's early comedies, might have attempted to reconfigure pioneering cinema's slapstick pacing with his (Sturges) later gift for writing dialogue.

The only creative snag with the comic pratfall parallels between Lloyd and Sturges is that the writer-director's first show business success came as a Broadway playwright with the hit *Strictly Dishonorable* (1929–30). In the theater, the play's words are sacred. But Sturges' early 1930s migration to Hollywood during the sound era gold rush (when the film capital was importing any East Coast writing talent for their suddenly "100% talking pictures"), the playwright soon learned that a film script was simply a starting blueprint for a movie production.[16] Sturges' eventual move to writing *and* directing, starting with *The Great McGinty* (1940), was in order to protect his writing. Thus, Sturges and Lloyd clashed over Sturges' seemingly sacred dialogue. In Tom Dardis' biography of the comedian, Lloyd discusses a *Sin* argument he had with the Sturges on this subject, filtered through the director's script obsession with Diddlebock buying a circus:

> There were so many themes that could have come in there. But he didn't want gags to come into it; he wanted this dialogue. But this [scene] called for [physical shtick] business, it just cried for it. I came to him with business, and he said, "Well, the business is too good for my dialogue!" I said, "Preston, this is terrible." He said, "It'll kill the dialogue." I said, "*Let* it kill the dialogue, what are we after? We're after entertainment, laughs."

To Sturges' credit, *Sin* showcases a great deal of slapstick, especially the film's framing device of opening with the comic conclusion of Lloyd's *The Freshman*, and ending with a revisionist homage to the comedian's signature thrill comedy. Conversely, Lloyd is also the recipient of some sparkling dialogue. One of the most inspired segments occurs in the bar run by character actor Edgar "slow burn" Kennedy, a frequent comic nemesis to many Laurel and Hardy screen misadventures, not to mention his tit for tat lemonade and peanut stand conflicts with Harpo and Chico Marx in *Duck Soup* (1933). After being fired, Harold has come in for the first drink in his life, which prompts bartender Kennedy to observe, "Yes, sir, you arouse the artist in me." Creating "The Diddlebock" drink for Harold, Kennedy waxes poetic, as only a Sturges supporting player can: "The cocktail should approach us on tiptoe, like a young girl, whose first appeal is innocence."

As this philosophy implies, "The Diddlebock" goes down too easily for Harold, the first time drinker. But alcohol energizes Lloyd's character, like Charlie Chaplin's Tramp after he accidentally sniffs cocaine in *Modern Times*. It also makes Harold periodically let out the strangest of yells. While Harold is unaware of being the source of this odd noise, the payoff for his character is suddenly having the ability to spout Sturges dialogue, too. A gravel-voiced Irish cop (Frank Moran) enters the bar to investigate that wild sound, and he has the following exchange with a still unknowing Lloyd:

> HAROLD: "To me it sounds like a Mongolian lynx and a wounded moose. Have you ever hunted a Mongolian lynx?"
> IRISH COP: "I have not."
> HAROLD: "How about a wounded moose?"
> IRISH COP: "Likewise."
> HAROLD: "You're probably better off."

The bottom line for this entertaining picture is that it had two chiefs ... but the one with the director's megaphone had the final say. So while Lloyd was disappointed with the movie's second half, *Sin* still plays as a successful Sturges film. Ironically, after the completion of the picture, Sturges would lose both final cut control of his footage, and even his general 1947 release. But prior to addressing that conflict, the Lloyd-Sturges collaboration, as it initially and briefly appeared to a few lucky viewers (before it was pulled from distribution), needs to be examined.

Exiting his former place of employment, Harold has gifted gorgeous Miss Otis (Sturges' then current lover) with a diamond ring, not as an engagement proposition, but as a farewell token. He has finally finished paying off the ring originally meant for, at various times, each of Miss Otis' lovely older sisters. Paradoxically, while Harold had recently planned to ask for her hand in marriage, fate had once again double-crossed him. Without a job, he would be unable to support her. But being ever the populist, Harold still wanted Miss Otis to have the diamond, so that her next suitor would neither be romantically delayed in saving for a ring, nor alibi that he could not afford one.

Out on the street, a goofy-looking little antihero named Wormy (Jimmy

Conlin) attempts to get a "loan" for the track (horse racing). Each request Wormy makes is denied by Harold with one of the practical, shopworn axioms with which he has previously led his life. But Conlin's comebacks are always more comically realistic:

> HAROLD: "A fool and his money are soon parted."
> WORMY: "Yeah, but think what beautiful memories he lays up." [Wormy requests money again but a reduced amount.]
> HAROLD: "He who lendeth money endeth friendship."
> WORMY: "That's all right. We ain't friends. I ain't even seen you before."

However, good things come of this chance encounter, since Harold eventually gives Wormy a tidy sum and the chronic gambler proposes that he buy his new benefactor a drink. The aforementioned "Diddlebock" drink experiment leads to a number of rash acts, from a new outfit (a loud checkered suit and cowboy hat), to Harold winning some huge longshot bets on the horses.

Sturges provides the obligatory montage of Harold at various nightclubs (including joining a line of beautiful French can-can dancers on stage), and a return to the track. The viewer next sees Harold waking up at the apartment of his sister Flora (Margaret Hamilton, the wicked witch actress from *The Wizard of Oz*, 1939). While he thinks it is merely the day after a wild drunken evening, the still "witchy" Hamilton (her signature type of supporting part), informs him that he was missing all-day Wednesday, too! The rest of the picture involves finding out just what happened on this "mad Wednesday," and then trying to fix it.

The most plot-pressing detail comes out rather quickly — Harold has purchased a circus! And with 37 lions, 14 tigers, and so on, he has to find either a buyer, or some food, quickly. But after he corners the original circus manager, played by Sturges regular E.L. Johnson (the cynical lawyer of *The Miracle of Morgan's Creek*), Harold comes to realize the difficulty of unloading this menagerie:

> CIRCUS MANAGER: "You couldn't make me an attractive offer, not if you got down on your bended knees knees and threw in a set of dishes."
> HAROLD: "I see."
> CIRCUS MANAGER: "You don't, but you will...."

And a trip to the "Kitty-Pooh Home for Hungry Cats," a shelter which also provides free pet food for owners down on their luck, is also a comic disaster ... after Harold and Wormy request three tons of liver! Yet, not withstanding Lloyd's aforementioned production complaint, that Sturges had not allowed enough of the comedian's persevering persona to resurface and solve things, the film does suggest the Harold character is again trying to take charge of his life:

> HAROLD: "Where there's a problem, there must be a solution. Where there's a mind, there must be thought. Do you follow me?
> WORMY: "Well, at a distance."

The inspiration Sturges writes for Harold even sounds more timely today. Mr. Diddlebock decides that since Wall Street banks are less than popular with the public, a good PR move for any of these financial institutions would be to buy his self-proclaimed "children's circus" and provide free passes for the young. Lloyd might have been disappointed, however, that his character's savvy business idea is minimized by the flamboyant way in which Sturges' script then sells the plan. The film cuts to a more lively Harold, decked out in that loud checkered suit — undoubtedly bolstered by a few "Diddlebock" drinks — bringing his circus idea to Wall Street with special flash: he is accompanied by a large lion (Jackie) on a leash.

Naturally, Harold and Jackie cause riots everywhere, but no immediate money offers are forthcoming, since it is hard to write a check when one is running. Worse yet, though good for the comedy, Jackie gets away and Harold's attempt to catch him lands both of them on a skyscraper ledge for some thrill comedy. Though the split-screen process shots are never so convincing that one is concerned about their plight, which eventually includes both Harold and Wormy dangling dangerously from a leash attached to the lion, for that very reason the viewer can simply enjoy this watered down tribute to the finish of Lloyd's *Safety Last*.

Once rescued, all three land in jail; even the lion is in an adjacent cell! Naturally, the incident makes all the New York papers, with one headline reading: "Lunatic with Lion Captured." But to paraphrase an old axiom, "There's no such thing as bad press, as long as they spell your name right." Sure enough, once the lovely Miss Otis bails them out, and some confusion is cleared up over just where Harold can be contacted, he is flooded with Wall Street offers for his "children's circus." The riot of wannabe owners comically rivals the pandemonium created by Harold's first promenade with Jackie the lion.

Ironically, among the certified checks coming Harold's way is one from his former boss. But just as the comedian's everyman character is about to pass out from excitement, he gets *the* offer. The simple note states: "Ringling Brothers Barnum & Bailey will TOP ALL BIDS." With Harold now getting that glassy-eyed fainting look, Edgar Kennedy's bartender is conveniently on hand to give the antihero a shot of the Diddlebock drink. Harold immediately lets out that sound of a "Mongolian lynx and a wounded moose" and the screen goes black.

He later comes to in his horse-drawn hansom cab (an enclosed carriage with a driver on top), which he had purchased on the aforementioned "mad Wednesday." With a nurse-like Miss Otis at his side, the two are leisurely traveling toward the end of the movie. Her look of beautiful wide-eyed innocence makes Miss Otis' explanation as to why Ringling Brothers Barnum & Bailey would pay such a record amount for a "children's circus" sound all the more satirically true — they did not like the idea of a "free circus," either for youngsters or the public in general!

Despite Miss Otis then giving Harold a huge check, the moment is ruined when he notices a wedding band on her finger. Paradoxically, now that he could actually support the last of the Otis family Miss Americas, she has already married. But Sturges immediately tops this twist by having the statuesque beauty suddenly getting the blues, too. It seems that "Mr. Diddlebock," as she still respectfully calls him, had married *her*, and goes on to explain:

> You mean you don't remember coming out to Flatbush in the middle of the night with a full orchestra and waking up the whole neighborhood while you told Mother it was about time you did something about [marrying] one of her daughters and then wrapping me in a long velvet ... window curtain and then galloping all the way back to New Jersey ... [for the ceremony]?

Her passionate but soft-spoken sexy revelation catches "Mr. Diddlebock" and the audience by surprise, and Harold speaks for everyone when he asks, "Are you sure of your facts, Miss Otis?"

When it is clear that these are the facts, Harold becomes apologetic, and implies concern about their twenty-plus year story age difference (thirty-plus years in real life) — stumbling over the phrase, "Looking at us together...." Yet, Harold cannot resist her loveliness, and finally alibis a modest defense which she parries with the most flattering of retorts:

> HAROLD: "Why didn't you resist me?"
> MISS OTIS: "Because you're irresistible."

The scene is comically poignant, and especially resonates with anyone who has lost his heart to a much younger partner. True or not, there is a need for an older lover to believe those "you're irresistible" words. Furthermore, one can assume author Sturges had more emotion invested in the scene than normal, since he was then romantically involved with Frances Ramsden (Miss Otis), and he was roughly Lloyd's age.

Yet, this is not simply a case of art imitating life. Sturges has always had a soft spot for portraying an older man's weakness around a young beauty. Indeed, Miss Otis' aforementioned revelation about Mr. Diddlebock serenading her with a full orchestra is reminiscent of Sturges' earlier *The Palm Beach Story* (1942), in which Rudy Vallee plays an older wealthy lover wooing a seemingly much younger Claudette Colbert character in the same way. And while it is a foregone conclusion that she will reconnect with her handsome, young, estranged husband (Joel McCrea), Sturges gerrymanders yet another surprise conclusion, when it is revealed that the couple each has an identical twin, and Vallee ultimately marries Colbert's clone of a sister!

In the case of *Sin*, Sturges makes Miss Otis' commitment to Harold quite passionate:

> It took you so long to make up your mind to join our family that now that we have you we don't think we better ever let you go ... I love you, Mr. Diddlebock.

Putting Miss Otis on the offense romantically makes the age difference more palatable, and anticipates a similar strategy by Cary Grant in the much later *Charade* (1963). Twenty-five years older than leading lady Audrey Hepburn, Grant had the script written so her character was the sexually aggressive one. To Grant, reversing the behavior would have appeared unseemly. Plus, a demonstratively supportive young lover can legitimize success and change in an older figure. For instance, years after *Sin*'s release, celebrated critic Andrew Sarris called it a "minor masterpiece," yet added the qualifier, "one cannot fully enjoy this film unless one shares Sturges' faith in the regenerative powers of middle age and in the motivational magic of a pretty girl like Frances Ramsden."[17]

"Motivational magic" or not, Sturges gives *Sin*'s close some romantic heat through dialogue innuendo. With the sale of his circus, Harold has become a wealthy man, and he tells the long-legged Miss Otis that "anything" he has is hers. Coming from what seems to have been an impoverished family background, her innocent yet suggestive reply promises more than the proverbial hope chest: "Everything that I have is yours, Mr. Diddlebock." Moreover, while their marriage has been revealed by Miss Otis early in the concluding hansom cab sequence, the growing sensuality of the scene makes Harold's epiphany-like final comment, after the obligatory movie closing kiss, ever so provocative: "That must be what I was doing all day Wednesday!"

(This is then followed by his mad Diddlebock drink-induced yell.) The safe reading of that end line is simply a reference to getting married. But the ultimately sexy mood of the entertainingly prolonged sequence suggests that Harold's sudden light bulb realization is that he and the gorgeous Miss Otis had been making love all day Wednesday.

Maybe Lloyd's later comments about Sturges not making the comedian's *Sin* character capable enough, despite some aforementioned evidence to the contrary, was anchored more in being incredulous over how his Harold could not remember doing the deed repeatedly with hot Miss Otis on that day, a time now synonymous with sex, à la "hump day"—a slang phrase first dating from this period. In fact, the provocative implication of the movie's new title, *Mad Wednesday*, might even have been a pop culture factor in creating (versus helping to disseminate) the phrase "hump day." Regardless, when *Sin* went into limited release in early 1947 the notices were strong, from the *Hollywood Reporter* headline, "'Diddlebock' Sturges Antic Sparked By Return of Harold Lloyd," to the opening of *Variety*'s review:

> Return to the screen of Harold Lloyd in almost any type of film vehicle would be a welcome note to film box office, and when the particular brand of Lloyd slapstick is combined with the zany touch of producer-director Preston Sturges ... box office in almost all situations [markets] can be expected to do top biz [business].[18]

And *Film Daily*'s rave review ultimately summarized, "This is an entertainment like what used to be in the old days."[19]

With all this promise, however, a strange thing then occurred. Producer Howard Hughes pulled the film from distribution. Sturges had made *Sin* through a partnership, California Pictures, with the millionaire aviator, businessman, filmmaker Hughes. The producer and director had become friends while Sturges was still at Paramount, and the world-classic eccentric would frequent the writer-director's night spot, The Player. Though there was a certain off-beat logic to their attraction — two multi-tasking iconoclasts who had succeeded in various fields outside of Hollywood — Sturges had to be aware of how Hughes' control tendencies had briefly derailed the careers of two other gifted movie directors, Leo McCarey and Howard Hawks.[20]

Hawks, who had had an earlier successful collaboration with Hughes on the gangster classic *Scarface* (1932), was unceremoniously sacked by the producer from *The Outlaw* (1943, the notorious "sex Western" that introduced Jane Russell). Though largely filmed by Hawks in 1941, Hughes would ultimately take the direction credit for a movie whose release was long delayed over censorship issues and the producer's reworking of the material. McCarey's interaction with Hughes never progressed to an actual production stage. But his contractual arrangement with Hughes, over the adaptation of a Hollywood exposé novel, contributed to a two-year lull before the release of a non–Hughes McCarey film.

Maybe Sturges thought his creative interaction with Hughes would be different. Or, possibly the writer-director was combining business with the further mining of the oddball millionaire for zany material, given that one Hughes biographer suggests Sturges drew part of his inspiration for *Sullivan's Travels* (1941) from the flyer turned film mogul's real life.[21] In Sturges' memoir he briefly suggests California Pictures was to be about artistic freedom for him, while allowing Hughes to remain financially involved in filmmaking during a period in which he was focusing on aviation interests.[22]

Regardless, the picture was not well-served by Hughes. Despite the positive 1947 reviews, the producer pulled the film from release until late 1950, when a re-edited version eleven minutes shorter appeared as *Mad Wednesday*, and now included a talking horse. The title change might have been the initial reason the producer had started his tweaking, given a May 1947 article in *Variety*: "Hughes reps [representatives] say the film was liked wherever it played but the title killed family trade since parents misinterpreted the word 'Sin.'"[23] The irony here is that Hughes would play the "family trade" card, after being most cinematically famous for making two movies which would purposely tested censorship code standards, *Scarface* and *The Outlaw*.

Sturges' original *Sin* title had been meant as a satirical punning title of Helen Hayes' Oscar-winning role in *The Sin of Madelen Chaudet* (1931), about a character who goes from simpleton to big city sophisticate ... before ending up in the gutter. But the comic connection was lost on most fans, despite the bumpkin to New York celebrity trajectory of Lloyd in Sturges' *Sin*—without the downer ending. Thus, in this one instance, Hughes' new title is possibly an improvement on the original. But all the producer's other changes are so much to the detriment of the film, that Hughes could be said to have broken the promise of Sturges' tongue-in-cheek motto for California Pictures: "Non Redolemus Pisce," Latin for "We Do Not Smell from Herring."[24]

The reviews for the *Mad Wednesday* release were mixed to good. For example, the *Saturday Review*'s Hallis Alpert wrote readers should tell their kids "they will have a comic experience far more rich and satisfying than anything Mr. [Bob] Hope and Danny Kaye could give them...."[25] In contrast, the *New York Times*' Thomas M. Pryor felt Hughes' version was "a curious mélange of ingenious comic spirit and lethargy," which sounds a lot like what happens when the editing is flawed.[26] *Cue* liked the film and even managed to add a positive sound bite from Lloyd: "I never retired. I just waited for the right story, and now I think I have it."[27]

Because Sturges' meteoric rise in the 1940s had just as quickly reversed itself by 1950, many of the follow-up reviews for *Mad Wednesday* seemed to key on simply being happy about having the great Lloyd return, from the aforementioned *Cue* review being entitled, "Harold's Back Again," to the *Los Angeles Examiner* critique heading, "Lloyd Film Laugh Maker."[28] Plus, maybe a new decade already weighed down by the communist witch-hunting of the conservative right merely relished even a truncated comedy anchored by the closing reel of a 1920's silent comedy. Otherwise, why would the aforementioned *Examiner* review feel compelled to request:

> We hope that those who are looking for subversives under every doorstep will not take the lines of this film literally [about kidding capitalistic Wall Street] but will accept them for the delightfully satirical nonsense they are.[29]

The *Los Angeles Times* even apologized for praising *Mad Wednesday*'s "crazy anachronistic" spirit.[30]

All in all, one has to love the original director's cut of a movie, in which a legendary comedy star suffers his first experience of camera shyness in the last scene of his final film ... for the most surprising of reasons. Lloyd is afraid of planting a closing kiss on this leading lady because he is worried about how her jealous lover *and* writer-director of *Sin* will respond! Yet, everything worked out okay for Lloyd. The delayed early 1950s re-emergence of the film, even in a flawed format, no doubt helped jump-start the

Lloyd shortly after receiving an honorary 1952 Oscar for lifetime achievement as a "master comedian and good citizen" (March 19, 1953).

push for the comedian to finally receive a lifetime achievement Oscar (1952). Fittingly, the citation for the award sounded like the beginning of a satirical line Sturges might have written for *Sin*: "Harold Lloyd, master comedian and good citizen." As the old axiom goes, "The truth is out there ... and it is funny."

10

BOB HOPE
My Favorite Brunette (1947)

Bob Hope's Brunette *opens with his character on San Quentin's death row: "This is the worst last meal I ever had." And when there is no word from the governor on commuting his sentence, he adds, "Well, I'll know who not to vote for next time."*

Given the amazing 1940s critical and commercial success of nonstop entertainer Bob Hope (1903–2003) in assorted media, as well as his standing as, to borrow a Will Rogers line, " a self-made [American] diplomat," one could arguably credit the comedian with being the decade's top box office funny man, too.[1] Thus, this text again examines one of his watershed films. But whereas an earlier chapter focused upon the best of his inspired teamings with Bing Crosby, the *Road to Utopia* (1946), *Brunette* is, for my money, Hope's most important movie ... in *any* decade.

While there is no denying the great chemistry between the sometimes team of Hope and Crosby, allowing the ski-nosed comedian to go it alone better showcases his versatility. The *Road* pictures, as brilliantly funny as they are, represent a dumbing down of Hope, as the smart aleck–antihero dichotomy delineated earlier factors out, with Crosby as the wise guy and Hope as the comic boob. Though this divide is not so extreme as that demonstrated by Bud Abbott and Lou Costello, once a Hope fan has savored his full comic range, anything less seems like a muting.

Brunette, however, remains anchored in what Hope does best — personality comedian meets parody. Consequently, while the *Road* movies spoof the broad umbrella category of action adventure films, or just movies in general, the comedian's best solo outings often derail a specific genre, from the haunted house horror target of *The Cat and the Canary* (1939), to *The Paleface* (1948) sideswiping the Western. *Brunette* is primarily a parody of film noir (literally, black cinema), a mystery thriller genre then at the height of its

The "Road" picture dumbing down of Bob Hope might best be represented by this comic *Road to Morocco* (1942) still, with Dorothy Lamour. In contrast, *My Favorite Brunette* (1947) finds him prepared to give tutorials on love.

popularity in 1947. (See also this text's chapter on *A Night in Casablanca*, 1946.)

Film noir is synonymous with the world weary, man-in-the-middle detective, such as Dashiell Hammett's seminal Sam Spade in the 1941 film adaptation of *The Maltese Falcon*, or novelist Raymond Chandler's equally significant Philip Marlowe in the 1946 movie take on *The Big Sleep*, with both private-eyes being played by Humphrey Bogart. (Though there are differences between Spade and Marlowe on the printed page, the deviations are blurred in *film* noir because Bogart played both roles in key screen adaptations.)

Period critics' praise for Hope's *Brunette* naturally made reference to this new (noir) variation on the detective mystery, with the occasional literary tie-in, too. For example, *Time* magazine said, "*Brunette* is a well-roasted rib of the fancy talk and fancy incident served up by Raymond Chandler and other authors of the rough and tough school [also labeled 'tough guy fiction'].[2] And *Newsweek* even laced its noir footnote with a satirical wit befitting the novelist: "[Hope's character is a variation of] Chandler's Philip Marlowe who has been raised on 'Winnie-the-Pooh'...."[3]

Chandler's usurping of Hammett in these reviews is probably because he had a higher mid–1940s presence in this emerging genre. Chandler was a more prolific novelist than Hammett and had also spectacularly adapted both his own original material to the screen (*The Blue Dahlia*, 1946) as well as another architect of noir, James Cain, whose novel, *Double Indemnity*, Chandler co-scripted with Billy Wilder. Plus, Hope's *Brunette* also indirectly footnotes Chandler in its use of an uncredited cameo by a diminutive blonde male star whose career was then largely defined by film noir—Alan Ladd.

Ladd's pivotal pre–*Brunette* noir pictures all had a Chandler connection. First, the actor's career was initially made with the screen adaptation of Graham Greene's *A Gun for Sale*—retitled *This Gun for Hire* (1942, a novel sometimes compared to Chandler's work). Next, Ladd's hit *The Glass Key* (1942) is from the Hammett novel of the same name. And the aforementioned *Blue Dahlia* also starred Ladd, with the love interest in all three pictures being played by the sultry blonde with the famous "peek-a-boo" hairstyle, Veronica Lake.

The *Brunette* scene juxtaposing Hope and Ladd, therefore, is the most inventive parody job in a picture peppered with imaginative moments. Besides the immediate comedy contrast between Hope's essentially cowardly figure and his attempts to be a tough guy, the two men have blatantly different acting styles. Hope is a fully animated, over-the-top comedian. Ladd, like most noir figures, embraces a minimalist, almost stuck-in-amber, sense of body and dialogue. If and when wordage does occur, it is ever so terse. Noir is an existentialist world in which protecting one's self means personally exposing very little. While the success of all the Hope spoofs is moored to being inappropriately silly in a serious genre, the veil of noir is the film world furthest from the expressive realm of the personality comedian. In addition, as critic David Thomson has so effectively sketched Ladd's screen persona, beyond the contrast with Hope, the noir actor's brief *Brunette* appearance somehow makes this parody seem more substantial than so many one-joke spoof movies:

> Ladd's calm slender ferocity makes it clear that he was the first American actor to show the killer as cold angel. He had a great voice, too, deeper than one expected.[4]

Ironically, Chandler privatively felt Bogart had a better noir persona. In a letter to his English publisher, Hammish Hamilton, Chandler wrote, "Ladd is hard, bitter and occasionally charming but he is after all a small boy's idea of a tough guy. Bogart is the genuine article."[5]

Still, that line, "a small boy's idea of a tough guy," is perfect for Hope's *Brunette*. His character is a baby photographer, Ronnie Jackson, whose studio is in the same building as Ladd's private-eye office. Ronnie mimics everything about Ladd's cool detective, Sam McCloud, from clothing to mannerisms, like a child hero-worshipping his father. Ladd humors this business neighbor to a point, allowing Hope to cover his phone when the detective is away on a case. As a then exiting McCloud puts on his standard cinema noir issue private eye trench coat, Ronnie still tries to tag along, reasoning: "I've got a coat just like that."

Brunette was especially important to Hope. It was the first movie product of Hope Enterprises, Inc., and it was made on a fifty-fifty basis with Paramount studio. The comedian was very happy to be his own boss: "When you're under contract to a certain studio you are obligated to do certain things whether you like it or not. Of course, they will fix it for you, but it is not the way to make pictures today."[6]

The private-eye picture was carefully chosen, possibly influenced by the fact that detective stories were Hope's favorite reading material. He spared no expense, using more than a million dollars of his own funds in the project. This added control paid off; the movie was one of the top box office hits of 1946–47.[7]

Being a detective is not a film noir requirement. But as demonstrated with *Brunette*, the genre's central male invariably ends up playing at least an amateur sleuth, regardless of his given screen trade. Thus, Hope's wannabe private-eye pays the bills with his struggling (children tend to bite him) photography job ... until his antihero stumbles into some detective work when a sexy woman (Dorothy Lamour — the *Road* picture heroine) mistakes him for Sam McCloud. Like James Thurber's celebrated short story, "The Secret Life of Walter Mitty," in which another everyman antihero daydreams himself into various scenes of action adventure heroics, Hope's Ronnie Jackson is bored with his dull life and fantasizes about being swashbuckling and brave, too.[8] Since most readers or viewers have at some time felt the same way, this readily helps the fan of funny to relate to these underdogs.

Through a twist of fate, however, Jackson's controlled daydream suddenly plunges him into a potentially comic nightmare — reality, film noir style. Still, the same nonchalant bravery in the face of death applies. For instance, *Brunette* opens with Hope's Jackson being calmly flippant on death row, while "The Secret Life" closes with Mitty imagining how he would heroically face a firing squad ... or maybe because he is so tired of his henpecking wife, death would simply be a relief. (The film adaptation of Thurber's story, with Danny Kaye as Mitty, would appear in theaters just a few months after *Brunette's* release, 1947.)

Straight noir, of course, has its own nightmare quality, with suffering and death the indifferent norm. The fatalism of 1920s German Expressionism, as well as its visual style (the city at night, shiny black reflective surfaces, unusual camera angles...) had a great influence on film noir. The noir genre, which flourished from the middle 1940s until the early 1950s (but continues to surface in movies like *Chinatown*, 1974, and *L. A. Confidential*, 1997), was also greatly impacted by several events which occurred both during and shortly after the end of World War II. Given *Brunette's* often almost clinical parody dissection of the genre, some of these additional noir primers merit footnoting.

First, noir's cynical worldview was reinforced by revelations about the Nazi Holocaust, the impact of America's use of atomic bombs on Japan, and the sudden segue from hot to "cold war" as the Soviets quickly went from World War II ally to global enemy. Second, many Jewish German filmmakers, who had been part of the aforementioned Expressionistic movement prior to fleeing Nazi-occupied Europe, eventually found themselves in Hollywood. Quite possibly, noir would have been influenced by the horrors of Expressionism anyway. But given the influx of these immigrants to the film capital, a group whose numbers included Fritz Lang and Billy Wilder, early architects of noir, the direct links between these two cinemas of desperation cannot be denied.

Third, "tough guy" fiction, à la Chandler, Hammett, Cain, and others, had been around since the 1930s. But Hollywood's censorship board was not as restrictive by the mid–1940s, which allowed screen adaptations which were closer to their provocative original stories. (After all the inhumanity to man stockpiled under the umbrella called "World War II," American moviegoers expected more adult fare.) Fourth, with so many men serving in the armed forces, women on the home front assumed many jobs previously held by men — the "Rosie the Riveter" phenomenon. When the war was over, there was sometimes a sexy tension in the marketplace between returning veterans and women who did not want to leave positions outside the home. Film noir tapped into this friction by having femme fatale type leading ladies.

Thematically, this genre undercuts the American Dream or the Horatio Alger story: people who seem to have achieved success have cheated along the way. The dream is just one more American myth. The genre also undercuts the traditional location of the American paradise — California, be it the 1849 gold rush, or the 1930s migration of Dust Bowl farmers. Thus, film noir invariably takes place in California, often in Los Angeles or San Francisco. Appropriately, the genre sometimes rubs shoulders with the film industry. Indeed, the movies are a metaphor for this negative worldview. That is, films are not what they seem to be, from the false-front buildings to stuntmen for the stars. The dark comedy, noir classic *The Player* (1992) is even about a film producer as an amateur sleuth.

Hope's *Brunette*, appearing in the genre's heyday, is the most thorough of noir parodies. Set in San Francisco's Chinatown, the movie unfolds in traditional noir terms — a story-long flashback with voiceover narration by the wannabe detective, as he awaits execution on death row for a mysterious crime yet to be explained. As the flashback mode takes the viewer to the story's beginning, *Brunette*, with its black and white photography and off-kilter camera angles, might double for the opening of any straight rendition of the genre. Soon further links to noir fall into place, including the aforementioned extended cameo of iconic noir actor Alan Ladd (as well as Hope's character mentioning his tough guy movie detective heroes — a list which includes *Ladd*!), the initially femme fatale look of Dorothy Lamour's catalyst sexy woman in black, and a villain (Peter Lorre) whose first international acting success was as the child-molesting murderer in Fritz Lang's riveting German Expressionistic film, *M* (1931).

Still, Hope establishes early in the flashback that his Ronnie is a comic boy among noir men. For example, during Hope's interaction with Ladd's detective, the baby photographer brags that he has already invented a keyhole camera ... which has gotten him kicked out of five hotels. The comedian so embraces a little boy's enthusiasm to be a private eye (a precursor to Will Ferrell's charmingly excitable but more innocent title character in *Elf*, 2003), that the viewer immediately "signs up" for the *Brunette* movie experience. Plus, Hope's every comic move and wisecrack plays as naturally as that child-like furor. *New York Herald Tribune* critic Howard Barnes said of this *Brunette* performance, "Bob Hope wanders through the show as though he were improvising every incident. Performing such as this is no trick. It is high artistry."[9]

Though the *Tribune*'s praise was a blanket endorsement of the picture, the scene in which Ronnie Jackson finds himself sitting at Sam McCloud's office desk, after the tough guy has gone, probably ranked high on the critic's praise meter. Hope's character tries to imitate Sam by downing a shot of McCloud's whiskey. To adequately describe the comedian's often underpraised visual shtick, as it applies here to some high octane he-man alcohol, one might recycle the response of another child-like antihero, Robert Benchley, to strong drink: "In ... seconds the top of the inhaler's head rises slowly and in a dignified manner until it reaches the ceiling where it floats, bumping gently up and down. The teeth then drop out and arrange themselves on the floor to spell 'Portage High School, 1930' ... and a strange odor of burning rubber fills the room."[10]

Fittingly, the heavily Hope-influenced Woody Allen creates a variation of this antiheroic drinking scene in his own film noir parody, *Play It Again, Sam* (1972). Allen's character is also trying to imitate a hard-drinking noir detective, Bogart as Sam Spade. As with Hope, Allen falls spoofingly short of his tough guy idol. In both cases, the scenes would be howlingly funny without any prior noir knowledge. Yet, the humor quotient skyrockets if one

The Hope-influenced Woody Allen does his own film noir parody in *Play It Again, Sam* (1972). Allen's frenzied movement here belies his attempt to be Humphrey Bogart cool.

realizes that excessive drinking is an intrinsic part of this genre. As another Bogart character observes in *Casablanca* (1942), when a Nazi officer asks him his identity, Bogart replies, "Drunkard."

As in most film noir, the catalyst for the hero's (or in this case, the antihero's) entry into the genre is by way of a beautiful, mysterious woman. The *New York Daily Mirror*'s Jack Thompson described it thus: "Hope with his confusion, double-takes, asides to the audience, and drooling pursuit of the sultry Dorothy Lamour, makes a highly agreeable detective."[11] Mobsters have kidnapped Lamour's scientist uncle, and she desperately wants help from Hope's Jackson, whom she mistakes for Ladd's McCloud. The comedian seems on the verge of spilling his real identity, like that old joke, "If I can be of any help — you're worse off than I thought." But he cannot resist having a working relationship with Lamour, or as *Variety* described the sex appeal of this "cinematic cutie": "[Her] attractiveness makes the Hope [story] scramble plausible."[12] The naughty naturalness of this noir temptation even inspired a rare witticism from the normally staid *New York Times* film critic Bosley Crowther:

> And, in the course of his fearful endeavor to stand between her [Lamour] and them [assorted villains] — and, at times, to reverse those positions — Mr. Hope gets into some [comically] screaming jams.[13]

For the modern viewer, *Brunette* plays as a brilliant but broad takeoff on film noir, not unlike the adventure movie spoofing of Hope and Crosby's *Road to Utopia*. But for period fans of *Brunette*, the movie sometimes demonstrated a more subdued comic approach that juggled comic deflation with an eventual reaffirmation of the subject under attack. These "parodies of reaffirmation" can produce a fascinating tension between genre expectations (in this case, noir's thriller aspect) and a parody that is comic without deflating the characters involved.[14]

While no one would now label *Brunette* with this more serious parody moniker, coupled as these modern "reaffirmation" pictures often are with the deaths of central figures, such as the title characters in *Butch Cassidy and the Sundance Kid* (1969) and *An American Werewolf in London* (1981), Hope's film still managed to score some serious noir points with 1940s audiences. This fact is reflected in period reviews. For example, the *Commonweal* critic observed, *Brunette* manages to have "suspense and excitement as well as jokes," while the *New York Daily Mirror* reviewer stated, "In addition to being hilariously funny, the picture is a genuine thriller."[15] And the *Hollywood Reporter* went so far as to claim: "Hope, Lamour and all the others concerned find themselves in wacky situations but they remain believable characters under [director Elliott] Nugent's control."[16]

Such serious period slants on *Brunette* merely document the enigmatic nature of genre study. While a formula of sorts exists for each type, one must allow for variations to occur over time. At the risk of sounding blasphemous, even pioneer genre writings by pivotal film critics such as Robert Warshow (on the Western and the gangster film) and James Agee (on comedy) are not without some limitations. Warshow has problems with *My Darling Clementine* (1946), *Kiss of Death* (1947), *High Society* (1956), and *Shane* (1953); Agee has reservations about comedy outside the silent era.[17] Genre criticism exists as a guide for the curious mind, highlighting recurring patterns of cultural significance in the arts, and not as a dictator of said patterns. As influential genre author John G. Cawelti has observed, "When genre critics forget that their super texts are critical artifacts and start treating them as prescriptions for artistic creation, the concept of genre becomes stultifying and limiting."[18] Consequently, *Brunette* remains a parody today but any period suggestions of reaffirmation, the aforementioned "genre thriller," have long since gone.

Continuing this examination of *Brunette* as broad parody, a passing comedy aside by *Newsweek*'s review—"anything Sherlock Holmes can do, Sherlock Hope can do better"—invites a connection between film noir and the antiheroic Hope.[19] The noir private eye is just the opposite of Sherlock Holmes. Sherlock is all-knowing; he can look at a footprint and tell how much change the suspect had in his pants and whether he preferred peach cobbler to pumpkin pie. With his brilliant deductions, the last page of the Holmes story has all the loose ends tied together. Now, the film noir detective is tough, but he is often no further ahead in solving the mystery than a member of the audience, and some questions even go unanswered. In arguably the greatest film noir, the revisionist *Chinatown*, Jack Nicholson's central character is never ahead of the viewer and ends up defeated by John Huston's figure of evil. But, though the "last page" of *Chinatown* is difficult to accept, one has enjoyed the equal ground nature of the "trip" to the end.

Bob Hope can only comically fill the film noir shoes of an Alan Ladd or Jack Nicholson, and thus film noir is parodied. Yet, it is appropriate that Hope should be spoofing a then-new, more vulnerable private eye. Hope's persona might be miles from the standard toughness of noir detectives, but they are all on the same page when it comes to a certain intellectual vulnerability. In contrast, cinema's most memorable Sherlock Holmes (Basil Rathbone, who played the cerebral character in 14 films and numerous radio mysteries) was sometimes described as a "brain in a tweed coat." Thus, neither Hope's Ronnie Jackson, nor the typical noir private ever provides the anticipated story-closing summation which was a Sherlock Holmes' signature. As the *New York Times* review of *Brunette* aptly added in its own near-summation, "As for [noir storyline] clarity, what would it want with such as that?"[20]

A period criticism point about *Brunette* sometimes fumbled, however, is the mistaken connection drawn between it and the similarly titled Hope picture *My Favorite Blonde* (1942), in which the comic is *not* in search of adventure. While some parallels exist, such as a pretty girl and an antihero with "delusions of courage,"[21] *Blonde*'s parody has a different pre-noir target — Hitchcock's political thriller *The 39 Steps* (1935). Hope's character in *Blonde* is hardly setting the entertainment world on fire — a secondary sidekick to a penguin in small-time variety theaters. But his lack of interest in getting involved (unlike Hope's wanna-be private eye in *Brunette*) is central to the

Despite Hope's visual kidding of Sherlock Holmes, his *My Favorite Brunette* character (with Dorothy Lamour) spoofs the much more vulnerable film noir detective.

parody success of *Blonde*, since *The 39 Steps* plays upon one of Hitchcock's favorite themes, a "wrong man" forced into involvement.

It is unfortunate that most people think only of Mel Brooks' spoof of the director — *High Anxiety* (1977) — when one mentions parody and Hitchcock. *Blonde* complements Brooks' work, since the Hope vehicle focuses on one Hitchcock movie, and *High Anxiety* takes a shotgun approach that attempts to refer to as many of the celebrated director's movies as possible. If truth be told, the Hope picture is the better spoof. Brooks' film, because of its broad comic attack, is often uneven in getting laughs. But comparison of these two affectionate but different spoofs of Hitchcock will have to be saved for some future study.

Brunette sometimes seems a model for Woody Allen. For instance, Hope's false bravado on death row (the framing device from which the flashback occurs) anticipates Allen's demeanor in *Love and Death* (1975) as he awaits execution; both characters anticipate a pardon. Consequently, these normally devout cowards act as calm wise guys. For instance, Hope's Ronnie Jackson, on the verge of his walk to San Quentin's gas chamber, sneers at a penitentiary that has not yet converted to electricity. Even this comment is topped with the closing reaction of the disappointed executioner (Bing Crosby) when Ronnie's last-second pardon arrives. Hope's character responds, "That guy will take any part." *Road* picture footnotes such as this, always at Crosby's expense, occur in many of Hope's solo films, including *Blonde*.

There is also an engrossing link between *Brunette* and Allen's dark comedy *Crimes and Misdemeanors* (1989), which shows Hope's continued influence on the comedian, even when parody is not the focus genre. In Hope's *Brunette* a confession that would clear the antihero of murder charges has been recorded. But a switch is made, and when Ronnie plays what he thinks will clear him, he hears a speeded-up version of Betty Hutton singing "Murder He Said," from the film *Happy Go Lucky* (1943), a comic surprise that seems to keep pointing the murder finger at Hope's Ronnie. In *Crimes* Allen has a dual-focus narrative, with a murder in one story and more comic frustration for his antihero in the other. And at precisely the moment when one character decides to murder, the film cuts to a theatrical screening of *Happy Go Lucky* and Hutton belting out "Murder He Said." It is an inspired surprise comic transition to the world of Allen's antihero character, a film fan at a revival house screening of the Hutton movie. Allen the director has set up the transition by an earlier scene with his character at the screening of another old film. Thus, one character plans a murder, while another merely toys with the idea in the safety of a darkened theater.

A good parody acts as a guide to a genre, and *Brunette* does just that. The film noir woman is sexually manipulative. When Dorothy Lamour's character, Carlotta Montay, mistakes Ronnie for a detective, he is reluctant to take her case. But she comes on to him, saying: "We Montays are generous. If you will just find my husband [actually, it is her uncle] I will be so grateful. You'll see." With that promise and the appropriate sexy body language, the word *no* drops out of Ronnie's vocabulary. Period reviews often treated Lamour as just another pretty face: "She is little more than a comely prop in a one-man [Hope] job of bumbling clowning."[22] Though being drop-dead gorgeous is certainly in the genre's femme fatale job description, Lamour goes beyond beauty as a plot catalyst. In part because of earlier *Road* pictures, as well as two other pre–*Brunette* screen teamings with the comedian, she and Hope have excellent film chemistry. And with no Bing Crosby in sight, save for the cameo, the viewer can safely assume the comedian will get the girl. Moreover, despite Carlotta's initial film noir–given manipulation, Lamour's many previous movie pairings with Hope convince the viewer they belong together.

Film noir oozes sexuality, and *Brunette* is saturated with it, starting with the comic given that Hope's screen persona both thinks of himself as God's gift to women, and is obsessed with sex in general. For instance, when his *Brunette* character finds out Carlotta is not married, he drools, "So he's not your husband. Well, did I quote you any rates? I may work cheaper, you know." When Hope's Ronnie is being chased and escapes through an apartment building, he buzzes nearly all the apartments to unlock the main door, repeating the line, "Hello, honey, this is Joe." Countless women replying in a "come hither" nature lead him to observe in the midst of his flight, "I must remember this address." This is simply a topper to Hope having fun with noir's male sexual fantasy–like showcase of seemingly endless available women, which is best demonstrated in straight renditions of the genre by the Bogart-starring *Big Sleep* (1946). Every sexy woman his Philip Marlowe character briefly encounters, including cigarette girls, a taxi driver, a bookstore clerk (Dorothy Malone), and his eventual lover's sister (Martha Vickers), is all ready to be bedded.

In fact, even general noir business can be full of sexual suggestion. For example, when Hope's Ronnie comes to after being knocked out, he says, "I was playing post office with the floor." Such comic patter after a concussion is also reminiscent of the noir classic *Murder, My Sweet* (1944, an adaptation of Chandler's novel *Farewell My Lovely*), in which Dick Powell as Philip Marlowe is forever responding with a quip after being knocked out by bad guys.

Sometimes there is an implication that noir's sexual permissiveness, with regard to the femme fatale's family, might be linked to mental instability, too. For instance, the provocatively strange behavior of the aforementioned Martha Vickers character in *The Big Sleep* has the bemused Bogart telling her butler, "Then she tried to sit on my lap while I was standing up." The orchid scene directly after this Bogart-Vickers interaction, in which one meets her elderly screen father, might be "read" to imply an incestuous family. But the era's censorship policy forbade anything that provocative. Only much later, when restrictions were dropped, could noir pictures like *Chinatown*, *The Grifters* (1990), and *Kiss Kiss, Bang Bang* (2005, a reaffirmation parody of the genre) deal directly with incest.

In *Brunette*, sex and insanity is front and center when Ronnie is told erotic Carlotta has mental problems and he asks, "Does she snap her cap very often?" Carlotta's waffling on just who is missing, her husband or her uncle, could also be construed as someone being a victim of, or having a propensity towards, incest. But the comedian defuses any controversy with self-deprecating humor: Ronnie has to rescue Carlotta from a mental sanitarium, and this requires Hope to act crazy, something he finds upsetting: "I think I do this too well."

Parody films frequently spoof specific films or genres in addition to the key genre under attack — rather a scatter-gun effect. *Brunette* is peppered with these film footnotes, such as when Ronnie is having difficulty climbing a tree in order to break into a second-story window, he mumbles, "It always looks so easy in those *Tarzan* pictures." Later, when he finds himself hanging from a chandelier during a chase, he discovers a bottle and immediately quips, "Ray Milland has been here." This is a reference to Milland's Oscar-winning performance as an alcoholic in *Lost Weekend* (1945), forever hiding bottles in odd places.

Film noir often also features a magnificent old mansion in which the decadent heavies reside, or at least appear to live. Ronnie says in voice-over, "It's the kind of house that looks like you can hunt quail in the hallway." But as in Hitchcock's later noir-ish *North By Northwest* (1959), the central character (in *Brunette*'s case, Ronnie) brings in authorities only to find the house empty of boarders. Things are seldom as they seem in film noir, and even the sanity of the lead figure appears to be in question. Whether occupied or not, such a mansion represents old money obtained in shady deals. The decay of such families is sometimes symbolized by ego and sickness. For example, in *The Big Sleep* a hothouse for plants is attached to the mansion, with the wheelchair-bound elderly patriarch constantly there. Though not as blatant as this,

Brunette manages to create that ambience, including a heavy pretending to use a wheelchair.

Even Ronnie's quips have a way of resurfacing in later noir films. For instance, when he finally manages to hold a gun on the diminutive, knife-obsessed Peter Lorre, he cracks, "One move and you're a dead midget." In *Chinatown*, Jack Nicholson's character makes the mistake of calling director Roman Polanski's knife-carrying cameo figure a midget and nearly loses his nose. And as *Chinatown*'s wounded private eye observes, "I like my nose and I like breathing through it."

This Nicholson crack, or Bogart's earlier riff about the nympho-like Martha Vickers *Big Sleep* character, entertainingly demonstrates that even the straight noir picture often has a lead capable of making like a comedian. Consequently, to effectively spoof the genre, the parody private eye has to be especially funny, something Hope's character more than accomplishes in *Brunette*. His most definingly antiheroic line occurs early in the film: "You see, I wanted to be a detective, too. It only took brains, courage, and a gun. And I had the gun." As the *Hollywood Reporter* critic observed, "Hope is in rare form with some really wise wisecracks...."[23]

In all these ways, Hope's *Brunette* manages to take apart film noir, one genre component after another — a perfect example of what is sometimes called "creative criticism."[24] That is, to create effective parody, one must be thoroughly versed in the subject under attack. Parody is the most palatable of critical approaches, offering insights through laughter. Though the fundamental goal of spoofing is to be *funny* (something that should never be lost on the scholar), this genre is also an educational tool. And Hope's *Brunette* is a noir tutorial.

Given that the film was helping launch Hope Enterprises, the comedian orchestrated the most star-studded premiere possible, including four MCs (Cary Grant, Jack Benny, Eddie Cantor, and Hope himself). Other show-stoppers who briefly entertained included Frank Sinatra, Red Skelton, Jimmy Durante, Al Jolson, Betty Hutton, and Dinah Shore. Additional musical support came from the Andrew Sisters singing "Beat Me Daddy," Danny Kaye applying his funny phonetics to "Begin the Beguine," and Desi Arnaz doing "Babalu." Besides having a hit movie, the *Los Angeles News* said the premiere "program was fast, funny and melodious."[25]

With this vaudeville-like show following Hope's movie, and being also billed as a "Damon Runyon [1884–1946] Benefit," for the late comically celebrated author of such quintessential New York loopy lowlifes as are depicted in *Guys and Dolls*, this was a sought-after ticket in filmland. (Hope would later have a huge Runyon-based film hit, more New York characters with big hearts, strange names, and imaginative speech patterns, in *The Lemon Drop Kid*, 1951.) And while one Los Angeles area newspaper keyed upon the *Brunette* premiere ability to raise money for cancer research, the publication still managed to title its review, "Bob Hope Big Hit In New Film Comedy," adding it is "An hilarious take-off on some of the recent and even contemporary 'private eye' films...."[26]

In contrast, the *Hollywood Citizen News* did same day individual pieces on each event: "Runyon Benefit Tops For Vaudeville Show" and "Bob Hope Big Hit in New Film Comedy."[27] Its movie review went on to add, "[This is] an hilarious take-off on some of the recent and even contemporary 'private eye' films...." All this entertainment firepower, both in the benefit and Hope's new picture, is possibly the real reason why producer Howard Hughes staged his own elaborate simultaneous premiere of the Preston Sturges–Harold Lloyd film *The Sin of Harold Diddlebock* (1947, see previous chapter) as far from Hollywood as possible — Miami, Florida.[28]

Regardless, *Brunette* was a critical and commercial smash, with the raves from both the *Hollywood Citizen News* and the *Los Angeles News* being typical. While a host of aforementioned critical sound bites attest to this fact, maybe the following *Variety* quote states it with the most universal affection: "You can say Hope, like Kilroy [the everyman American soldier] was here before.... [But] score up the concoction for surefire b.o."[29]

11

CHARLIE CHAPLIN
Monsieur Verdoux (1947)

Shortly before killing one of his victims, Henri Verdoux (Charlie Chaplin) observes, "When the world looks grim and dark, then I think of another world." Thus, the normal populist spirit of Chaplin's immortal Tramp has been turned on its ear.

While Charlie Chaplin's previous picture, *The Great Dictator* (1940), had also been a controversial dark comedy, *Monsieur Verdoux* was even more of a test for period audiences. At least *Dictator*, with Chaplin showcased in dual roles, both skewered a universally despised villain (Hitler), and retained a semblance of the comedian's beloved Tramp in the Jewish barber. But *Verdoux* finds Chaplin playing a title character who marries and murders little old ladies for a profit. His dapper Parisian character was inspired by the "career" of Frenchman Henri Landru, better known as the "modern Bluebeard," who was guillotined in 1922 for liquidating ten of his girlfriends.

Although both films had didactic antiwar tendencies, a message fueled by the negativism of a Hitler-like dictatorship is much more palatable in the United States than a warning about the potentially murderous inclinations of domestic big business and big government. In 1941, Orson Welles had originally approached Chaplin about the role of Landru in a series of simulated documentaries the young director was contemplating. But Chaplin's often macabre sense of humor was more drawn to a fictionalized, darkly comic treatment of the material. The artist's Verdoux might also be seen as simply a lethal update of the caddish womanizer he wrote for Adolphe Menjou in *A Woman of Paris* (1923).

Regardless, *Verdoux* would be released at a time when Chaplin had suffered through years of public persecution from the conservative right over sexual scandals and idealistically naïve liberal political activity. Ironically, this was nothing new. The comedian had always bedded young women; his first two marriages were hurried-up affairs precipitated by that very fact. And the post–World War II accusations about Chaplin being a communist sympathizer, which had begun with his Second Front support for the Soviet Union during the conflict, had antecedents in the "Red" scare following World War I. Indeed, in the comedian's 1922 book, *My Trip Abroad*, Chaplin even included a reporter asking if he was a Bolshevik. His vulnerable-for-attack sound bite response was not unlike the cavalier comments that would get him in greater political hot water during the 1940s: "I am an artist. I am interested in life. Bolshevism is a new phase of life. I must be interested in it."[1]

The difference, however, between these periods — the quarter century from the publishing of *My Trip Abroad* and the release of *Verdoux*— was that the public's perpetual forgiveness of Chaplin's past provocative personal actions was predicated upon there always being another Charlie the Tramp film about to open. But by the late 1940s, Chaplin's "little fellow," as he called his screen alter ego, had long been in retirement. Moreover, the artist compounded the public's sense of loss by replacing the lovable antiheroic Tramp with a "Lady Killer" (the working title of the *Verdoux* script).

Still, to briefly back up the 1940s tabloid bus, what events leading up to the release of *Verdoux* had so tarnished Chaplin's reputation? For starters, the early years of the decade would briefly find him involved in two sex scandals. One would produce lurid headlines for years, while the other was eventually recognized as the sort of unique reciprocated love that his Charlie persona should have found at the bittersweet close of *City Lights* (1931). The first case involved a beautiful but unstable young woman named Joan Barry, with whom Chaplin had become professionally and romantically involved during the early 1940s. (The comedian and his third wife, actress Paulette Goddard, had amicably separated in 1941 and were said to have been divorced in 1942, but their Mexican decree was just as vague as their earlier marriage claims.)

Chaplin felt that Barry, a beautiful redhead, would be a perfect fit for a film adaptation of Paul Vincent Carroll's Irish play *Shadows and Substance*, about an unschooled girl who sees visions of a saint. Paradoxically, the instability one might associate with such a character was actually part of Joan Barry's personality. When Chaplin ended his contact (1942) with the actress over her lack of professionalness, she began to harass him, doing everything from breaking windows in his house to actually *breaking in* and holding him at gunpoint. The following year (1943) Barry named Chaplin in a paternity suit, which was followed in 1944 by a Federal grand jury indictment of the comedian for violation of the Mann Act (the transfer of a woman across a state line for sexual intentions). The latter accusation, also allegedly involving Barry, was soon shown to be ludicrous, and the charge was dropped. But the paternity suit was upheld in court through the slanderous melodramatics of Barry's lawyer, despite a blood test that proved conclusively that Chaplin could not have been the father. (Blood tests were not then accepted as positive proof in California court cases ... but this miscarriage of justice would help change the law.)

The second "scandal" would normally not have been pigeonholed as such but it became inevitable because of its timing and Chaplin's proven proclivity toward young women. Thus, at approximately the same time as the paternity suit was filed, the comedian quietly married eighteen-year-old Oona O'Neill, daughter of playwright Eugene O'Neill. Chaplin was fifty-four. And though this fourth marriage would become *the* success of his private life, lasting as it did until his 1977 death and producing a family of Victorian size (eight children), the union only intensified the ballyhoo against him in 1943. In an otherwise very romantic, hidden-away honeymoon in Santa Barbara, California, Chaplin would later confess:

> Occasionally I would sink into a deep depression, feeling that I had the acrimony and the hate of a whole nation upon me and that my film career was lost.[2]

The preceding examples were merely the most prominent of Chaplin's 1940s controversies. Additional problems included tax differences with the government and a continued tendency in post–World War II America to antagonize the political right and some moderates with such actions as his support of Henry Wallace. Wallace, the former third-term vice-president under Franklin Roosevelt, had been President Truman's Secretary of Commerce until a falling out over Truman's "get tough" policy with the Soviets. Wallace felt world peace could be maintained only by better relations with the Soviet Union; he opposed such presidential actions as the Truman Doctrine and the Marshall Plan. In 1948 Wallace ran for president on the Progressive Party ticket, which supported closer ties with the Soviets. He finished last in a four-way race ultimately won by Truman. Candidate Wallace and supporter Chaplin might best be described today as idealistically naïve liberals who underestimated the disruptive nature of the Soviets in Europe after World War II.

Chaplin did not always even have to do something to be controversial. For example, he was widely criticized during the 1940s and early 1950s for not relinquishing his British passport and becoming an American citizen, because he had lived in this country since 1913. Chaplin's defense, that he felt himself a citizen of the world, did not fall on many sympathetic ears, though there were countless other unhounded artists in Chaplin's position. One such individual was his celebrated understudy from Karno days, Stan Laurel. Biographer John McCabe notes that Laurel, who kept his British citizenship throughout a fifty-four-year residency in the States, was forever irked that Chaplin should be so singled out.[3]

With these frustrations as a backdrop, Chaplin's decision to make another dark comedy statement film seems most logical. But one must keep in mind that the comedian's initial interest in what became *Verdoux* predated all the aforementioned public travail. As early as December 8, 1941, the *Hollywood Reporter* carried a brief but amusing front page story on the subject, which opened with the statement:

> Charlie Chaplin is apparently serious about playing Landru, the French Bluebeard, in his next picture, and towards that end has grown a Van Dyke beard, and is mugging in the mirror and getting the opinion of friends on how he'd photograph minus his trademarked midget mustache. [The comedian eventually decided against the beard, and went with more of a pencil-thin dandy's mustache.][4]

Of course, one could argue that while Chaplin was flirting with the *Verdoux* scenario before the Barry case, the vindictiveness of this unstable woman might have been an added catalyst for getting it produced. Like most artists, the comedian labored over many projects which never came to fruition, from the aforementioned *Shadows and Substance*, to a film about Napoleon.

Before more fully addressing Chaplin's pioneering use of dark comedy in *Verdoux*, one must document a final public humiliation for the comedian just as the picture was going into general release. United Artists, the studio which Chaplin had co-founded decades before, and through which *Verdoux* was produced and distributed, held a press conference for the picture in New York City on April 12, 1947, the day after its premiere. The transcript of the proceedings reads like a scenario on how to conduct a witch hunt. Chaplin was rudely questioned on a number of "patriotic" topics, from his foreign citizenship to his controversial friendships. The only bright spot in the inquisition was the tribute paid to him by author and critic James Agee, who posed an ironically rhetorical question on just what having a free country meant. In a voice trembling with anger over Chaplin's mistreatment, Agee asked:

> What are people who care a damn about freedom — who really care for it — [to] think of a country and the people in it, who congratulate themselves upon this country as the finest on earth and as a "free country," when so many of the people in this country pry into what a man's citi-

zenship is, try to tell him his business from hour to hour and from day to day and exert a public moral blackmail against him for not becoming an American citizen — for his political views and for not entertaining troops in the manner — in the way that they think he should. What is to be thought of a general country where those people are thought well of?[5]

A very appreciative Chaplin thoughtfully but tactfully acknowledged Agee's kindness without opening himself up to further barbs from the political right: "Thank you very much — but I have nothing to say to that question." Agee would go on to write a passionate three-part celebration of *Verdoux* in *The Nation*, which will be addressed shortly. As an Agee biographer would later write, "He became its [the film's] self-appointed champion and defended *Monsieur Verdoux* as vehemently as if he himself had made it."[6]

Charlie Chaplin's dapper French Bluebeard of a title character, *Monsieur Verdoux* (1947).

Paradoxically, while Chaplin's ambush press conference — at which the actual merits of the movie became lost in the shuffle — was probably unavoidable given the period political climate, history seems to have forgotten an added factor in the vindictiveness. Shortly before United Artist's post-premiere press debacle, the studio also sponsored a similar Chaplin conference for foreign correspondents, with the understanding that said interview bites were limited to the various overseas bureaus. But through a snafu, many of the comedian's comments were actually published in newspapers across America ... the day *before* his New York roasting. Some of Chaplin's innocently cavalier comments, not so unlike his Bolshevik observation quoted earlier, provided fresh ammunition for his next day's domestic critics. For example, the comedian's "good paying guest" embellishment on his normally non-nationalist reason for not becoming an American citizen was one of his foreign press quotes with which he was especially skewered at the follow-up New York press conference:

> I am not a nationalist. Seventy percent of my income is derived from outside the United States and 30 percent from this country. The United States takes 100 percent of that income for taxation purposes. I am a very good paying guest.[7]

Seventeen years after this volatile period, upon the 1964 re-issuing of *Verdoux*, *New York Times* critic Bosley Crowther said the picture's original release resulted in "the most antagonistic critical and public reception ever accorded a Chaplin film."[8] But as a testament to the comedian's storied career, even *Verdoux*'s period reviews — if one avoids the extreme polemical publications — sometimes included positives. For example, though Crowther's 1947 *New York Times* critique found *Verdoux* too "serious and bitter," he still credited the movie with being "screamingly funny in spots — funny as only the old Chaplin is able to make a comic scene...."[9] The *New York Post*'s Archer Winsten felt *Verdoux*'s ending was an emotional and intellectual downer, yet there are "acts of comic creation no one but Chaplin could give us. They make it a picture to be seen."[10] The *New York Daily Mirror* called *Verdoux* an

> uneven but continuously interesting film. Though it's not off Chaplin's top shelf, it comes from a higher perch than more of the pictures you will enjoy in a season.[11]

The subject around which these semi-friendly notices danced was addressed more directly by *Variety*: "Comedy based on the characterization of a modern Parisian Bluebeard treads dangerous shoals indeed.... Chaplin generates little sympathy."[12] The *Hollywood Reporter*'s panning added, "Only confusion results from his injecting [black humor] 'messages' and pseudo-political observations into the comedy."[13] The *New York Herald Tribune*'s Howard Barnes said, "It [dark comedy] is a strange notion he [Chaplin] has had for discarding [the Tramp's] baggy pants and adopting straight dialogue."[14]

In the United States, however, credit for keeping the critical reputation of *Verdoux* alive until a time when black humor was more acceptable, and the public could better judge a work as separate from an artist's life was greatly assisted by Agee's three-part championing of the film in *The Nation*. The critic's first *Verdoux* essay focused upon various complaints about the movie, from it not being funny, to asking why retire the Tramp? One might best summarize this defensive piece with the critic's bald comment:

> Disregard virtually everything you may have read about the film. It is of interest but chiefly as a definitive measure of the difference between the thing a man of genius puts before the world and the things the world is equipped to see in it.[15]

Agee's second *Verdoux* essay tackles the key thrust of the film, what the critic feels is Chaplin's "greatest" theme thus far: "the bare problem of surviving at all in such a world as this."[16] Granted, Verdoux's predecessor (the Tramp) had been all about surviving, too — an Everyman to whom it was easy to relate. But Agee's insightful vision of Verdoux as a "metaphor for the modern personality" is a frightfully fitting take on the evolution of Chaplin's persona.[17] As critic Robert Warshow would suggest later in 1947, prior to *Modern Times* (1936), the Tramp and society often were at odds, but there seemed to be no real threat to the continued independence of a professional free spirit like Chaplin's Charlie. Yet, with the Great Depression of the 1930s (a subject at the heart of *Verdoux*, too), changes in society had created a condition that represented an ongoing threat to the individual. Not surprisingly, the machine world of *Modern Times*, as well as the fascist one of *The Great Dictator*, quite literally threaten the life of Chaplin's alter ego.[18] *Verdoux* is the direct result of this threat ... à la, kill or be killed.

The third Agee *Nation* piece on *Verdoux* further explores why this character became a murderer. Moving beyond the "metaphor for the modern personality" and the big picture satirical attacks upon the profitable business of war, the critic wishes Chaplin had also embellished some basic "bottom causes" for criminality. Though Agee continues to call the picture "one of the few indispensable works of our time," he implies that the comedian might also have suggested such nefarious activity would be grounded in fundamental human weakness, exacerbated by Verdoux's desperate need to support an invalid wife and young child.[19]

Agee goes on to state that Chaplin's dichotomy of good and evil — the murderous Verdoux of the marketplace versus the homefront's loving husband and father, who must support his vulnerable family in style — predetermines the killings. Yet, Agee's essay ends with high praise for both Verdoux and Chaplin's iconic Charlie, whom the critic movingly and provocatively describes as "the most humane and most nearly complete among the religious figures our time has evolved...."[20] But Agee's lengthy run-on sentence close also posits the stimulating idea that if the artist's Bluebeard figure had fully embraced his beloved handicapped wife in a marriage of equals, content to exist in a milieu of Charlie the Tramp poverty, a more contented relationship, sans murder, would have evolved.

Running with Agee's suggestion, his revisionist *Verdoux* might have played as *City Lights, II*, if the film's blind heroine had not regained her eyesight, and been dependent upon the Tramp supporting them. Obviously, Chaplin's codependent comedy was often predicated by his outsider screen persona being attracted to a vulnerable, needy leading lady. A *City Lights, II*, if gifted with even a modicum of the comedian's genius, would have been a blockbuster. In fact, when Chaplin nervously revived *City Lights* on Broadway, just three years after the *Verdoux* debacle, the movie was a critical and commercial hit yet again. *Life* magazine said the two-decades-old *City Lights* was the year's best picture, while *Time* magazine declared the film "so eloquently visual that it makes most sound movies seem like the stunted products of a half-forgotten art."[21]

One could quibble, however, with Agee's notion that Chaplin's screen alter ego, in the critic's proposed new take on *Verdoux*, would not eventually revert to his proactive nature. After all, the original *City Lights* might have ended on a happy note, had the Tramp not taken it upon himself to find the money which enabled the blind girl to have her miraculous operation. Though it was the right thing to do, gifting her with eyesight was a predictable threat to an already tangential relationship ... which is borne out by the movie's gut-wrenching close.

In addition, since the main message of *Verdoux* is tied to modern times' murderous mores, what would be more fitting (or sadly *natural*), than to have a title character succumb to society's increasingly violent norm? Chaplin's individualized test case is made all the more poignant, given that Verdoux still exhibits so many of the Tramp's secular humanist sensitivities. That is, a Charlie-like character could come to this. Moreover, as Chaplin noted at the time, "Things are in just as much of a mess now [as during World War II] and I could hardly come on again in baggy pants, pretending that life is still all Santa Claus."[22] Still, Agee's inventive "What if" hypothesis, a rational vote against mayhem in the arts, is thought provoking—the goal of all good criticism. *But* one could read it as more of a smokescreen (reinforcing Agee's conscientious responsible critic credentials) in order for him to exit the article with his own tongue-in-cheek variation on Chaplin's shock theater tactics: "[The comedian has given] his century its truest portrait of the upright citizen."[23]

Much of what drives Agee's lengthy combative celebration of *Verdoux* in *The Nation* is the protective rage which first exploded at the aforementioned United Artists press conference. Paradoxically, just prior to the first installment of this series, Agee wrote a more conventional, less harried *Verdoux* review for *Time* magazine, the other major national publication for which the prolific critic wrote in much of the 1940s. In this piece Agee even confesses that some of Chaplin's philosophical musings might seem "inadequate, muddled and highly arguable—too highbrow for general audiences, and too naïve for the highbrows."²⁴ One is reminded of critic Parker Tyler's biting crack about *Verdoux*: "The Tramp's lack of familiarity with speech seems to have given Chaplin a proportionately exaggerated faith in it ... [coupled with] a natural concomitant for pathological murder."²⁵ Still, Agee's *Time* piece honors Chaplin's artistic bravery in avoiding any ploy for sympathy while presenting his provocative argument through a then groundbreaking character:

> Unlike most of the few films which try with any honesty to say anything remotely worth saying, this one does not, in its last reel or so, duck out from under ... Chaplin still has his sure virtuosity; his is one of the most beautiful single performances ever put on film.²⁶

Agee's praise for Chaplin's attempt to raise Hollywood's artistic bar is foreshadowed in the close to one of the critic's earliest reviews, when he vents his frustration at the film capital's inability to intellectually engage its audience:

> Why did they bother to make the film at all? Why, for that matter, do they bother to make any? Surely, not twice in any hundred thousand feet [of film] can they flatter themselves that they qualify to.²⁷

Fittingly, like Orson Welles' title character in *Citizen Kane* (1941), when Agee started his career in print journalism, he had also written a quality credo for himself.²⁸ *Verdoux*, therefore, allowed Agee to elevate his game — like an airborne fiddler in a Chagall painting. Yet, when it comes to controversial cinema, whatever the time or genre, too often "the subject matter was reviewed and" not the picture.²⁹ But Agee keeps things focused. In addition, he brings to mind an old axiom of the arts — the need to create is sometimes the only way to make sense of one's self. Thus, if orchestrating *Verdoux* also enabled Chaplin to work through a personally turbulent period, so much the better.

While *Verdoux* would soon be withdrawn from distribution in the United States, given the conservative backlash against Chaplin, the movie was an immediate critical and commercial success in Europe. And one of *Verdoux*'s most interesting analyses came from French theorist and critic André Bazin. A proponent of realistic cinema's long take and long shot, which maximizes the magic of the comedian's pantomime (editing would suggest trickery), a large emphasis of Bazin's writing on Chaplin focuses on the myth of Charlie — how a huge public relates to him as a twentieth-century Ulysses.³⁰ But Bazin makes his thesis even more provocative when it is applied to movies in which the comedian did *not* play the archetypal Charlie, such as the iconoclastic *Verdoux*, discussed in the theorist's "The Myth of Monsieur Verdoux."³¹

By pushing this cult of a comic myth into less-studied Chaplin territory, Bazin is able to provide both insight and an explanation for why there might be viewer identification with a Bluebeard, 1947 America notwithstanding:

> It is the character [of Charlie in *Verdoux*] that we love, not his qualities or defects. The audience's sympathy for Verdoux is focused on the myth [of Charlie], not on what he stands for morally. So when Verdoux, with the spectator on his side, is condemned, he is doubly sure of victory because the spectator condemns the condemnation of a man "justly" condemned by society. Society no longer has any emotional claim on the public conscience.[32]

Moreover, while one did not identify with Chaplin's title character from *The Great Dictator*, the catalyst for a definite viewer fascination with the Hitler-like Hynkel was undoubtedly also anchored in the remnants of Charlie that remained. For instance, the ease with which the crazed dictator climbs his drapery is reminiscent of the frightened Tramp's unexpected facility for going up that pole in *The Circus* (1928). And Hynkel's mesmerizing balletic interaction with the world globe (a comic tutorial on a dictator's lust for power), brings to mind Charlie's dancer-like movements when threatened by the neighborhood gang in *Easy Street* (1917), or his grace on roller skates in *The Rink* (1916) and *Modern Times* (1936). But critic Parker Tyler makes a more biting Charlie link between the *Dictator* and *Verdoux*:

> Hynkel had cried: "Democratia shtunk!" It is what the sly bourgeois into which the Tramp was converted in *Monsieur Verdoux* sincerely came to believe. He came to believe it as the simple-minded rationalization of the desperate democrat that the Chaplinesque Landru was.[33]

Of course, despite the shock value Verdoux's behavior might have elicited from a conservative 1940s viewer, the murderous methodology of Chaplin's title character now seems standard fare for the modern fan of dark comedy. The comedian's *Dictator* and *Verdoux* were groundbreakers for the genre. Both demonstrate black humor's three interrelated themes: man as beast, the absurdity of the modern world, and the omnipresence of death.[34]

Fleshing these components out, with regard to *Verdoux*, demonstrates the provocative innovativeness of Chaplin. For example, "man as beast" is not just about comically undercutting any concept of human dignity by way of finding humor in death. Dark comedy often also derails giving any lasting significance to man's lofty ideals when serious subjects of concern are frequently displaced by sex. The metaphorical "animal" (beast-like) nature of sex represents an absence of control — a sense of chaos consistent with black

While flowers, for Chaplin, normally symbolize the fragility of love and relationships, in *Monsieur Verdoux* they are just one more killing component of his character's ongoing mix of marriage and murder (Chaplin and Barbara Slater).

humor. Decades later, Luis Buñuel, a Chaplin friend and arguably the most acclaimed foreign director of this genre, would even observe, "in a rigidly hierarchical society, sex — which represents no barriers and obeys no laws — can at any moment become an agent of chaos."[35] Though period censorship put limits on what any 1940s filmmaker could reveal in his or her work, Chaplin's widow-shopping Verdoux was playing a sexual card in preying upon lonely older women of means. Undoubtedly against their better judgments, they literally got in bed with their executioner.

Second, *Verdoux* also demonstrates how institutionalized absurdity eventually means man's chaos-making abilities attain irrevocable steamroller proportions. Chaplin's ironic conclusion has his title character going to the guillotine for crimes eclipsed a millionfold by world governments' murders. As Verdoux dryly observes late in the film, "Numbers sanctify." Or, business profits simply justify *anything*. To illustrate, shortly before the ending, Verdoux meets a young woman whose life he once spared, unbeknownst to her. Now she is rich from a marriage to a munitions manufacturer, and Chaplin's Bluebeard states, "That is the business I should have been in. It will be paying big dividends soon!" (The film's story ends on the verge of World War II.)

One can see the direct link between Chaplin's seminal *Verdoux* pronouncement about the murderous money-driven institutionalized absurdity of big-business and governments and Mike Nichol's 1970 adaptation of Joseph Heller's classic dark comedy novel *Catch-22* (1961). Milo (Jon Voight) is the perfect example of this phenomenon. His creation and direction of "M and M Enterprises" turns World War II into the most profitable of businesses, and the source of methodical absurdity. These enterprises range from taking all the camp parachutes because he could obtain a good price on silk, to a Milo deal which has Americans bombing their own base in exchange for the German enemy's helping Milo liquidate his unloadable stockpile of cotton. Fittingly, late in the movie Voight's character paraphrases the famous old General Motors big-business axiom — "What's good for M and M Enterprises is good for the world."

Along similar roots-in-*Verdoux* lines, another later hallmark of dark comedy, the Paddy Chayefsky–written *Network* (1976), has television mogul Arthur Jensen (Ned Beatty) stating: "There is no America, no democracy, there is only ... [corporation after corporation named]. Those are the nations of the world." As if the metaphor needed further expansion, he goes on to add, "The world is a business; it has been since man crawled out of the slime." But whereas *Network* was a critical and commercial smash in America, with a multitude of Oscars (including Chayefsky's script), *Verdoux* was unappreciatively ahead of its time. (As an Oscar sidebar to the year *Verdoux* was released, the Academy Award ceremony occurred just a month before the opening of Chaplin's dark comedy. And instead of *Verdoux*'s use of World War II as fuel for black humor, the big Oscar winner that night was William Wyler's *Best Years of Our Lives*, which took home seven statuettes. A moving chronicle of three war veterans readjusting to civilian life, co-star Harold Russell brought down the Academy house ... twice. An actual war veteran who had lost his hands, Russell won a Best Supporting Actor Oscar, and a special statuette for "bringing hope and courage to his fellow veterans." The groundbreaking *Verdoux* could not have been more out-of-step with the then tenor of the times.)

The third hallmark of dark comedy, the omnipresence of death, is constantly front and center in *Verdoux*. But the most dramatic examples could be likened to bookends, at the beginning and end of the picture. Black smoke opens *Verdoux*—disposal of the latest wife cannot help but remind the viewer of the Nazi concentration camp ovens, accented by the film's close historical proximity to these atrocities. Couple this with Verdoux's chilling courtroom comment after he has been sentenced to death: "I shall see you all soon — very soon!"

Though an old axiom of dark comedy declares the genre's "message is there is no message," its obsession with death reaffirms several terrible absurdities about life. For instance, how can a once vital curious, passionate, thinking human suddenly be reduced to so much "garbage" (Heller's term) in death? Chaplin toys with this concept near the conclusion of *Verdoux*. Here is a title character so alive that moments before his walk to the guillotine he accepts a glass of rum (after first refusing) because "I've never tasted rum."

Another absurdity of death in dark comedy is the frequency with which suicide occurs. It represents that rare activity where the individual can initiate the event instead of being the random recipient. How paradoxically appropriate, however, that this act results in the total negation of the individual. Moreover, life is full of pain, and suicide provides a way around this. Certainly this is the key to Verdoux's suicide-like surrender to the police and certain death. In fact, his personal and professional travail, even before assuming his career as a Bluebeard, and escalating thereafter, ultimately results in his ceasing to care about anything. Consequently, Verdoux observes, just before giving himself up, "Despair is a narcotic; it lulls the mind into indifference." One recalls the theme song to the later celebrated black comedy *M*A*S*H** (1970): "Suicide Is Painless."

In addition, on a metaphorical level, suicide is an apt phrase for the literal implementation of the death-like tendency of modern man to seemingly rush towards an apocalypse of his own making. This is reminiscent of Herring's (Billy Gilbert) joy in the *Dictator* when a new poison gas has been discovered: "It will kill *everybody!*" Chaplin revisits a variation of this scene in *Verdoux*, when a pharmacist friend of his Bluebeard innocently shares information about a new killing drug whose results would simply suggest a heart attack.

Dark comedy suicides, or the attempts, often also reveal that randomness is just as strong in suicides (and the genre in general) as the unhappy lives the acts seek to end. For example, Verdoux initially escapes the authorities through some energetic physical comedy in the spirit of an early Charlie getaway film like *The Adventurer* (1917). But maybe this was just an "Artful Dodger" force of habit, because he immediately turns around and gives himself up.

An effective dark comedy sometimes utilizes its wave of death to implicate the viewer in its temptation to murder. That is, if a comic character in harm's way is made deliciously obnoxious enough, one might root for his or her demise. Such is the case with Martha Raye's Annabelle Bonheur, the only wife Verdoux forever fails to kill. A later Chaplin biographer perfectly described her as "The vulgarian with the braying laugh."[36] Even such a critically negative opening review as that found in the *Hollywood Reporter* found time to add, "Featured in support of the star is Martha Raye, at her best in rowdy and boisterous moments, such as the boat ride when she narrowly escapes being drowned [by Verdoux]."[37]

A final lesson to be drawn from dark comedy's obsession with death, especially as personified by *Verdoux*, is mankind's growing callousness to shock. While viewers tend initially to be surprised, in-film characters have a complacency towards death succinctly captured in the later famous anthem of Kurt Vonnegut's novel *Slaughterhouse-Five* (1969): "and so it goes." Yet, this ho-hum attitude is central to the pioneering *Dictator* and *Verdoux*. In the former, Chaplin's title character notes, after yet another death of a war-related guinea pig inventor, "Herring, why do you waste my time like this?" Along similar lines, Verdoux minimizes his murders: "Mass killings — does not the world encourage it? ... I'm an amateur in comparison."

This "growing callousness" to the depiction of death for comic purposes is ultimately best demonstrated by juxtaposing *Verdoux*'s aforementioned initial (1947, unprepared for dark comedy) critical reception in American with how most of the fourth estate treated the movie upon its re-release. The 1964 glowing review from the *New York Times*' Bosley Crowther also indirectly paid service to the invaluable early appreciation of *Verdoux* by a minority few (including Agee, Warshow, and Bazin) when it declared:

> The engagement now permits all those people who did not get to see it 17 years ago and all those who have been hearing about it as one of the great Chaplin films through all the years to see for themselves what a superior sardonic comedy it is — and also to estimate how unjust was the bitter discrimination against it.[38]

Judith Crist, then reviewing for the *New York Herald Tribune*, crowned *Verdoux* a genre "prototype of the lovable-murderer comedy."[39] Oh how times had changed, a transformation also assisted by the release earlier that year of *Dr. Strangelove: Or, How I Learned to Stop Worrying and Love the Bomb* (1964). Dark comedy had now moved to center stage.

12

RED SKELTON
A Southern Yankee (1948)

"The paper's in the pocket of the boot with the buckle, the map is in the packet in the pocket of the jacket."
— Red Skelton's title character in A Southern Yankee

Red Skelton's greatest film revisits a comedy scenario not unlike Bob Hope in the *Road to Utopia* (1946)—a personality comedian spoofing an action adventure genre. But whereas *Utopia* casts Hope and *Road* companion Bing Crosby as hucksters off to a late nineteenth century Klondike, Skelton's misadventure chronicles his Civil War evolution from bellhop to spy. Moreover, what makes Skelton's parody distinctly his own, the aforementioned tongue-twisting opening notwithstanding, are the comedian's pantomime skills, arguably the greatest of any screen comedian whose career began in the sound era.[1] This unique status was undoubtedly further bolstered by the tutelage of Buster Keaton—a relationship to be fleshed out shortly.

While Skelton's comedy legacy is neglected today, he was one of America's favorite clowns when *A Southern Yankee* was released. Though he had obtained late 1930s headliner status in the last vestiges of vaudeville, two events during 1941 launched his major star status: the movie *Whistling in the Dark*, and his new radio program, the *Red Skelton Scrapbook of Satire*, or simply the *Red Skelton Show*.

By the time Skelton went into World War II military service (1944), his radio program was virtually in a Hooper-Nielsen ratings dead heat with the era's two perennial favorites: *Fibber McGee and Molly* and the *Bob Hope Program*.[2] Skelton had even comfortably passed the still very popular *Jack Benny Program* and *Abbott and Costello*. His MGM war-era films were also hits, though the studio was not as comedy-friendly as Paramount, so Skelton's humor sometimes seemed almost rationed in all-star productions like *DuBarry Was a Lady* (1943). But when a movie property was hand-tailored to his skills, such as the sequels: *Whistling in Dixie* (1942) and *Whistling in Brooklyn* (1943), the comedian entertainingly carried the films.

After Skelton's time in uniform, he effortlessly resumed his popular radio program, but MGM initially struggled with his post-war pictures. Indeed, the studio would later be embarrassed that Skelton's first bona fide hit, after sixteen months in the army, was a loan out to Columbia, *The Fuller Brush Man* (1948). In fact, the professional humiliation was intensified by *Brush* being a genuine box office smash.[3]

Well before this, in early 1947, however, the comedian was putting pressure on MGM for better material. For example, in May syndicated columnist and Skelton crony Bob Thomas would write, "All is not peaches and cream between Red Skelton and MGM. The comic is still unhappy over 'Morton of the Movies' [a soon to be 1947 misfire] which already has undergone considerable re-shooting. He complains the studio is not publicizing him, and is even talking of playing [taking] his film talents elsewhere. 'I've got them licked,' [Skelton claims], pointing to a radio microphone, 'as long as I've got this.'"[4]

"This," for Skelton, meant his radio career, a medium that gave him greater creative control and more money. (Raleigh Cigarettes, his radio sponsor, had even paid him $1,000 a week throughout his army tour just to ensure his postwar services.[5]) MGM soon realized this was not a bluff on Skelton's part, and others within the film industry were supportive of the comedian's need for better scripts. For instance, in a collaboration with Bob Thomas, celebrated funnyman Joe E. Brown soon included Skelton in his all-time top ten list of screen comedians, with the not so subtle suggestion to MGM, "he [Brown] thinks Skelton could be the greatest of them all, if given different material."[6]

Skelton's lobbying for stronger movies eventually paid off. In late summer 1947 famed Hollywood columnist Louella Parsons wrote, under the headline "Skelton Gets Break He Has Earned," that MGM was teaming the comedian with producer Paul Jones and the writing duo of Norman Panama and Melvin Frank.[7] For 1940s film comedy, this trio represented the gold standard. Jones had produced such Preston Sturges classics as *The Great McGinty* (1940), *The Lady Eve* (1941), *Sullivan's Travels*, and *The Palm Beach Story* (both 1942). He had also been in charge of the best two Hope and Crosby *Road* pictures: *The Road to Morocco* (1942) and *The Road to Utopia*. In addition, Jones produced such imaginative Hope solo outings as *My Favorite Blonde* (1942) and *Monsieur Beaucaire* (1946). Continuing this Hope connection, writers Panama and Frank started out collaborating on radio scripts for the ski-nosed comedian in 1938. By the time their names were first linked with Skelton in 1947, their most notable successes were the Hope-Jones pictures *My Favorite Blonde* (story), *Road to Utopia* (script), and *Monsieur Beaucaire* (script).

Jones' greatest gift as a producer was anchoring a film in good writing and then simply letting creative people do their thing with minimal interference. With the most elaborate story treatment from Panama and Frank, what would become *A Southern Yankee* was off to a solid start. While most story preludes to a script only run ten to twenty pages, Panama and Frank's contribution ran a whoppingly brilliant seventy pages.[8]

Indeed, for all inspired parody of an action adventure movie provided by Panama and Frank, their most creative touch, an "alternate ending," went unused. But this was probably because Skelton's antihero would not have gotten the girl, Sally Ann (Arlene Dahl). The writing team had proposed that Skelton's character lost touch with her as the Civil War wound down. Then, a chance encounter at the close finds Ann married to a Mr. Butler — Rhett Butler, with a show-stopping cameo by Clark Gable, as he briefly reprises his *Gone With the Wind* (1939) role.

Such a delightfully dizzy deviation had much to recommend it, beyond comic surprise. First, with Skelton often borrowing parody pages from Bob Hope, losing the girl in the final reel to Crosby was often the *Road* norm for the comedian — further underlining that antiheroic persona. Second, nothing says parody more entertainingly than cameos by actors associated with a film related to the genre being spoofed.[9] Third, because both Skelton and Gable were MGM stars, one would assume something could have been worked out. Indeed, Gable's widow would later reveal that Skelton was one of the actor's favorite entertainers.[10]

An added irony to this missed Gable opportunity, and maybe partly fueled by it, MGM would soon use clips of the actor for comic effect in the upcoming Skelton film — *Watch the Birdie* (1950, a loose remake of Buster Keaton's *The Cameraman*, 1928). The comedian plays multiple parts in the picture, including both a "Grandpop" and a shy grandson (Rusty) in need of a cinema tutorial on romance. Besides escalating the laugh quotient, the added footage doubled as a commercial for two of the studio's most macho male stars, Gable and close friend Robert Taylor. Thus, the amusing juxtapositioning of milquetoast Rusty and Hollywood machismo occurred with the comedian's character "studying" Gable's *Boom Town* (1940) and Taylor's *Johnny Eager* (1942). The topper to this — beyond two Skeltons interacting — is that Grandpop encourages Rusty to mimic the now politically incorrect rough-with-the-ladies style of Gable and Taylor. Not surprisingly, timid young Skelton asks old Skelton, "What if she slaps back?" A knowing Grandpop comically answers, "That, my boy [chuckling pause], is marriage."

A final pitch for Panama and Frank's suggestion to include a Gable cameo in *Yankee* comes from a former teaching colleague and *Gone With the Wind* scholar, Conrad Lane. Based upon his one-man-show as the husband of *Wind* author Margaret Mitchell, he assures me that the work's still multitude of fans would enjoy even a playful suggestion of what happened to the post— "Frankly, my dear, I don't give a damn" Rhett Butler. (Along related comic lines, Skelton joked at the time that *Yankee* would be another *Gone With the Wind* but should be called *Back With the Breeze*.)

Despite the inventive Panama and Frank original story foundation and the opportunity to draw from Buster Keaton's own Civil War reaffirmation parody, *The General* (1927), there were creative problems on the *Yankee* production. In Keaton's autobiography, he chronicles being called in as a troubleshooter because the movie "had received disappointing receptions when previewed."[11] But other sources suggest he was diplomatically toiling on the

Skelton and his romantic *Southern Yankee* co-star, Arlene Dahl.

film much earlier. For example, Marion Meade's Keaton biography includes this comment from Skelton's *Yankee* co-star, Arlene Dahl: "Whatever ideas Buster had were given sotto voce, so as not to hurt Red's feelings. He [Keaton] was a quiet presence who always knew what worked and what didn't. [But] You never would have imagined he was one of the great comedians of all time."[12] Keaton's early involvement was undoubtedly assisted by the *Yankee* director being the comedian's old working crony Edward Sedgwick, who megaphoned several of Keaton's MGM films, including the memorable *Spite Marriage* (1929, remade by Skelton as *I Dood It*, 1943). And when it came to collaborations between Keaton and Sedgwick, film historians tend to give the lion's share of credit to the silent clown.

Buster Keaton was a major influence on Red Skelton's film career, and especially *A Southern Yankee* (1948). Keaton is pictured here in his own comic Civil War saga, *The General* (1927).

Before exploring Keaton's major impact upon Skelton and *Yankee*, a comedy back story needs to be told. While MGM must be credited for bringing the two comedians together, the studio missed the proverbial golden opportunity to make the duo a production team—a separate comedy unit. Keaton so liked Skelton, both personally and professionally, that, as later chronicled by the older comedian's friend and pivotal biographer, Rudi Blesh, Keaton "went to bat for him [Skelton] as if he were his own son—or an extension of himself from [before] the disastrous past [when personal problems derailed an amazing career] into a restored future. He went straight to [MGM chief Louis B.] Mayer.... In the inner sanctum he surprised himself with an eloquence he had never been able to summon in his own behalf:

> "Let me take Skelton," he said, "and work as a small company within Metro [MGM]—do our own stories, our gags, our production, our direction. Use your resources but do it our way—the way I did my best pictures. I'll guarantee you hits," he said. "I won't take a cent of salary until they have proved themselves at the box office."[13]

A supportive Skelton also "offered to work without salary" (no small task for the money-conscious comedian) if he could team up with Keaton.[14] Paradoxically, Keaton's proposal merely paralleled (or was it inspired by?) the separate musical comedy niche producer Arthur Freed had created at MGM.

Sadly, but not surprisingly given Mayer and MGM's less-than-enlightened perspective on personality comedy during the 1930s and 1940s, a special Keaton and Skelton production unit did not happen. Besides the amazing comedy this might have produced, some cinematic autonomy could have also recharged Skelton's interest in film. As it was, the older comedian was sometimes frustrated over Skelton's lack of passion for pictures, though Keaton leaves the goldbricker unnamed in his memoir: "Another great comic would not even watch the scenes in his pictures that he did not appear in. He was more interested in getting back to his dressing room so he could write jokes for his radio show."[15]

How does one know Keaton was referring to Skelton? His widow, Eleanor Norris Keaton, confirmed this to me at a later film festival in her husband's honor.[16] But the comedian had also put a name to this "great comic" in an obscure documentary broadcast after his death:

> Skelton's first love was radio and yet nobody could do a better scene on the screen than Skelton without opening his trap.... [But] he'd go to his dressing room on the stage between scenes and he wasn't worrying about what he'd do in the next scene. He'd go in there and start writing gags for [his radio] "Little Junior" [character] to say, or something for his radio script.[17]

But one could argue that Skelton's obsession over writing Junior sketches was more a product of having total control on radio, versus feeling like a mere hired hand in film. In fact, Skelton invariably defined himself as a pantomimist.[18] Regardless, the result was the same for Keaton—a struggle to maximize the screen talent of his gifted young friend.

Yet, neither comedy connoisseurs nor regular film fans have anything to complain about with the finished *A Southern Yankee*. Skelton's execution of several Keaton-devised sketches is so effortlessly funny they seem almost improvised. Chronicling the older comedian's earliest involvement on the production would also explain how Keaton's most inspired contribution to *Yankee*, the two-sided flag scene, is included in Harry Tugend's script material prepared for the picture.[19] The Tugend pages were filed *after* the earliest documented Keaton involvement on *Yankee*.[20] However, because there are some questions about dates cited on the original Yankee script material in the Cinema-Television Library at the University of Southern California in Los

Angeles, it is possible that the idea for the battle scene with the two-sided flag and uniform originated with Tugend but was not initially shot. Later, Keaton recognized the scene's significance and orchestrated the material's inclusion in the finished film.

Still, this pivotal scene is one of the few *Yankee* contributions for which the otherwise modest Keaton takes credit in his memoir. And like Skelton's first mentor, Clarence Stout, Keaton's chronicling of past events usually rings true, as opposed to Skelton's often "creative" reminiscences. Thus, here is the older comedian's detailed account of the two-sided scene, and why it proved to be such a comedy highlight:

> [I] contributed the gag in which Red was shown walking between the Union Army and the Confederate Army, with both armies cheering him madly. The reason was that Red was wearing half of a Union Army hat and uniform on the side facing the Northern soldiers and a Southern hat and uniform on the other. In addition, he had sewed together the flags of the two opposing sides so that the boys in blue saw a Union flag and the Southerners only the flag of the Confederacy. Both sides cheer him wildly until a sudden gust of wind reverses the flag, showing both sides the game he is playing. As Red turns around to straighten the flag they discover his half-and-half uniform [too].[21]

This scene is easily the most brilliant in the Skelton filmography and merits inclusion in any cinema pantheon of legendary comedy routines. The material is also perfectly consistent with the Keaton oeuvre — the darkly comic ludicrousness of life. That is, Skelton's character's foray into the contested space between the two opposing armies is initially a great success — a success predicated upon the most knee-jerk of responses — blindly jingoistic, flag-waving patriotism. Such rigid behavior is what comedy theorist Henri Bergson refers to as "mechanical inelasticity."[22] This is comedy more reflective of the cerebral Keaton than the heart-directed emotion of Chaplin.

Though the scene was initially conceived as having the two flags sewn together, and was first maybe even shot that way, the Hays censorship office would not allow it — too disrespectful! Consequently, in the finished picture Skelton carries *two* flags between the opposing armies, with both the Union and Confederate soldiers initially seeing only their own flags. (Paradoxically, many viewers "remember" the sequence as having the flags sewn together. In fact, that had been my childhood memory of the bit, until I rescreened the movie for a later Skelton biography)

Nevertheless, this Keatonesque *Yankee* scene is predicated upon the older comedian's formalistic tendencies. For instance, the contrasting camera placements which make both armies think one of their own is bravely carrying the flag through no-man's land. But Skelton's ruse, to extricate himself from being pinned down between two armies, is short-lived. Yet, even this sudden change is classic Keaton. For Keaton, the absurdity of modern life is often triggered by natural forces, be it the rock slide of *Seven Chances* (1925) or the tornado of *Steamboat Bill, Jr.* (1928). In Skelton's *Yankee* a simple change in the wind wreaks comic disaster. Now each army sees the enemy's flag, and as Skelton struggles to control these symbols in the wind, the two-sided nature of his uniform becomes apparent, also. A *change in the wind*—what a wonderful metaphor for how easily man's grand plans are derailed.

There are several additional Keaton bits documented in the *Yankee* files at the USC archives. The most entertaining example is an inventive exercise in Keaton minimalism, which is again driven by camera placement—and a small pine cone (another bow to provocative Mother Nature). After a lengthy horseback ride, Skelton's character stops to dismount. The Keaton-authored material (with Sedgwick) was shot as follows:

> Aubrey [Skelton] glances around for a place to rest his sore posterior. He spies a tree stump. The minute his rump touches the stump, Aubrey jumps with pain. He needs something softer to sit on. He looks about for a moment; then, gathering an armful of pine needles on the ground, he places them on the tree stump for matting. He sits down and this time he fairly flies off [the stump] with pain. As he turns around we see that a pine cone which was concealed in the needles is still stuck to the seat of his pants. Aubrey, feeling about in the pine needles where the cone was concealed, and discovering nothing that should have caused such sharp pain, sits down [on the stump] again. Of course, he sits right on the pine cone. Once again he leaps with pain. He glances about suspiciously—unable to understand what it is that is causing the trouble.[23]

Skelton's battle with the invisible-to-him pine cone is yet another exercise in Keaton basics. The seemingly wild-goose-chase futility of life is reduced to a pesky pine cone, out of Skelton's line of vision. As with the two-sided flag and uniform scene, this second Keaton-constructed routine is predicated on the positioning of the lens. Indeed, Red's first pine cone-induced jump off the stump is initially a mystery to the viewer, too, until the comedian turns around. Also, like the *change in the wind* catalyst from the earlier sketch, the pine cone represents Keaton's fatalistic use of Mother Nature to cause a comic character grief. And having Skelton "suspiciously" looking around, as if there were a conspiracy going on underlines yet again the cerebral nature of Keaton's art, as opposed to the emotional, heart-directed orientation of Chaplin's films: the two poles of silent comedy upon which Skeleton drew.

Either the pine cone scene, or the *change in wind* routine could qualify for what director Mike Nichols calls the "controlling metaphor"— the idea that defines a film.[24] That is, Skelton's character is trying to be a spy in a world where an inanimate object can mystify him and a variable summer breeze could kill him. Based upon this comic everyman, therefore, what chance does any of us have? Yet, Skelton's *Yankee* somehow "soldiers" through, thus providing hope ... *or* anticipating by decades the darkly comic message of so many later Cohen Brothers films: the dumbing down of America provides a certain protection — nothing seems to matter. If one embraces the latter "reading" of *Yankee*, an alternate ending even better than the proposed Rhett Butler twist, would be to borrow the ironic close of Keaton's *College* (1927), where the persevering comedian's happy ending romantic winning of the heroine is immediately qualified by a series of brief epilogue dissolves that negate the preceding celebration of love.

Additional Keaton-authored *Yankee* material (on file at USC) which surfaced on screen included sketches in which Skelton seemingly attempts to carry half the luggage available during the Civil War, as well as several routines tied to avoiding enemy capture by way of hiding in a doghouse, and behind linen on a clothesline, and an accidental visit to a dentist. Keaton was also responsible for the scrapping of early *Yankee* footage showcasing Skelton acting like an "imbecile." The older filmmaker explained:

> As the comedian and leading man, Red lost the audience's sympathy by behaving too stupidly. If you act as screwy as he was doing, the people out front would not care what happened to the character you were playing.... [The scenes were reshot], toning down Red's nutty behavior."[25]

Keaton had an excellent handle on the comedic fine line between the intellectually challenged and the village idiot. One of the ways in which MGM had mismanaged

Toning down Red Skelton's gift for inspired stupidity in *A Southern Yankee*.

Keaton's career was to take his initially slow (but quick to adapt) silent screen character and turn him into a sound film boob.

Skelton's *Yankee* figure, like most movie clowns, is closer to dunce-like than erudite, but Keaton was correct in somewhat lessening the dumb-squared factor. Besides making Skelton's figure into someone with whom it would be easier to identify (as Keaton has suggested), modestly upgrading the intelligence of the *Yankee* title character also makes his occasional alternating between antiheroic physical comedy and smart aleck verbal wit more palatable.

In the final analysis, Skelton's *Yankee* character is a comically self-made man who is not as well made as he might have been but who (like most of us) is coping. The beauty of Skelton's performance is that he mixes the input of Keaton, and Panama and Frank (à la the split-comedy personality of a Bob Hope), with his own Chaplinesque tendencies. For example, whereas the minimalism of Keaton's "Great Stone Face" would have given *Yankee*'s *change in the wind* sequence a greater existentialism absurdity, Skelton's demonstrative look of comic shock and fear is more poignantly real to most viewers. But Keaton's cerebral influence helps balance the younger comedian's proclivity to sometimes overplay Chaplin pathos, as Skelton later does in the entertaining yet mawkish *The Clown* (1953).

At Skelton's best, as personified by his *Yankee* role, the funnyman has an endearing vulnerability which makes the viewer want to reach out to protect him or, to recycle a phrase of which film critic David Thomson is fond — "to put an umbrella over his head." Skelton's *Yankee* character anticipates the comedian's later most beloved television figure, Freddie the Freeloader. This inspired comic creation, sort of a cross between Chaplin's Tramp and Emmett Kelly's Weary Willie, was the most fully realized character in Skelton's eccentric small screen menagerie. Of course, even here one must acknowledge a Keaton touch, if for no other reason than Weary Willie's signature routine is the haunting untiring attempt to sweep up a circle of light — cast from an off-camera circus spotlight. All such modern comic futility is best called Keatonesque, be it Buster caught on the treadmill-like paddle-wheel steamer of *Daydreams* (1922), or devising the elusive pine cone sketch for Skelton's *Yankee*.

To carry the *Yankee*–Freddie the Freeloader analogy a step further, one might best link Skelton's antiheroic Civil War character's ingenuity in stitching the two-sided uniform and flag to a later description of Freddie by one of Skelton's television writers, Larry Rhine:

> Freddie was our [the writers'] favorite. There was depth to this lovable rogue. Chaplinesque. A have-not but in his mind a have-everything. A soul in a discarded tin can.... Freddie is a poet, philosopher, make-doer.[26]

Red Skelton as his later pivotal television character, Freddie the Freeloader (circa 1965).

Mixing the comic existentialism of Keaton (yet losing the latter comedian's minimalism) with Chaplin's frantic enthusiasm, such as his Tramp's skidding corners on his celebrated "east-west feet," Skelton's Yankee is often as busy as a nurse at an earthquake. If his sometimes seemingly running only from the knees down movement is reminiscent of a *Life* magazine description of baseball contemporary Yogi Berra's gait, "like a fat girl in a skirt," Skelton was paid to make us laugh.[27] Of all the funnymen chronicled in this text, Skelton's human comedy frailties in *Yankee* seem the most naturally presented, as if he were unaware of (Harry Langdon–like) all the muses which assisted this performance. Consequently, his shenanigans embraced comedy's ephemeral magic elixir — to either be spontaneous ... or appear so (artfully artless).

Thanks to *Yankee*, MGM finally had a post-war critical and commercial hit for their often under-utilized comedy star. The all-important *Variety* stated:

> It's as wild and raucous a conglomeration of gags and belly-laughs as Skelton's recent [Columbia movie] "The Fuller Brush Man." The kiddies, the family and the general film fan will find it bait for the risibility and respond with hearty ticket window payoff.[28]

The *Hollywood Reporter* said, "Skelton, well on his road to becoming a really great clown, makes the most of every line."[29] The *Los Angeles Daily News* added:

> Red Skelton fans are going to love this one. It has everything Skelton does best — the pratfall, the delayed gag, the double-take, the mugging, the [spoofing] cowardice, and all the rest.[30]

Cue, with an intuitive sense of the uncredited Keaton, noted, "With gags borrowed from old time silent movies, and slapstick stunts adapted from his [Skelton's] own and others' comedies, Red Skelton romps dizzily through this wacky Civil War comedy."[31] But the critical pièce de resistance came from *Motion Picture Daily*, which called the film the "fastest, funniest comedy of this or any recent year."[32]

Despite such superlative reviews for Skelton's greatest picture, history has done a disservice to *Yankee*'s critical reception. Sadly, much of this problem can be attributed to Arthur Marx's Skelton book, the first biography of the comedian, which claimed the *Yankee* critiques were "lukewarm."[33] Worse yet, Marx suggested "lukewarm" was an appropriate take on this neglected masterpiece. Marx had a proclivity to limit his review research to the *New York Times*, a publication that had panned *Yankee*.[34] But a close reading of this *Times* critique reveals more of an ongoing attack on MGM's mishandling of Skelton's career than simply a slam of the picture.

Granted, a period *Hollywood Reporter* article suggested *Yankee* had not been well received by New York critics.[35] Yet, there were many positive Gotham reviews, too. For instance, the *New York Morning Telegraph* said, "For Skelton fans ... this is the gravy train. They'll no doubt go rolling down the aisles with [comic] hysterics."[36] Moreover, it was obvious that the general New York viewer was pleased with the picture. The *Motion Picture Herald* documented:

> Even when [*Yankee* was] previewed in a hot New York theatre — the air-conditioning engineers were on strike — the sweltering audience had itself a great time as Skelton ... mimicked and drawled his way through 90 minutes of pure fun. [And the two-sided uniform scene resulted in] the theatre howling with uproarious laughter.[37]

Or, to put the picture's ongoing comedy uniqueness more succinctly, one might simply close with a quote from contemporary film historian Leonard Maltin, "*A Southern Yankee* is superior Skelton all the way."[38]

Epilogue

"Even if the world were perfect," Yogi Berra once said, "it wouldn't be."

As baseball great Yogi Berra, the surrealist wordsmith of derailed cracker-barrel axioms implies, life at best is a human comedy. Our favorite clowns simply underline that fact. Thus, if one's day-to-day existence seems like the proverbial "circular firing squad," our favorite personality comedians comfort us through laughter, and remind us that no one is immune and that we are still probably better off than our favorite antiheroes.

Most genres are predicated upon what poet Samuel Coleridge (1772–1834) called a "willing suspension of disbelief." For instance, where would the musical be if viewers did not accept performers suddenly bursting into song, or what would become of the action adventure film if fans did not embrace heroes effortlessly vanquishing scores of villains with minimal strain. Obviously, that same "suspension" applies equally to personality comedians, whether W. C. Fields as a "bank dick" or Charlie Chaplin's Tramp being mistaken for a "dictator." But having said that, cinema clowns tap into so much universal angst, forever the outsiders peeking through the window at normalcy, that the genre often seems more realistic.

Unlike my earlier comedian decade book, *Film Clowns of the Depression* (2007), however, where everyone but Chaplin avoided acknowledging the economic crisis of the 1930s, the text in hand documents how World War II cast a much more obvious shadow on 1940s screen clowns. Fully half of the films featured herein have a direct war contact: Chaplin's take on Hitler in *The Great Dictator* (1940), Abbott & Costello accidentally becoming *Buck Privates* (1941), Jack Benny battling Nazi in *To Be or Not to Be* (1942), Eddie Bracken's dream to join the military in *The Miracle of Morgan Creek* (1944), the Marx Brothers continuing to fight escaped Nazis in the post-war *A Night in Casablanca* (1946), and Chaplin again applying the business side of war to the private sector in *Monsieur Verdoux* (1947).

Moreover, half of the text's six remaining pictures have indirect tie-ins with the war. For example, Red Skelton's title character struggles with cowardice as a Civil War soldier in *A Southern Yankee* (1948). While Bob Hope and Bing Crosby's *Road to Utopia* (1946) is the best film in their celebrated *Road* escapades, the series' signature globetrotting still managed to play upon the public's new found war-era fascination with all points around the world. And Hope's solo outing spoof of film noir in *My Favorite Brunette* (1947), like the Marxes' *Night*, was dependent upon the horrors of World War II being *the* central factor in spawning this target genre of fatalistic despair.

American cinema's take upon the personality comedian is usually obsessed with the little man sideswiped by the heartless (but often mundane) absurdity of the modern world. Chaplin has been the ongoing exception, from his groundbreaking World War I comedy *Shoulder Arms* (1918, at a time when friends and colleagues were strongly counseling against such a risky subject), to his aforementioned singularly unique shish kebab of the Depression when that seemed an equally verboten topic. Undoubtedly, Chaplin ushering in the 1940s with the then controversial *Great Dictator* contributed to war having a higher profile in that decade's clown comedies. Still, not to be outdone, his later *Monsieur Verdoux* gave viewers a second comic tyrant also based upon a real life monster but without the *Dictator*'s dual focus narrative safety valve inclusion of the Tramp-like Jewish barber.

Another commonality of these anything-but-common seminal films is that, ironically, for an era associated with "radio comedians" (the majority of the funnymen featured in this text were radio dial regulars sometime during the 1940s), these movies are often anchored to the world of silent comedy. For instance, besides this book's three-picture representation of original silent comedians Chaplin and Fields, Preston Sturges' showcase satire of *Safety Last* (1923) icon Harold Lloyd in *The Sin of Harold Diddlebock* (1947) even opened with the closing reel of the silent funnyman's *The Freshman* (1925). Plus, the then new comedy stars Danny Kaye and Eddie Bracken were perceived and first packaged as updated Harold Lloyd characters, with Kaye's *Kid From Brooklyn* even being a Lloyd remake. Most of Red Skelton's best films, including his watershed *A Southern Yankee* (1948), were greatly impacted by the work of legendary silent great Buster Keaton. Skelton benefited from both new material from then MGM gag writer Keaton, as well as simply remaking the older comedian's pictures. Indeed, *Yankee* itself is sometimes called a loose remake of Keaton's Civil War dark comedy *The General* (1927), though Buster's influence has much more to do with special material he wrote specifically for Skelton.

While the often inspired comic lines or dialogue of this text's highlighted movies will be addressed shortly, it bears noting that the 1940s upgrade of silent comedy's legacy was not limited to these pictures. If giving a semblance of the Tramp another final bow in *Dictator* was not enough pump-priming, Chaplin simply dusted off a ready-made catalyst for this revisionism. That is, when the comedian reissued his acclaimed *Gold Rush* (1925) in early 1942, with a voiceover narration and modest editorial changes, it was a critical and commercial sensation, including a record ten-week run at New York City's Globe theater.[1] The *Hollywood Reporter*'s rave review included comments conducive to also salvaging other sadly neglected silent films and artists:

> The comedy ... boasts highlights even funnier than our fondest memories of them — the deathless eating of a boiled shoe, the to-this-day unduplicated dance of the French rolls, the kidding of thrill climaxes.... The picture's reissue at this time is another master stroke by a master showman.[2]

Though Chaplin, Keaton, Lloyd, Fields, and the sometimes surrogates Skelton, Kaye, and Bracken helped give new 1940s energy to slapstick's ageless form, the Marxes' *A Night in Casablanca* provided the mad mute (Harpo) with yet another platform for his inventive visual shtick, too. These routines ranged from his combination dueling and eating scene, to a musical chairs–like hotel room hiding sketch. But the picture's biggest laugh is generated by an opening sight gag surprise — a building's collapse is seemingly caused by a sarcastic cop asking the leaning-against-a-wall Harpo whether this most surreal of the Marxes thinks he is holding up the structure ... which proves to be the case.

While *Night* was the last Marx Brothers movie with the traditional trio of Groucho, Harpo, and Chico, a follow-up film (*Love Happy*, 1949) further accented the visual slant by keying upon Harpo and his team-mate within the team, Chico. While Groucho provides some early voiceover narration and a brief picture-closing cameo, *Love Happy* is essentially a Harpo vehicle, with the comedian playing a tramp figure which some Marx biographers have likened to Chaplin's "little fellow."[3] Still, *Love Happy* suffers from a lack of Groucho. *Night* is a stronger Harpo movie because, as humor historian Neil Schmitz notes of the non-speaking Marx, who periodically pops up in a film without necessarily being of the film:

> [As] the haphazard narrative goes on around him ... he is never found in the purity of mime. His silence rather is a silence that is in relation to a particular brilliance of [a Groucho] speech.[4]

Though most personality comedians of any age are defined by some degree of silent visual humor, even if it is no more than simply "looking funny," 1940s film comedy was often enriched by a greater appreciation and sometimes last artistic utilization of pioneering silent funny men. But just as Harpo's *Love Happy* did not make the cut as one of this book's featured films, several other once prominent pantomimist, ranging from Harry Langdon to Laurel and Hardy, also generated some late career interest which one could couple with the 1940s renewal of interest in yesteryear comedy.

Undoubtedly, the best of the bunch was Laurel and Hardy, though their work during the decade, with the possible exception of *Jitterbugs* (1943), in which Stan and Ollie come to the antiheroic rescue of yet another put-upon heroine, pales in comparison to their earlier classics.[5] One of the team's first film historian champions, William Everson, was fond of calling *Jitterbugs* an "oasis" in an otherwise desert landscape of their 1940s films. Still, I would chart a middle ground. The movies are disappointing but even Laurel and Hardy in decline have their moments.

A third link for this study's pivotal pictures, and in stark contrast to the previous physical and visual comedy component, is that these movies are also often gifted with brilliantly funny lines or dialogue. Granted, in any given decade of American film comedy one can usually zero in on some legitimate classics of sight or sound, but the 1940s were verbally special for no other reason than the word "Sturges," an artistic second cousin to Oscar Wilde and arguably American cinema's best writer of witty repartee.

Preston Sturges' mercurial writer-director career in Hollywood was limited to the 1940s, but its short-lived brilliance might best be described by a few lines from Edna St. Vincent Millay's poem "First Fig" (1920): "My candle burns at both ends; it will not last the night; but ah ... it gives a lovely light." Sturges' *The Miracle of Morgan Creek* and *The Sin of Harold Diddlebock* are two such artistic candles burning at both ends, providing both casts with a wealth of verbal and visual shtick. As the *New York Journal American* critic said of *Miracle*, "They could run this Preston Sturges daffy-dilly as a silent, or simply give you the sound track. It would be hilarious in either case."[6] Such praise applies equally to *Diddlebock*. An observation Sturges later made in his memoir, about an older man thinking back on his life, also nicely describes both these films and the human comedy in general:

> a Mardi Gras, a street parade of masked, drunken, hysterical, laughing, disguised, travestied, carnal, innocent, and perspiring humanity of all sexes, wandering aimlessly, but always in circles, in search of that of which it is a part: life.[7]

Maybe the most provocative paradox of Sturges' enigmatic life is that his art could so successfully link polar opposites. For example, *Miracle* and *Did-*

dlebock not only mix memorable slapstick and laugh-out-loud dialogue, both pictures satirize small-town values while still somehow making the viewer nostalgic for that same populist feel good milieu ... which maybe never existed beyond the film world of silent comedians like Lloyd and 1930s humanists like Frank Capra.

Kaye's *The Kid from Brooklyn* operates on that same comically bipolar Sturges level, celebrating a yesteryear innocent (à la Lloyd and Bracken) but ultimately making it obvious that modern success is not based upon old-fashioned hard work but a new twist on deus ex machina — comic absurdity to the rescue. And while W. C. Fields' *The Bank Dick*, which he scripted as Mahatma Kane Jeeves, offers no populism praise as it skewers small-town life, the ending predates these other "miracle" conclusions in its cynical suggestion that happy endings are strictly a matter of long shot chance.

While the verbal banter of *Miracle, Diddlebock, Brooklyn,* and *Dick* sideswiped the former status quo, Chaplin and Ernst Lubitsch used the 1940s spoken world to help launch an even more iconoclastic enterprise — a dark comedy genre for mainstream cinema. Ironically, while *Dictator* and *To Be* applied black humor to save what remained of a seemingly innocent populist world, *Monsieur Verdoux*'s use of the genre aligned itself more with Sturges and suggested hypocrisy reigns. But Chaplin granted no last minute personality comedian rescue, and Verdoux goes to the guillotine.

Though the Marxes' *Night* and Hope's *Brunette* are never so deep-dish *Verdoux*-like in their entertaining verbal patter, the fact that both movies parody the darkly comic world of film noir still links these spoofs to the murderous macabre transitions being made by Chaplin and Lubitsch. When society goes through cataclysmic change, such as a world war and a holocaust, even the popular arts invariably reflect these shifts, whether in dead-on dark comedies or in the border skirmish style of two noir parodies.

The funny lines of the remaining focal films are anchored in other mediums: Abbott and Costello's polished sketches in *Buck Privates* are slickly recycled from their stage work. The brilliant wordsmithing of both *Road to Utopia* and *A Southern Yankee* come courtesy of two former Bob Hope radio writers, Norman Panama and Melvin Frank. And at times this latter duo almost matches Sturges' pointed drollness. For instance, when *Utopia*'s Hope forgets he is supposed to be tough in a Yukon frontier bar and orders a lemonade, Panama and Frank rescue him with the now famous rejoinder to the bartender, "in a dirty glass!"

As Tom Stoppard suggests in his *Rosencrantz and Guildenstern Are Dead* (1966, filmed 1990) — a story which might be described as theater of the absurd as a party game, or Laurel and Hardy meet Hamlet: "Every exit is an entrance someplace else." Consequently, while the majority of comedians herein chronicled would never again creatively surpass these films (Danny Kaye's Panama and Frank-written *Court Jester*, 1956, would be the only obvious exception), these pictures foreshadowed the shape of much comedy to come. Painting in broad strokes, by the 1960s, dark comedy would be a mainstream genre. Kaye and Eddie Bracken both created screen personae by way of a groundbreaking cinema schizophrenia that obviously impacted *the* personality comedian of the 1950s — hello dementia Jerry Lewis, who was best showcased early while teamed (balanced) by the casually cool Dean Martin.

Bob Hope's equally influential comic split persona (antihero and smart aleck) would continue to serve him well in several 1950s screen comedies, in addition to being a model for countless modern (post–1960) film funnymen, including the greatest comedy auteur (writing, directing, starring) since Chaplin — Woody Allen. Plus, during the 1950s both Hope and Jerry Lewis would take greater creative advantage of a comic writer-director who was first making a name for himself behind the screen in memorable 1940s films like *A Night in Casablanca*— Frank Tashlin, the author of the aforementioned Harpo collapsing building bit which opens that movie.

All in all, personality comedians still often focus on the little things in life, such as the *Dictator* scene in which Chaplin's Jewish barber loses himself in shaving a customer in exacting time to a radio broadcast of Brahms' "Hungarian Dance No. 5," despite the lingering threat of a concentration camp. But whereas day-to-day comic minutiae used to be an antiheroic dodge from life's more crushing worries, frequently even these once mundane safety zones can now be a minefield for modern comedy. As author and *New York Times* critic David Gates wrote in 2009, "[Today's] chitchat sometimes achieves the lunatic inconsequence of an [absurdist] play by Beckett or Pinter."[8] And if any 1940s viewers shocked by the then extremes of Chaplin and Lubitsch were to be pinballed through time to the dark comedy clown excesses of today, they "would assume an expression somewhere between a Jack Benny stare and the stoic grimace of a 13th-century saint being burned alive at the stake."[9] But then as now, life goes on ... forever assisted by those who make us laugh. As Chaplin was fond of saying, "In the end, everything is a gag."

Filmography

1940   *The Great Dictator* (United Artist, 128 minutes).
Director and Screenplay: Charles Chaplin. Stars: Chaplin, Paulette Goddard, Jack Oakie, Henry Daniell, Reginald Gardiner, Billy Gilbert, Maurice Moskovich.

1940   *The Bank Dick* (Universal, 74 minutes).
Director: Edward Cline. Screenplay: Mahatma Kane Jeeves [W. C. Fields]. Stars: Fields, Cora Witherspoon, Una Merkel, Evelyn Del Rio, Jessie Ralph, Franklin Pangborn, Shemp Howard, Richard Purcell, Grady Sutton.

1941   *Buck Privates* (Universal, 77 minutes).
Director: Arthur Lubin. Screenplay: Arthur T. Horman ("special material" credit: John Grant). Stars: Abbott and Costello, Lee Bowman, Alan Curtis, Andrews Sisters, Jane Frazee, Nat Pendleton.

1942   *To Be or Not to Be* (United Artists, 108 minutes).
Director: Ernst Lubitsch. Screenplay: Edwin Justus Mayer, from a Lubitsch and Melchior Lengyel story. Stars: Jack Benny, Carole Lombard, Robert Stack, Felix Bressart, Lionel Atwill, Stanley Ridges, Sig Ruman, Tom Dugan, Charles Halton.

1944   *The Miracle of Morgan's Creek* (Paramount, 99 minutes).
Director and Screenplay: Preston Sturges. Stars: Eddie Bracken, Betty Hutton, Diana Lynn, William Demarest, Porter Hall, Emory Parnell, Al Bridges, Julius Tannen, Vic Potel, Brian Donlevy, Akim Tamiroff.

1946   *Road to Utopia* (Paramount, 90 minutes).
Director: Hal Walker. Screenplay: Norman Panama and Melvin Frank (uncredited material from Bob Hope and Bing Crosby gag writers). Music and lyrics: Johnny Burke and Jimmy Van Heusen. Stars: Bob Hope, Bing Crosby, Dorothy Lamour, Robert Benchley, Hillary Brooke, Douglass Dumbrille, Jack LaRue.

1946 *The Kid from Brooklyn* (Samuel Goldwyn Production, released through RKO, 113 minutes).
Director: Norman Z. McLeod. Screenplay: Grover Jones, Frank Butler, and Richard Connell, from the Lynn Root and Harry Clork play *The Milky Way*, adapted by Don Hartman and Melville Shavelson. Music and lyrics: Julie Styne and Sammy Cahn (words and music of Kaye's "Pavlova": Sylvia Fine and Max Liebman). Stars: Danny Kaye, Virginia Mayo, Vera-Ellen, Steve Cochran, Eve Arden, Walter Abel, Lionel Stander, Fay Bainter, Clarence Kolb, Jerome Cowan, Don Wilson.

1946 *A Night in Casablanca* (United Artists, 85 minutes).
Director: Archie L. Mayo. Screenplay: Joseph Fields and Roland Kibbee (additional material: Frank Tashlin). Music and lyrics: Ted Snyder, Bert Kalmar, and Harry Ruby. Stars: Marx Brothers (Groucho, Harpo, and Chico), Siegfried Rumann, Lesette Verea, Charles Drake.

1947 *The Sin of Harold Diddlebock* (California Pictures, released through United Artists, 90 minutes).
Director and Screenplay: Preston Sturges. Stars: Harold Lloyd, Frances Ramsden, Jimmy Conlin, Raymond Walburn, Edgar Kennedy, Franklin Pangborn, Rudy Vallée, Lionel Stander, Margaret Hamilton.

1947 *My Favorite Brunette* (Paramount, 87 minutes).
Director: Elliott Nugent. Screenplay: Edmund Beloin and Jack Rose. Stars: Bob Hope, Dorothy Lamour, Peter Lorre, Lon Chaney, John Hoyt, Charles Dingle, Reginald Denny, Jim Thorpe.

1947 *Monsieur Verdoux* (United Artists, 123 minutes).
Director and Screenplay: Charles Chaplin. Stars: Chaplin, Martha Raye, Isobel Elsom, Marilyn Nash, Robert Lewis, Mady Correll, Allison Roddan, Marjorie Bennett, Bernard J. Nedell, Charles Evans, William Frawley.

1949 *A Southern Yankee* (MGM, 90 minutes).
Director: Edward Sedgwick. Screenplay: Harry Tugend, from a story by Melvin Frank and Norman Panama (loosely inspired by Buster Keaton's *The General*, 1927; additional gags were created by Keaton for *Yankee*). Stars: Red Skelton, Brian Donlevy, Arlene Dahl, George Coulouris.

CHAPTER NOTES

Preface and Acknowledgments

1. Steve Lopez, *The Soloist* (New York: Berkley Books, 2008), 9–10.
2. Melissa Burdick Harmon, "Noel Coward and His Jamaican Paradise," *Biography*, (October 1998), 78.
3. Christopher Buckley, *Losing Mum and Pup: A Memoir* (New York: Twelve: Hachette Book Group, 2009), 68.
4. Bill Russell (with Alan Steinberg), *Red and Me: My Coach, My Lifelong Friend* (New York: HarperCollins, 2009), 145.
5. "Right Up There: Red Skelton's Back on Top and Here Are [the] Reasons Why," *TV Guide*, April 28, 1956, 6.
6. Marco R. della Cava, "Conan Brings a New Vibe to 'Tonight,'" *USA Today*, May 29–31, 2009, 2A.

Introduction

1. John Lahr, *Coward: The Playwright* (1982; rpt. New York: Discus Book, 1983), 162.
2. Hilton Als, "Intruder in the Wings," *The New Yorker*, May 26, 2008, 82.
3. Marco R. della Cava, "Conan Brings a New Vibe to 'Tonight,'" *USA Today*, May 29–31, 2009, 2-A.
4. Mark Harris, "Twilight of the Tummlers," *New York*, June 1, 2009, 35.

Chapter 1

1. *The Tramp and the Dictator*, 2002, a Kevin Brownlow film.
2. Howard Barnes, "The Screen [column]," *New York Times*, June 22, 1941.
3. Bosley Crowther, "In 'The Great Dictator,' Charlie Chaplin Reveals Again the Greatness in Himself," *New York Times*, October 20, 1940.
4. "The Current Cinema: Charlie's Hitler," *The New Yorker*, October 26, 1940.
5. Carl Combs, "'The Great Dictator' In Carthay Premiere," *Hollywood Citizen-News*, November 15, 1940.
6. *The Great Dictator* review, *Variety*, October 16, 1940.
7. "Chaplin: A Bewildered 'Little Feller' Bucking Modern Times," *Newsweek*, February 8, 1936, 19.
8. Robert Van Gelder, "Chaplin Draws a Keen Weapon," *New York Times Magazine*, September 8, 1940, 8.
9. "Charlie Chaplin," in *Current Biography 1940*, ed. Maxine Block (New York: H. W. Wilson, 1940), 158.
10. See the author's "Chaplin and the Progressive Era: The Neglected Politics of a Clown," *Indiana Social Studies Quarterly*, Fall 1981 (Ball State University), 10–18.
11. See Steve Lipman's *Laughter in Hell: The Use of Humor During the Holocaust* (1991; rpt. Northvale, New Jersey: Jason Aronson, 1993).
12. Rich Cohen, "Becoming Adolf," *Vanity Fair*, November 2007, 239–40.
13. Charles Maland, *Chaplin and American Culture: The Evolution of a Star Image* (Princeton, New Jersey: Princeton University Press, 1989), 177.
14. "Chaplin Says He Just Had to Make That Speech," *New York World Telegram*, October 19, 1940, 7.

15. Ibid.
16. David Robinson, *Chaplin: His Life and Art* (New York: McGraw-Hill, 1985), 493.
17. Ilan Avisar, *Screening the Holocaust: Cinema's Images of the Unimaginable* (Bloomington: Indiana University Press, 1988), 135.
18. "Chaplin Says He Had to Make That Speech," 7.
19. Charles J. Maland, *Chaplin and American Culture: The Evolution of a Star Image*, 171.
20. "The Great Dictator," *Sidney Morning Herald*, November 5, 1940, Women's Supplement section, 7.
21. Reginald Gardiner, "*The Great Dictator*: Charlie Chaplin's Gift of Humor and Satire to the Totalitarian State," *New York Herald Tribune*, September 16, 1940.
22. Charles Chaplin, *My Autobiography* (1966; rpt. New York: Pocket Books, Inc., 1966), 426.
23. Theodore Huff, *Charlie Chaplin* (1951; rpt. New York: Arno Press & *New York Times*, 1972), 272.
24. "Mr. Chaplin Answers His Critics," *New York Times*, October 27, 1940, section 9, 5.
25. Deborah Crawford, *Franz Kafka: Man Out of Step* (New York: Crown Publishers, 1973), 99.
26. Ibid., 72–73.
27. Otis Ferguson, *The Great Dictator* review, *The New Republic*, November 4, 1940.
28. "Chaplin Strikes Back at New York Critics," *Los Angeles Times*, January 5, 1941.
29. John Mosher, "The Current Cinema: Charlie's Hitler," *The New Yorker*, October 26, 1940, 78.
30. Louella Parsons (syndicated), "Old, New Chaplin in 'Dictator' Film," *New York Journal American*, January 29, 1939.
31. Kevin Thomas, "'Great Dictator' in Re-release," *Los Angeles Times*, June 23, 1972.

Chapter 2

1. See the author's *W. C. Fields: A Bio-Bibliography* (Westport, Connecticut: Greenwood Press, 1984); *Groucho & W. C. Fields: Huckster Comedians* (Jackson: University Press of Mississippi, 1994).
2. Andre Sennwald, "W. C. Fields: Buffoon," *New York Times*, January 13, 1935, section 9, 5.
3. Nicholas Yanni, *W. C. Fields* (New York: Pyramid Publications, 1974), 111.
4. Gerald Mast, *The Comic Mind: Comedy and the Movies* (Indianapolis: Bobbs-Merrill, 1973), 290.
5. Steve Seidman, *Comedian Comedy: A Tradition in Hollywood* (Ann Arbor: University of Michigan Research Press, 1981), 153.
6. See the author's "*Mr. B" Or, Comforting Thoughts About the Bison: A Critical Biography of Robert Benchley* (Westport, Connecticut: Greenwood Press, 1992), 8, 10.
7. [W. C. Fields], Mahatma Kane Jeeves, *W. C. Fields in The Bank Dick Script* (1940; rpt. New York: Simon and Schuster, 1973), 10.
8. James Agee, *The Miracle of Morgan Creek* review, *Nation*, February 5, 1944.
9. James Curtis, *W. C. Fields: A Biography* (New York: Alfred A. Knopf, 2003), 419.
10. *W. C. Fields Speaks* (Los Angeles: Price/Stern Publishers, 1981), 52.
11. Carlotta Monti (with Cy Rice), *W. C. Fields & Me* (1971; rpt. New York: Warner Books, 1973), 184.
12. William K. Everson, *The Art of W. C. Fields* (New York: Bonanza Books, 1972), 201.
13. Maude Cheatham, "Juggler of Laughs," *Silver Screen*, April 1935, 30.
14. Curtis, *W. C. Fields: A Biography*, 339.
15. Charles Chaplin, *My Autobiography* (1966; rpt. New York: Pocket Books, Inc., 1966); see also the author's *Charlie Chaplin: A Bio-Bibliography* (Westport, Connecticut: Greenwood Press, 1983).
16. Charles Chaplin, Jr. (with N. and M. Rau), *My Father, Charlie Chaplin* (New York: Random House, 1960), 93.
17. Ibid., 196.
18. [W. C. Fields] Mahatma Kane Jeeves, *W. C. Fields in the Bank Dick Script*, 69.
19. Jack Grant, "That Nose of W. C. Fields," *Movie Classic*, February 1935, 60.
20. Monti (with Cy Rice), *W. C. Fields & Me*, 48, 51.
21. Charles Dickens, *David Copperfield* (1848–1849; rpt. New York: Penguin Books, 1981), 143.
22. Ibid., 192.
23. Cheatham, "Juggler of Laughs" 62.
24. [W.C. Fields] Mahatma Kane Jeeves, *W. C. Fields in The Bank Dick Script*, 46.

25. Robert Lewis Taylor, *W. C. Fields: His Follies and Fortunes* (1949; rpt. New York: Signet Books, 1967), 83.
26. Eddie Cantor (with Jane Kesner Ardmore), *Take My Life* (New York: Doubleday, 1957), 140.
27. Bram Dijkstra, *Idols of Perversity* (New York: Oxford University Press, 1986), 18–19, 83, 111, 366.
28. P. T. Barnum, *Struggles and Triumphs; Or, Forty Years' Recollections of P. T. Barnum* (1855; rpt. New York: Penguin Classics, 1987).
29. Mark Twain and Charles Dudley Warner, *The Gilded Age: A Tale of Today* (1873; rpt. New York: New American Library, 1969).
30. Richard Stengel, "The Mark of Twain," *Time*, July 14, 2008, 4.
31. Curtis, *W. C. Fields: A Biography*, 418.
32. "The New Pictures," *Time*, December 30, 1940, 35.
33. Bosley Crowther, *The Bank Dick* review, *New York Times*, December 13, 1940: 29.
34. *The Bank Dick* review, *Daily Variety*, November 29, 1940.
35. Kevin Thomas, "'Bank Dick' in Fields Film Fest," *Los Angeles Times*, August 18, 1971.
36. Leonard Maltin, *The Great Movie Comedians* (New York: Crown, 1978), 150.
37. "Cline Direction Powerful Asset," *Hollywood Reporter*, November 29, 1940.
38. John Mosher, "The Current Cinema: Mahatma Fields," *The New Yorker*, December 14, 1940, 122.
39. Ibid., 123.
40. James Agee, *A Death in the Family* (1957; rpt. New York: Bantam Books, 1972), 19.
41. W. C. Fields, "The Mountain Sweep Stakes," Library of Congress, (W. C. Fields Papers), March 21, 1919, 1.
42. Sara Redway, "W. C. Fields Pleads for Rough Humor," *Motion Picture Classic*, September 1925, 33.
43. *The Bank Dick* review, *Variety*, December 4, 1940.
44. Howard Barnes, *The Bank Dick* review, *New York Herald Tribune*, December 13, 1940, 26.
45. W. C. Fields, *Fields for President* (New York: Dodd, Mead, 1940).
46. *Fields for President* review, *Newsweek*, April 22, 1940, 41.
47. Richard Schickel, "Nothing Stronger Than Gin Before Breakfast," *New York Times Book Review*, March 30, 2003, 11.

Chapter 3

1. Chris Costello (with Raymond Strait), *Lou's on First: A Biography* (New York: St. Martin's Press, 1981), 55.
2. Cobbett Steinberg, *Reel Facts: The Movie Book of Records* (New York: Vintage Books, 1978), 404.
3. Bob Thomas, *Bud & Lou: The Abbott and Costello Story* (New York: J. B. Lippincott, 1977), 80.
4. David Thomson, *The New Biographical Dictionary of Film* (New York: Alfred A. Knopf, 2003), 3.
5. Frank Capra, *The Name Above the Title* (New York: Macmillan, 1971), 64.
6. Leonard Maltin, *The Great Movie Comedians* (New York: Crown, 1978), 177–78.
7. Maxine Block (ed.), "Abbott & Costello," in *Current Biography 1941* (New York: H. W. Wilson, 1942), 1.
8. Moe Howard, *Moe Howard & The Three Stooges* (Secaucus, New Jersey: Citadel Press, 1977), 67.
9. "*Buck Privates'* Program Notes," "Abbott & Costello File," Margaret Herrick Library, Academy of Motion Picture Arts and Sciences, Beverly Hills, California.
10. Thomas, *Bud & Lou: The Abbott and Costello Story*, 130.
11. *Buck Privates* review, *Variety*, February 5, 1941.
12. Don Eddy, *Buck Privates* review, *American Magazine*, January 1943.
13. Philip K. Scheuer, "'Buck Privates' Hilarious Comedy of Army Life," *Los Angeles Times*, February 28, 1941.
14. *Buck Privates* review, *New York Times*, February 14, 1941, 15.
15. *Buck Privates* review, *Hollywood Reporter*, January 29, 1941.
16. Dorothy Manners, "'Buck Privates' Brings Riot of Laughs," *Los Angeles Examiner*, February 28, 1941.
17. Gerald Mast, *The Comic Mind: Comedy and the Movies* (Indianapolis: Bobbs-Merrill, 1973), 281.
18. Kathryn Bernheimer, *The 50 Funniest Movies of All Time* (Secaucus, New Jersey: Citadel Press, 1999), 155–58.

19. Leonard Maltin, *Movie Comedy Teams* (1970; rpt. New York: Signet, 1974), 275.
20. John Montgomery, *Comedy Films, 1894–1954* (1954; rpt. London: George Allen & Unwin, 1968).
21. Anthony Lane, "Vanity Cases: 'Tropic Thunder,'" *The New Yorker*, August 25, 2008, 84.
22. Maltin, *The Great Movie Comedians*, 181.
23. William Boehnel, *Buck Private* review, *New York World Telegram*, February 14, 1941.

Chapter 4

1. *To Be or Not to Be* revisionist review/appreciation, *Cinemaphile*, April 1976, 3.
2. "Jack Benny," in *Current Biography 1941*, ed. Maxine Block (New York: H. W. Wilson, 1941), 68.
3. Scott Eyman, *Ernst Lubitsch: Laughter in Paradise* (New York: Simon Schuster, 1993), 293.
4. Jack Benny and daughter Joan Benny, *Sunday Nights at Seven: The Jack Benny Story* (New York: Warner Books, 1990), 150.
5. Joe Franklin, *Joe Franklin's Encyclopedia of Comedians* (Secaucus, New Jersey: Citadel Press, 1979), 51.
6. Steve Allen, *The Funny Men* (New York: Simon and Schuster, 1956), 61.
7. Noel F. Busch, "A Loud Cheer for the Screwball Girl," *Life*, January 26, 1942, cover article; Also see the author's *Carole Lombard: The Hoosier Tornado* (Indianapolis: Indiana Historical Society Press, 2003).
8. "'To Be or Not to Be' Very Funny Anti-Nazi Comedy," *Hollywood Reporter*, February 18, 1942.
9. Irving A. Fein, *Jack Benny: An Intimate Biography* (1976; rpt. New York: Pocket Books, 1977), 72.
10. Robert Stack (with Mark Evans), *Straight Shooting* (1980; rpt. New York: Berkley Books, 1981), 105.
11. Scott Eyman, *Ernst Lubitsch*, 295.
12. David Thomson, *The New Biographical Dictionary of Film* (New York: Alfred A. Knopf, 2003), 72.
13. Eyman, *Ernst Lubitsch*, 294.
14. Archer Winsten, "'To Be or Not to Be' Opens at the Rivoli Theatre," *New York Post*, March 7, 1942.
15. Kathryn Bernheimer, *The 50 Funniest Movies of All Time* (New York: Citadel Press, 1999), 70.
16. Nancy Franklin, "Conventional Wisdom," *New Yorker*, September 15, 2008, 84.
17. See the author's *American Dark Comedy: Beyond Satire* (Westport, Connecticut: Greenwood Press, 1996).
18. Bernheimer, *The 50 Funniest Movies of All Time*, 71.
19. Bosley Crowther, *To Be or Not to Be* review, *New York Times*, March 7, 1942, 13.
20. Bosley Crowther, "Against a Sea of Troubles," *New York Times*, March 22, 1942, section 8, 3.
21. Ernst Lubitsch, "Mr. Lubitsch Takes the Floor for Rebuttal," *New York Times*, March 29, 1942, section 8, 3.
22. Rose Pelswick, "Lubitsch Blends Farce, Drama Into Film," *New York Journal-American*, March 7, 1942, 14.
23. Lee Mortimer, "'To Be or Not to Be' A Memorable Finale," *New York Mirror*, March 7, 1942, 19.
24. "'To Be or Not to Be' Very Funny Anti-Nazi Comedy," *Hollywood Reporter*.
25. "The New Pictures: *To Be or Not to Be*," *Time*, March 16, 1942, 90.
26. *To Be or Not to Be* review, *Variety*, February 18, 1942.
27. Ibid.
28. George Ross, "New Film at Rivoli Amusing," *New York World-Telegram*, March 7, 1942, 5.
29. Ibid.
30. Mary Benny and Hilliard Marks (with Marcia Borie), *Jack Benny* (Garden City, New York: Doubleday, 1978), 135.
31. Terrence Rafferty, "David Lean, Perfectionist of Madness," *New York Times*, September 14, 2008, Arts and Leisure, 22.
32. Andy Borowitz, "Nazis Say the Darnedest Things," *The New Yorker*, May 22, 2006, 47.

Chapter 5

1. Anthony Lane, "Ants in His Pants: Preston Sturges....," *The New Yorker*, September 14, 1998, 86.
2. Anna Rothe (ed.), "Eddie Bracken," in *Current Biography 1944* (New York: H. W. Wilson, 1945), 65.

3. James Agee, *The Miracle of Morgan Creek* review, *Nation*, February 5, 1944.
4. James Ursini, *Preston Sturges: An American Dreamer* (New York: Curtis Books, 1973), 133–34.
5. Richard Schickel, "Frank Capra," in *The Men That Made the Movies* (New York: Antheneum, 1975), 87–88.
6. Eric Jonsson, "Preston Sturges and the Theory of Decline," *Film Culture*, Fall 1962, 20.
7. Andrew Sarris, *The American Cinema: Directors and Directions, 1929–1968* (New York: E. P. Dutton, 1968), 113.
8. "Word of Mouth," *Miracle of Morgan's Creek* segment with Eddie Bracken, Turner Classic Movies (TCM), rebroadcast November 4, 2008.
9. James Curtis, *Between Flops: A Biography of Preston Sturges* (New York: Harcourt Brace Jovanovich, 1982), 181.
10. Wes D. Gehring, interview with Eddie Bracken (Muncie, Indiana), October 5, 1982.
11. Bosley Crowther, *Miracle of Morgan Creek* review, *New York Times*, January 20, 1944, 15.
12. *Miracle of Morgan Creek* review, *Variety*, January 5, 1944.
13. Agee, *Miracle of Morgan Creek* review.
14. John McManus, "Mr. Sturges' Merry Miracle," *PM* (January 20, 1944), 24.
15. Alton Cook, "Miracle of Morgan's Creek Has Audience in Stitches," *New York World Telegram*, January 20, 1944, 15.
16. G. E. Blackford, "'Miracle of Morgan's Creek': Paramount Film by Preston Sturges," *New York Journal American*, January 20, 1944, 10.

Chapter 6

1. Ronald L. Smith, *Who's Who in Comedy* (New York: Facts on File, 1992), 219.
2. William Robert Faith, *Bob Hope: A Life in Comedy* (New York: G. P. Putnam's Sons, 1982), 185.
3. *Road to Singapore* review, *Hollywood Reporter*, February 21, 1940, 3.
4. Bob Hope, *They Got Me Covered* (Hollywood: privately published, 1941), 72.
5. *Road to Utopia* review, *The New Yorker*, March 2, 1946, 81.
6. Jack Moffitt, "Back to Utopia," *Esquire*, April 1946, 63.
7. *Road to Utopia* review, *New York Herald Tribune*, February 28, 1946.
8. Moffitt, "Back to Utopia."
9. Brooks Riley, "Words of Hope," *Film Comment*, May-June 1979, 24.
10. Robert Benchley and Nathaniel Bentley, *The Benchley Roundup* (1954; Chicago: University of Chicago Press, 1983).
11. Bing Crosby (with Pete Martin), *Call Me Lucky* (New York: Simon and Schuster, 1953), 95.
12. Bob Hope (with Melville Shavelson), *Don't Shoot, It's Only Me* (New York: G. P. Putnam's Sons, 1990), 34.
13. Ibid.
14. Moffitt, "Back to Utopia," 63.
15. Bosley Crowther "The Eyes Have It," *New York Times*, March 10, 1946.
16. Frank Tashlin, "*Son of Paleface* Went Thataway," *New York Times*, October 5, 1952, section 2, 5.
17. Faith, *Bob Hope*, 183.
18. Otis L. Guernsey, Jr., "The Playbill: Miss Lamour, Bing and Bob," *New York Herald Tribune*, April 2, 1944, 1.
19. *Road to Utopia* review, *New York Herald Tribune*.
20. Frederick C. Othman, "Hope Fades for Hope as He Sees Bear," *Hollywood Citizen-News*, January 29, 1944, 4, 5.
21. Frederick C. Othman, "Reindeer Search Tough Job," *Hollywood Citizen-News*, December 20, 1943.
22. "Hope Springs Eternal in *Road to Utopia*," *Cue*, February 28, 1946, 14.
23. "Last of a Series," *Los Angeles Daily News*, December 21, 1943.
24. "Production Notes on 'Road to Utopia,'" Paramount *Road to Utopia* Press Kit, April 28, 1944, in the "*Road to Utopia* Clipping File," Margaret Herrick Library, Academy of Motion Picture Arts and Sciences, Beverly Hills.
25. Cobbett Steinberg, *Reel Facts: The Movie Book of Records* (New York: Vintage Books, 1978), 405.
26. Bosley Crowther, *Road to Utopia* review, *New York Times*, February 28, 1946.
27. Ruth Waterbury, "'Utopia' Film Full of Fun," *Los Angeles Examiner*, March 22, 1946.
28. Jack D. Grant, *Road to Utopia* review, *Hollywood Reporter*, December 5, 1945.

29. *Road to Utopia* review, *Variety*, December 5, 1945.
30. Lowell E. Redelings, "Crosby and Hope Score Another Hit in 'Road to Utopia' Film," *Hollywood Citizen-News*, March 22, 1946.
31. *Road to Utopia* review, *Cue*, March 3, 1946.
32. Leonard Maltin, *The Great Movie Comedians: From Charlie Chaplin to Woody Allen* (New York: Crown, 1978), 186.
33. Steve Allen, *The Funny Men* (New York: Simon and Schuster, 1956), 211.

Chapter 7

1. Maxine Block (ed.), "Danny Kaye," in *Current Biography 1941* (New York: H. W. Wilson, 1942), 460.
2. Anna Rothe and Evelyn Lohr (eds.), "Danny Kaye," in *Current Biography 1952* (New York: H. W. Wilson, 1953), 299.
3. Leonard Maltin, *The Great Movie Comedians: From Charlie Chaplin to Woody Allen* (New York: Crown, 1978), 198.
4. John McCarten, "The Current Cinema: One Up For Kaye...," *The New Yorker*, April 20, 1946, 85.
5. Dennis Lim, "Unsettling Goofiness of the Divided Mind," *New York Times*, December 28, 2008, Arts & Leisure section, 17, 20.
6. Original Jerry Lewis *Nutty Professor* poster art, collection of the author.
7. "The Kid from Brooklyn ... and Quite a Kid, Too," *Motion Picture Herald* March 23, 1946.
8. This was Stan Laurel's description of "Stand and Ollie." See the authors: *Laurel & Hardy: A Bio-Bibliography* (Westport, Connecticut: Greenwood Press, 1990).
9. See the author's *Leo McCarey: From Marx to McCarthy* (Lanham, Maryland: Scarecrow Press, 2005).
10. David Thomson, "Danny Kaye," in *The New Biographical Dictionary of Film* (New York: Alfred A. Knopf, 2003), 456.
11. Alan Dale, *Comedy Is a Man in Trouble: Slapstick in American Movies* (Minneapolis: University of Minnesota Press, 2000), 28.
12. Jim Knipfel, *Quitting the Nairobi Trio* (2000; rpt. New York: Berkley Books, 2001), 277.
13. Martin Gottfried, *Nobody's Fool: The Lives of Danny Kaye* (New York: Simon & Schuster, 1994).
14. Michael J. Bandler, "Magical Misfit: A Review," *Louisville Courier-Journal*, February 18, 1995, A-13.
15. Steve Allen, *The Funny Men* (New York: Simon and Schuster, 1956), 145.
16. Jeremy McCarter, "Method and Madness," *New York Times*, January 4, 2009, Book Review section, 12.
17. Bosley Crowther, *The Kid from Brooklyn* review, *New York Times* (April 19, 1946), 25.
18. McCarten, "The Current Cinema: One Up for Kaye...."
19. *The Kid from Brooklyn* review, *Variety*, March 20, 1946.
20. Cobbett Steinberg, *Reel Facts: The Movie Book of Records* (New York: Vintage Books, 1978), 343.
21. Dorothy Master, "'Brooklyn Kid' Rates High," *Los Angeles Examiner*, July 5, 1946.
22. Ibid.
23. "'The Kid from Brooklyn' ... and Quite a Kid, Too."
24. "'Kid' Spectacular, Corny," *Hollywood Reporter*, March 20, 1946, 3.
25. *The Kid from Brooklyn* review, *Time*, April 22, 1946, 101.
26. Henry Jenkins, *What Made Pistachio Nuts?* (New York: Columbia University Press, 1994), 150.
27. For example, see *The Kid from Brooklyn* print ad, *New York Journal American*, April 17, 1946, 15.
28. Alton Cook, "A Good Time for All in Danny Kaye Film," *New York World Telegram*, April 18, 1946, 30.
29. John McManus, "The Kid Wins By a Decision," *PM*, April 19, 1946, 6.
30. Rose Pelswick, "Danny Kaye Film Opens," *New York Journal American*, April 19, 1946, 9.
31. "The Brooklyn Kid," *New York Times*, April 21, 1946.

Chapter 8

1. Jim Marshall, "The Marx Menace," *Colliers*, March 16, 1946, 71.
2. Arthur Marx, *Life With Groucho: A*

Son's-Eye View (New York: Simon and Schuster, 1954), 264.
    3. Richard Rowland, "American Classic," *Hollywood Quarterly*, now known as *Film Quarterly*, April 1947, 264.
    4. The Groucho letter dated "May 31, 1945," in "The Groucho Marx Papers," Box 1, Folder 3 (Correspondence with Dr. Samuel Salinger, 1928–1938), State Historical Society of Wisconsin Archives, Madison, Wisconsin.
    5. Groucho Marx, *The Groucho Letters: Letters From and To Groucho Marx* (New York: Simon and Schuster, 1967), 13–18.
    6. Ibid., 14.
    7. The Groucho letter dated "May 31, 1945."
    8. Paul G. Wesolowski, "Brother Against Brother," *The Freedonia Gazette*, Winter 1983, 4.
    9. Joe Adamson, *Groucho, Harpo, Chico and Sometimes Zeppo* (New York: Simon and Schuster, 1973), 396.
    10. See the author's *The Marx Brothers: A Bio-Bibliography* (Westport, Connecticut: Greenwood Press, 1987); *Groucho & W. C. Fields: Huckster Comedians* (Jackson: University Press of Mississippi, 1994); *Laurel & Hardy: A Bio-Bibliography* (Westport, Connecticut: Greenwood Press, 1990); and *Film Clowns of the Depression: Twelve Defining Comic Performances* (Jefferson, North Carolina: McFarland, 2007).
    11. Edgar Allan Poe, "Diddling: Considered as One of the Exact Sciences," in *The Complete Tales and Poems of Edgar Allan Poe* (New York: Random House, 1938), 367, 369.
    12. Susan Kuhlmann, *Knave, Fool, and Genius: The Confidence Man as He Appears in Nineteenth Century American Fiction* (Chapel Hill: University of North Carolina Press, 1973), 6.
    13. Stephen Matterson, Introduction to Herman Melville's *The Confidence-Man* (1857; rpt. New York: Penguin Classics, 1990), xviii.
    14. Ibid.
    15. Louis Chavance, "The Four Marx Brothers As Seen by a Frenchman," *The Canadian Forum*, February 1933, 175.
    16. Harpo Marx (with Rowland Barber), *Harpo Speaks!* (1961; rpt. New York: Freeway Press, 1974), 58.
    17. "Marx 'Casablanca' Riotous," *Hollywood Reporter*, April 15, 1946, 3.
    18. *A Night in Casablanca* review, *Variety*, April 17, 1946.
    19. James Agee, "Films: 'A Night in Casablanca,'" *Nation*, May 25, 1946, 636.
    20. Ibid.
    21. "The New Pictures: *A Night in Casablanca*," *Time*, May 20, 1946, 89.
    22. Ibid.
    23. D. Mosdell, "Film Review: 'A Night in Casablanca,'" *Canadian Forum*, September 1946, 138.
    24. Ibid., 139.
    25. Thomas M. Pryor, *A Night in Casablanca* review, *New York Times*, August 12, 1946, 17.
    26. Bosley Crowther, "Those Marx Men," *New York Times*, August 18, 1946, section 2, 1.
    27. Pare Lorentz, *Horse Feathers* review, *Vanity Fair* (October 1932).
    28. Eileen Creelman, *A Night in Casablanca* review, *New York Sun*, August 12, 1946, 14.
    29. Leonard Maltin, *The Great Movie Comedians: From Charlie Chaplin to Woody Allen* (New York: Crown, 1978), 141.
    30. Crowther, "Those Marx Men."

Chapter 9

    1. James Agee, "Comedy's Greatest Era," *Life*, September 3, 1949.
    2. Mae Tinée, "Harold Lloyd's Latest Comedy Is Delightful," *Chicago Tribune*, March 7, 1936, 15.
    3. Richard Watts, Jr., "On the Screen: 'The Milky Way'—Paramount," *New York Herald Tribune*, March 26, 1936, 15.
    4. "Lloyd Slaps Suits Against Columbia," *Hollywood Reporter*, March 7, 1946, 1.
    5. Richard Schickel, *Harold Lloyd: The Shape of Laughter* (Boston: New York Graphic Society, 1974), 214.
    6. William Cahn, *Harold Lloyd's World of Comedy* (London: George Allen and Unwin, 1966), 175.
    7. John Belton, "Harold Lloyd: The Man and His Times," in *Harold Lloyd: The King of Daredevil Comedy*, ed. Adam Reilly (New York: Collier Books, 1977), 198.
    8. Harold Lloyd (with Wesley W. Stout), *An American Comedy* (1928; rpt. New York: Dover Publications, 1971), 97–118.

9. Preston Sturges, *Preston Sturges*, ed. Sandy Sturges (1990; rpt. New York: Touchstone Book, 1991).
10. Frank Nugent, "Genius with a Slapstick," *Variety*, February 7, 1945, 2, 23.
11. Bosley Crowther, "When Satire and Slapstick Meet," *New York Times Magazine*, August 27, 1944, 14–15.
12. "Preston Sturges," *Look*, October 3, 1944, 64.
13. Maxine Block (ed.), "Preston Sturges," in *Current Biography 1941* (New York: H. W. Wilson, 1942), 845.
14. Joseph McBride (ed.), *Hawks on Hawks* (Los Angeles: University of California Press, 1982), 69.
15. Manny Farber and W. S. Poster, "Preston Sturges: Success in the Movies," in *Negative Space* (1954)(New York: Frederick Praeger, 1972), 96.
16. The phrase a "100% talking picture" was a promotional blurb indiscriminately used in the selling of many early sound pictures. Initially, the public obsessed with the new phenomenon.
17. Andrew Sarris, "Nostalgic Gamble," *Village Voice*, October 15, 1979.
18. "'Diddlebock' Sturges Antic Sparked By Return of Harold Lloyd," *Hollywood Reporter*, February 18, 1947, 3; *The Sin of Harold Diddlebock* review, *Variety*, February 19, 1947.
19. *The Sin of Harold Diddlebock* review, *Film Daily*, February 20, 1947.
20. See the author's *Leo McCarey: From Marx to McCarthy* (Lanham, Maryland: Scarecrow Press, 2005).
21. Charles Higham, *Howard Hughes: The Secret Life* (1993; rpt. New York: St. Martin's Press, 2004), 67.
22. Sturges, *Preston Sturges*, 304.
23. "'Harold Diddlebock' Getting New Name," *Variety*, May 26, 1947.
24. James Curtis, *Between Flops: A Biography of Preston Sturges* (New York: Harcourt Brace Jovanovich, 1982), 201.
25. Hallis Alpert, "The Middle Years of Harold Diddlebock," *Saturday Review*, November 4, 1950.
26. Thomas M. Pryor, *Mad Wednesday* review, *New York Times*, January 25, 1951, 21.
27. "Harold's Back Again," *Cue*, November 18, 1950.
28. Shirle Duggon, "Lloyd Film Laugh Maker," *Los Angeles Examiner*, November 27, 1950, section 2, 7.
29. Ibid.
30. Philip K. Scheuer, "Harold Lloyd Back in 'Mad' Waggery," *Los Angeles Times*, November 27, 1950.

Chapter 10

1. Will Rogers, *Letters of a Self-Made Diplomat to His President* (New York: Albert & Charles Boni, 1926).
2. *My Favorite Brunette* review, *Time*, March 31, 1947, 99–11.
3. "Everybody's Favorite Hope," *Newsweek*, March 31, 1947, 92.
4. David Thomson, *The New Biographical Dictionary of Film* (New York: Alfred A. Knopf, 2003), 485.
5. Frank MacShane (ed.), *Selected Letters of Raymond Chandler* (1981; rpt. New York: Delta, 1987), 75.
6. Charles Thompson, *Bob Hope: Portrait of a Superstar* (New York: St. Martin's Press, 1981), 78–79.
7. Cobbett Steinberg, *Reel Facts: The Movie Book of Records* (New York: Vintage Books, 1978), 343.
8. James Thurber, "The Secret Life of Walter Mitty," in *My World—And Welcome To It* (New York: Harcourt, Brace and Company, 1942), 72–81.
9. Howard Barnes, *My Favorite Brunette* review, *New York Herald Tribune*, March 20, 1947.
10. Robert Benchley, "Carnival Week in Sunny Las Los," in *The Treasurer's Report and Other Aspects of Community Singing* (New York: Grosset and Dunlap, 1930), 41.
11. Jack Thompson, *My Favorite Brunette* review *New York Daily Mirror*, March 30, 1947, 16.
12. *My Favorite Brunette* review, *Variety*, February 19, 1947.
13. Bosley Crowther, *My Favorite Brunette* review, *New York Times*, March 20, 1947, 38.
14. See the author's *Parody as Film Genre: "Never Give a Saga an Even Break"* (Westport, Connecticut: Greenwood Press, 1999).
15. *My Favorite Brunette* review, *Commonweal*, April 4, 1947, 614; Thompson, *My Favorite Brunette* review.

16. Jack D. Grant, "'Brunette' Funny Bob Hope," *Hollywood Reporter*, February 18, 1947, 3.
17. Robert Warshow, "The Gangster as Tragic Hero" (1948) and "Movie Chronicle: The Westerner" (1954), in *The Immediate Experience*, ed. Sherry Abel (New York: Atheneum, 1962), 127–33, 135–54; James Agee, "Comedy's Greatest Era," *Life*, September 3, 1949.
18. John G. Cawelti, "The Question of Popular Genres," *Journal of Popular Film and Television*, Summer 1985, 55–56.
19. "Everybody's Favorite Hope."
20. Crowther, *My Favorite Brunette* review.
21. *My Favorite Brunette* review, *Time*.
22. Barnes, *My Favorite Brunette* review.
23. Grant, "'Brunette' Funny Bob Hope."
24. Joe Lee Davis, "Criticism and Parody," *Thought*, Summer 1951, 180.
25. Virginia Wright, "Brunette," *Los Angeles Daily News*, March 20, 1947.
26. *My Favorite Brunette* review, incomplete Hollywood newspaper citation (March 20, 1947), *Brunette* file, Margaret Herrick Library, Academy of Motion Picture Arts and Sciences, Beverly Hills, California.
27. Lloyd L. Sloan, "Runyon Benefit Tops For Vaudeville Show," *Hollywood Citizen News*, March 20, 1947; "Bob Hope Big Hit in New Film Comedy," *Hollywood Citizen News*, March 20, 1947.
28. See also "Hughes Selects Miami for Lloyd Premiere," *Motion Picture Herald*, February 8, 1947.
29. *My Favorite Brunette* review, *Variety*.

Chapter 11

1. Charlie Chaplin, *My Trip Abroad* (New York: Harper & Brothers, 1922), 8.
2. Charles Chaplin, *My Autobiography* (1964; rpt. New York: Pocket Books, Inc., 1966), 458.
3. John McCabe, *Charlie Chaplin* (Garden City, New York: Doubleday, 1978), 203.
4. "Chaplin Sprouting 'Landru' Spinach," *Hollywood Reporter*, December 8, 1941, 1.
5. "Charlie Chaplin's [1947] *Monsieur Verdoux* Press Conference," *Film Comment*, Winter 1969, 39.
6. Geneviève Moreau, *The Restless Journey of James Agee* (New York: William Morrow, 1977), 216.
7. "UA Double-Crosses Itself On Interview With Chaplin," *Hollywood Reporter*, April 11, 1947, 6.
8. Bosley Crowther, *Monsieur Verdoux* revisionist review, *New York Times*, July 4, 1964, 8.
9. Bosley Crowther, *Monsieur Verdoux* review, *New York Times*, April 12, 1947, 11.
10. Archer Winsten, *Monsieur Verdoux* review, *New York Post*, April 12, 1947.
11. *Monsieur Verdoux* review, *New York Daily Mirror*, April 12, 1947.
12. *Monsieur Verdoux* review, *Variety*, April 16, 1947.
13. "'M. Verdoux' Disappointing," *Hollywood Reporter*, April 14, 1947, 3, 9.
14. Howard Barnes, *Monsieur Verdoux* review, *New York Herald Tribune*, April 12, 1947, 8.
15. James Agee, "Monsieur Verdoux — I," *The Nation*, May 31, 1947.
16. James Agee, "Monsieur Verdoux — II," *The Nation*, June 14, 1947.
17. Ibid.
18. Robert Warshow, "Monsieur Verdoux" (1947), in *The Immediate Experience* (1962; rpt. New York: Antheneum, 1972), 208.
19. James Agee, "Monsieur Verdoux — III," *The Nation*, June 21, 1947.
20. Ibid.
21. *City Lights* review, *Time* magazine, April 17, 1950, 38.
22. Theodore Huff, *Charlie Chaplin* (1951; rpt. New York: Arno Press & the *New York Times*, 1972), 296.
23. Agee, "Monsieur Verdoux — III."
24. James Agee, *Monsieur Verdoux* review, *Time* magazine, May 5, 1947.
25. Parker Tyler, *Chaplin: Last of the Clowns* (1947; rpt. New York: Horizon Press, 1972), 174.
26. Agee, *Monsieur Verdoux* review, *Time*.
27. James Agee, *The Human Comedy* review, *The Nation*, March 20, 1943.
28. James Agee, "[A New Critic]," *The Nation*, December 26, 1942.
29. Martin Gottfried, *All His Jazz: The Life and Death of Bob Fosse* (1990; rpt. New York: Da Capo Press, 1998), 423.
30. André Bazin, "Charlie Chaplin," in *What Is Cinema?*, vol. 1, selected and trans.

Hugh Gray (1958; rpt. Los Angeles: University of California Press, 1967), 52.
31. André Bazin, "The Myth of Monsieur Verdoux," in *What Is Cinema?*, vol. 2, selected and trans. Hugh Gray (1958; rpt. Los Angeles: University of California Press, 1971), 102–03.
32. Ibid., 111–13.
33. Tyler, *Chaplin: Last of the Clowns*, 145.
34. See the author's *American Dark Comedy: Beyond Satire* (Westport, Connecticut: Greenwood Press, 1996).
35. Luis Buñuel, *My Last Sigh*, trans. Abigail Israel (1982; rpt. New York: Random House, 1984).
36. Kenneth S. Lynn, *Charlie Chaplin and His Times* (New York: Simon & Schuster, 1997), 454.
37. "'M. Verdoux' Disappointing."
38. Crowther, *Monsieur Verdoux* revisionist review.
39. Judith Crist, "Mirth and Murder," *New York Herald Tribune*, July 26, 1964, 27.

Chapter 12

1. See the author's *Red Skelton: The Mask Behind the Mask* (Indianapolis: Indiana Historical Society Press, 2008); *Seeing Red ... The Skelton in Hollywood's Closet: An Analytical Biography* (Davenport: Robin Vincent, 2001); *I, Red Skelton: Exit Laughing* (a novelized memoir) (Indianapolis: New Century Press, 2009).
2. Harrison B. Summers, ed., *A Thirty-Year History of Programs Carried on National Radio Networks in the United States, 1926–1956* (New York: Arno Press, 1971), 115.
3. Cobbett Steinberg, *Reel Facts: The Movie Book of Records* (New York: Vintage Books, 1978), 344.
4. Bob Thomas (syndicated Hollywood columnist), "Hollywood," *Burlingame Advance*, May 26, 1947.
5. "Radio Notes," *Newsweek*, September 24, 1945, 26.
6. Bob Thomas (syndicated Hollywood columnist), "Ten Best Film Comics Picked by Joe E. Brown," *Long Beach Press Telegram*, August 20, 1947.
7. Louella Parsons (syndicated Hollywood columnist), "Skelton Gets Picture Break He Has Earned," *San Diego Union*, August 22, 1947.

8. Norman Panama and Melvin Frank, *The Spy*, August 12, 1947, *A Southern Yankee* script material folder number 1, University of Southern California Cinema-Television Library, Los Angeles, California.
9. See the author's *Parody as Film Genre: "Never Give a Saga an Even Break"* (Westport, Connecticut: Greenwood Press, 1999).
10. Kathleen Gable, *Clark Gable: A Personal Portrait* (Englewood Cliffs, New Jersey: Prentice-Hall, 1961), 79.
11. Buster Keaton (with Charles Samuels), *My Wonderful World of Slapstick* (Garden City, New York: Doubleday, 1960), 261.
12. Marion Meade, *Buster Keaton: Cut to the Chase* (New York: HarperCollins, 1995), 239.
13. Rudi Blesh, *Keaton* (1966: reprint, New York: Collier Books, 1971), 354.
14. Frank Miller, *Leading Men: The 50 Most Unforgettable Actors of the Studio Era* (San Francisco: Chronicle Books, 2006), 115.
15. Keaton, *My Wonderful World of Slapstick*, 261.
16. Eleanor Norris Keaton, conversation with author, Piqua, Kansas (Buster Keaton's birthplace), late 1980s.
17. *Telescope: Deadpan (Buster Keaton)*, CBS Canada, broadcast April 14, 1966, video collection of the Museum of Television and Radio, Beverly Hills, California.
18. Conversations with the author during performing visits to Ball State University (Muncie, Indiana) during the 1980s.
19. Harry Tugend, *A Southern Yankee* script material (filed July 19, 1948), *Yankee* script material folder number 1, USC Cinema-Television Library.
20. Buster Keaton and Edward Sedgwick, *A Southern Yankee* "retakes" (April 20, 1948), *Yankee* script folder number 4, USC Cinema-Television Library.
21. Keaton, *My Wonderful World of Slapstick*, 264.
22. Henri Bergson, "Laughter," in *Comedy*, Wylie Sypher, ed. (Garden City, New York: Doubleday and Company, 1956), 105.
23. Buster Keaton and Edward Sedgwick, *A Southern Yankee* "retakes" (April 27, 1948), *Yankee* script folder number 4, USC Cinema-Television Library.
24. Charles McGrath, "Mike Nichols, Master of Invisibility," *New York Times* (April 12, 2009), Arts & Leisure section: 1, 9.

25. Keaton, *My Wonderful World of Slapstick*, 264.
26. Larry Rhine, correspondence with the author (November 16, 1998).
27. Allen Barra, *Yogi Berra: Eternal Yankee* (New York: W. W. Norton & Company, 2009).
28. *A Southern Yankee* review, *Variety* (August 11, 1948), 8.
29. "Top Notch Comedy Won't Miss at BO [box office]," *Hollywood Reporter* (August 6, 1948).
30. Darr Smith, *A Southern Yankee* review, *Los Angeles Daily News*, in the *A Southern Yankee* file, Margaret Herrick Library, Academy of Motion Picture Arts and Sciences, Beverly Hills, California.
31. *A Southern Yankee* review, *Cue* (November 27, 1948).
32. William R. Weaver, *A Southern Yankee* review, *Motion Picture Daily* (August 6, 1948).
33. Arthur Marx, *Red Skelton* (New York: E. P. Dutton, 1979), 140.
34. *A Southern Yankee* review, *New York Times*, November 25, 1948, 47.
35. "'Yankee' Verdict Is Generally Negative Among N.Y. Critics," *Hollywood Reporter*, December 1, 1948.
36. Leo Mishkin, *A Southern Yankee* review, *New York Morning Telegraph*, November 25, 1948.
37. Fred Hift, *A Southern Yankee* review, *Motion Picture Herald*, August 7, 1948.
38. Leonard Maltin, *The Great Movie Comedians: From Charlie Chaplin to Woody Allen* (New York: Crown, 1978), 211.

Epilogue

1. "'Gold Rush' Plays To 306,000 In N. Y. Run," *Hollywood Reporter*, June 30, 1942, 1.
2. "Classic Chaplin 'Gold Rush' Glorious Fun In Reissue," *Hollywood Reporter*, March 3, 1942, 4.
3. For example, please see: Allen Eyles' *The Marx Brothers: Their World of Comedy* (New York: Paperback Library, 1971), 178.
4. Neil Schmitz, *Of Huck and Alice: Humorous Writing in American Literature* (Minneapolis: University of Minnesota Press, 1983), 20.
5. See the author's *Laurel & Hardy: A Bio-Bibliography* (Westport, Connecticut: Greenwood Press, 1990); and *Film Clowns of the Depression: Twelve Defining Performances* (Jefferson, North Carolina: McFarland, 2007).
6. G. E. Blackford, "'Miracle of Morgan's Creek': Paramount Film by Preston Sturges," *New York Journal American*, January 20, 1944, 10.
7. Preston Sturges, *Preston Sturges*, ed. Sandy Sturges (1990; rpt. New York: Touchstone Book, 1991), 339.
8. David Gates, "The Visit," *New York Times*, May 17, 2009, Book Review section: 6.
9. One Christopher Buckley description of his father, William F., in the son's *Losing Mum and Pup: A Memoir* (New York: Twelve: Hatchette Book Group, 2009), 55.

BIBLIOGRAPHY

Books

Adamson, Joe. *Groucho, Harpo, Chico and Sometimes Zeppo.* New York: Simon and Schuster, 1973.

Allen, Steve. *The Funny Men.* New York: Simon and Schuster, 1956.

Avisar, Ilan. *Screening the Holocaust: Cinema's Images of the Unimaginable.* Bloomington: Indiana University Press, 1988.

Barnum, P. T. *Struggles and Triumphs; Or, Forty Years' Recollections of P. T. Barnum.* 1855; rpt. New York: Penguin Classics, 1987.

Barra, Allen. *Yogi Berra: Eternal Yankee.* New York: W. W. Norton, 2009.

Benny, Jack and daughter Joan. *Sunday Nights at Seven: The Jack Benny Story.* New York: Warner Books, 1990.

Benny, Mary Livingstone, and Hilliard Marks (with Marcia Borie). *Jack Benny.* Garden City, New York: Doubleday, 1978.

Bernheimer, Kathryn. *The 50 Funniest Movies of All Times.* Secaucus, New Jersey: Citadel Press, 1999.

Blesh, Rudi. *Keaton.* 1966; rpt. New York: Collier Books, 1971.

Buckley, Christopher. *Losing Mum and Pup: A Memoir.* New York: Twelve: Hatchette Book Group, 2009.

Buñuel, Luis. *My Last Sigh.* Trans. Abigail Israel. 1982; rpt. New York: Random House, 1983.

Cahn, William. *Harold Lloyd's World of Comedy.* London: George Allen and Unwin, 1966.

Cantor, Eddie (with Jane Kesner Ardmore). *Take My Life.* New York: Doubleday, 1957.

Capra, Frank. *The Name Above the Title.* New York: Macmillan, 1971.

Chaplin, Charles. *My Autobiography.* 1964; rpt. New York: Pocket Books, 1966.

Chaplin, Charles, Jr. (with N. and M. Rau). *My Father, Charlie Chaplin.* New York: Random House, 1960.

Chaplin, Charlie. *My Trip Abroad.* New York: Harper & Brothers, 1922.

Costello, Chris (with Raymond Strait). *Lou's on First: A Biography.* New York: St. Martin's, 1981.

Crawford, Deborah. *Franz Kafka: Man Out of Step.* New York: Crown, 1973.

Curtis, James. *Between Flops: A Biography of Preston Sturges.* New York: Harcourt Brace Jovanovich, 1982.

_____. *W. C. Fields: A Biography.* New York: Alfred A. Knopf, 2003.

Dale, Alan. *Comedy Is a Man in Trouble: Slapstick in American Movies.* Minneapolis: University of Minnesota Press, 2000.

Dickens, Charles. *David Copperfield.* 1848–49; rpt. New York: Penguin Books, 1981.

Dijkstra, Bram. *Idols of Perversity.* New York: Oxford University Press, 1986.

Everson, William K. *The Art of W. C. Fields.* New York: Bonanza Books, 1972.

Eyles, Allen. *The Marx Brothers: Their World of Comedy.* New York: Paperback Library, 1971.

Eyman, Scott. *Ernst Lubitsch: Laughter in Paradise.* New York: Simon & Schuster, 1993.

Faith, William Robert. *Bob Hope: A Life in Comedy.* New York: G. P. Putnam's Sons, 1982.

Fein, Irving A. *Jack Benny: An Intimate Biography.* 1976; rpt. New York: Pocket Books, 1977.

Fields, W. C. *Fields for President.* New York: Dodd, Mead, 1940.

[Fields, W. C.] Mahatma Kane Jeeves. *W. C. Fields in The Bank Dick Script*. 1940; rpt. New York: Simon and Schuster, 1973.

Franklin, Joe. *Joe Franklin's Encyclopedia of Comedians*. Secaucus, New Jersey: Citadel, 1979.

Gable, Kathleen. *Clark Gable: A Personal Portrait*. Englewood Cliffs, New Jersey: Prentice-Hall, 1961.

Gehring, Wes D. *American Dark Comedy: Beyond Satire*. Westport, Connecticut: Greenwood, 1996.

_____. *Carole Lombard: The Hoosier Tornado*. Indianapolis: Indiana Historical Society Press, 2003.

_____. *Charlie Chaplin: A Bio-Bibliography*. Westport, Connecticut: Greenwood, 1983.

_____. *Film Clowns of the Depression: Twelve Defining Comic Performances*. Jefferson, North Carolina: McFarland, 2007.

_____. *Groucho & W. C. Fields: Huckster Comedians*. Jackson: University Press of Mississippi, 1994.

_____. *I, Red Skelton: Exit Laughing* (a novelized memoir). Indianapolis: New Century Press, forthcoming.

_____. *Laurel & Hardy: A Bio-Bibliography*. Westport, Connecticut: Greenwood, 1990.

_____. *Leo McCarey: From Marx to McCarthy*. Lanham, Maryland: Scarecrow, 2005.

_____. *The Marx Brothers: A Bio-Bibliography*. Westport, Connecticut: Greenwood, 1987.

_____. *"Mr. B" Or, Comforting Thoughts About the Bison: A Critical Biography of Robert Benchley*. Westport, Connecticut: Greenwood, 1992.

_____. *Parody as Film Genre: "Never Give a Saga an Even Break."* Westport, Connecticut: Greenwood, 1999.

_____. *Red Skelton: The Mask Behind the Mask*. Indianapolis: Indiana Historical Society Press, 2008.

_____. *Seeing Red ... The Skelton in Hollywood's Closet: An Analytical Biography*. Davenport: Robin Vincent Publishing, 2001.

_____. *W. C. Fields: A Bio-Bibliography*. Westport, Connecticut: Greenwood, 1984.

Gottfried, Martin. *All His Jazz: The Life and Death of Bob Fosse*. 1990; rpt. New York: Da Capo, 1998.

_____. *Nobody's Fool: The Lives of Danny Kaye*. New York: Simon & Schuster, 1994.

Higham, Charles. *Howard Hughes: The Secret Life*. 1993; rpt. New York: St. Martin's, 2004.

Hope, Bob. *They Got Me Covered*. Hollywood: privately published, 1941.

Howard, Moe. *Moe Howard & The Three Stooges*. Secaucus, New Jersey: Citadel Press, 1977.

Huff, Theodore. *Charlie Chaplin*. 1951; rpt. New York: Arno Press & the New York Times, 1972.

Jenkins, Henry. *What Made Pistachio Nuts?* New York: Columbia University Press, 1994.

Keaton, Buster (with Charles Samuels). *My Wonderful World of Slapstick*. Garden City, New York: Doubleday, 1960.

Knipfel, Jim. *Quitting the Nairobi Trio*. 2000; rpt. New York: Berkley, 2001.

Kuhlmann, Susan. *Knave, Fool, and Genius: The Confidence Man as He Appears in Nineteenth Century American Fiction*. Chapel Hill: University of North Carolina Press, 1973.

Lahr, John. *Coward: The Playwright*. 1982; rpt. New York: Discus Book, 1983.

Lipman, Steve. *Laughter in Hell: The Use of Humor During the Holocaust*. 1991; rpt. Northvale, New Jersey: Jason Aronson, 1993.

Lloyd, Harold (with Wesley W. Stout). *An American Comedy*. 1928; rpt. New York: Dover, 1971.

Lynn, Kenneth S. *Charlie Chaplin and His Times*. New York: Simon & Schuster, 1997.

MacShane, Frank, ed. *Selected Letters of Raymond Chandler*. 1981; rpt. New York: Delta, 1987.

Maland, Charles. *Chaplin and American Culture: The Evolution of a Star Image*. Princeton, New Jersey: Princeton University Press, 1989.

Maltin, Leonard. *The Great Movie Comedians*. New York: Crown, 1978.

_____. *Movie Comedy Teams*. 1970; rpt. New York: Signet, 1974.

Marx, Arthur. *Life with Groucho: A Son's-Eye View*. New York: Simon and Schuster, 1954.

_____. *Red Skelton*. New York: E. P. Dutton, 1979.

Marx, Harpo (with Rowland Barber). *Harpo Speaks!* 1961; rpt. New York: Freeway Press, 1974.

Mast, Gerald. *The Comic Mind: Comedy and the Movies.* Indianapolis: Bobbs-Merrill, 1973.
Matterson, Stephen. *The Confidence-Man.* Author Herman Melville. 1857; rpt. New York: Penguin Classics, 1990.
McBride, Joseph, ed. *Hawks on Hawks.* Los Angeles: University of California Press, 1982.
McCabe, John. *Charlie Chaplin.* Garden City, New York: Doubleday, 1978.
Meade, Marion. *Buster Keaton: Cut to the Chase.* New York: HarperCollins, 1995.
Miller, Frank. *Leading Men: The 50 Most Unforgettable Actors of the Studio Era.* San Francisco: Chronicle Books, 2006.
Monti, Carolotta (with Cy Rice). *W. C. Fields & Me.* 1971; rpt. New York: Warner Books, 1973.
Moreau, Geneviève. *The Restless Journey of James Agee.* New York: William Morrow, 1977.
Rogers, Will. *Letters of a Self-Made Diplomat to His President.* New York: Albert & Charles Boni, 1926.
Sarris, Andrew. *The American Cinema: Directors and Directions, 1929–1968.* New York: E. P. Dutton, 1968.
Schickel, Richard. *Harold Lloyd: The Shape of Laughter.* Boston: New York Graphic Society, 1974.
Schmitz, Neil. *Of Huck and Alice: Humorous Writing in American Literature.* Minneapolis: University of Minnesota Press, 1983.
Seidman, Steve. *Comedian Comedy: A Tradition in Hollywood.* Ann Arbor: University of Michigan Research Press, 1981.
Smith, Ronald L. *Who's Who in Comedy.* New York: Facts on File, 1992.
Stack, Robert (with Mark Evans). *Straight Shooting.* 1980; rpt. New York: Berkley, 1981.
Steinberg, Cobbett. *Reel Facts: The Movie Book of Records.* New York: Vintage, 1978.
Sturges, Preston. *Preston Sturges.* Ed. Sandy Sturges. 1990; rpt. New York: Touchstone Books, 1991.
Summers, Harrison B., ed. *A Thirty-Year History of Programs Carried on National Radio Networks in the United States, 1926–1956.* New York: Arno Press, 1971.
Taylor, Robert Lewis. *W. C. Fields: His Follies and Fortunes.* 1949; rpt. New York: Signet Books, 1967.
Thomas, Bob. *Bud & Lou: The Abbott and Costello Story.* New York: J. B. Lippincott, 1977.
Thompson, Charles. *Bob Hope: Portrait of a Superstar.* New York: St. Martin's, 1981.
Thomson, David. *The New Biographical Dictionary of Film.* New York: Alfred A. Knopf, 2003.
Twain, Mark, and Charles Dudley Warner. *The Gilded Age: A Tale of Today.* 1873; rpt. New York: New American Library, 1969.
Tyler, Parker. *Chaplin: Last of the Clowns.* 1947; rpt. New York: Horizon Press, 1972.
Ursini, James. *Preston Sturges: An American Dreamer.* New York: Curtis Books, 1973.
W. C. Fields Speaks. Los Angeles: Price/Stern/Sloan, 1981.
Yanni, Nicholas. *W. C. Fields.* New York: Pyramid, 1974.

Shorter Works

"Abbott & Costello." In *Current Biography 1941.* Ed. Maxine Block. New York: H. W. Wilson, 1942.
Agee, James. "Comedy's Greatest Era." *Life,* September 3, 1949.
——. *A Death in the Family.* 1957; rpt. New York: Bantam Books, 1972.
——. "Films: 'A Night in Casablanca.'" *Nation,* May 25, 1946, 636.
——. *The Human Comedy* review. *The Nation,* March 20, 1943.
——. *The Miracle of Morgan Creek* review. *Nation,* February 5, 1944.
——. "Monsieur Verdoux" (3 parts). *The Nation,* May 31, 1947; June 14, 1947; June 21, 1947.
——. *Monsieur Verdoux* review. *Time* magazine, May 5, 1947.
——. "[A New Critic]." *The Nation,* December 26, 1942.
Alpert, Hallis. "The Middle Years of Harold Diddlebock." *Saturday Review,* November 4, 1950.
Als, Hilton. "Intruder in the Wings." *The New Yorker,* May 26, 2008, 82.
Bandler, Michael J. "Magical Misfit: A Review." *Louisville Courier-Journal,* February 18, 1995, A-13.
The Bank Dick review. *Daily Variety,* November 29, 1940.

The Bank Dick review. *Variety*, December 4, 1940.
Barnes, Howard. *Monsieur Verdoux* review. *New York Herald Tribune*, April 12, 1947, 8.
_____. *My Favorite Brunette* review. *New York Herald Tribune*, March 20, 1947.
_____. *A Night in Casablanca* review. *New York Herald Tribune*, August 12, 1946, 12.
_____. "The Screen [column]." *New York Herald Tribune*, June 22, 1941.
Bazin, André. "Charlie Chaplin." In *What Is Cinema?* vol. 1, selected and trans. Hugh Gray. 1958; rpt. Los Angeles: University of California Press, 1967.
_____. "The Myth of Monsieur Verdoux." In *What Is Cinema?* vol. 2, selected and trans. Hugh Gray. 1958; rpt. Los Angeles: University of California Press, 1971.
Belton, John. "Harold Lloyd: The Man and His Times." In *Harold Lloyd: The King of Daredevil Comedy*. Ed. Adam Reilly. New York: Collier Books, 1977.
Benchley, Robert. "Carnival Week in Sunny Las Los." In *The Treasurer's Report and Other Aspects of Community Singing*. New York: Grosset and Dunlap, 1930.
Bergson, Henri. "Laughter." In *Comedy*, Wylie Sypher, ed. Garden City, New York: Doubleday, 1956.
Blackford, G. E. "'Miracle of Morgan's Creek': Paramount Film by Preston Sturges." *New York Journal American*, January 20, 1944, 10.
"Bob Hope Big Hit in New Film Comedy." *Hollywood Citizen News*, March 20, 1947.
Boehnel, William. *Buck Privates* review. *New York World Telegram*, February 14, 1941.
_____. "W. C. Fields Frolics at RKO Palace." *New York World Telegram*, December 13, 1940, 28.
Bradley, Bill. "Life Coach." *New York Times*, June 7, 2009, Book Review section, 10.
"The Brooklyn Kid." *New York Times*, April 21, 1946.
"Buck Privates' Program Notes." In the "Abbott & Costello File." Margaret Herrick Library. Academy of Motion Picture Arts and Sciences. Beverly Hills, California.
Buck Privates review. *Hollywood Reporter*, January 29, 1941.
Buck Privates review. *New York Times*, February 14, 1941, 15.
Buck Privates review. *Variety*, February 5, 1941.

Busch, Noel F. "A Loud Cheer for the Screwball Girl," *Life*, January 26, 1942.
Cawelti, John G. "The Question of Popular Genres." *Journal of Popular Film and Television* (Summer 1985).
"Chaplin: A Bewildered 'Little Feller' Bucking Modern Times." *Newsweek*, February 8, 1936, 19.
"Chaplin Says He Just Had to Make That Speech." *New York World Telegram*, October 19, 1940, 7.
"Chaplin Sprouting 'Landru' Spinach." *Hollywood Reporter*, December 8, 1941, 1.
"Chaplin Strikes Back at New York Critics." *Los Angeles Times*, January 5, 1941.
"Charlie Chaplin." In *Current Biography 1940*. Ed. Maxine Block. New York: H. H. Wilson, 1940.
"Charlie Chaplin's [1947] *Monsieur Verdoux* Press Conference." *Film Comment* (Winter 1969).
Chavance, Louis. "The Four Marx Brothers As Seen by a Frenchman." *The Canadian Forum*, February 1933, 175.
Cheatham, Maude. "Juggler of Laughs." *Silver Screen*, April 1935.
City Lights review. *Time* magazine, April 17, 1950, 38.
"Classic Chaplin 'Gold Rush' Glorious Fun In Reissue." *Hollywood Reporter* March 3, 1942, 4.
"Cline Direction Powerful Asset." *Hollywood Reporter*, November 29, 1940.
Cohen, Rich. "Becoming Adolf." *Vanity Fair*, November 2007, 239–40.
Combs, Carl. "'The Great Dictator' In Carthay Premiere." *Hollywood Citizen-News*, November 15, 1940.
Cook, Alton. "Chaplin Lays an Egg in His High Hat." *New York World Telegram*, April 12, 1947, 6.
_____. "Danny Kaye's Inspired Idiocy Runs Riot at Music Hall." *New York World Telegram*, March 3, 1944, 16.
_____. "A Good Time for All in Danny Kaye Film." *New York World Telegram*, April 18, 1946, 30.
_____. "*Miracle of Morgan's Creek* Has Audience in Stitches." *New York World Telegram*, January 20, 1944, 15.
Creelman, Eileen. *The Miracle of Morgan's Creek* review. *New York Sun*, January 20, 1944, 21.
_____. "Two Slapstick Comedies, 'Monsieur

Verdoux' and 'Buck Privates Come Home.'" *New York Sun*, April 12, 1947, 5.

Crist, Judith. "Mirth and Murder." *New York Herald Tribune*, July 26, 1964, 27.

Crowther, Bosley. *The Bank Dick* review. *New York Times*, December 13, 1940, 29.

_____. "The Eyes Have It." *New York Times*, March 10, 1946.

_____. "In 'The Great Dictator,' Charlie Chaplin Reveals Again the Greatness in Himself." *New York Times*, October 20, 1940.

_____. *The Kid from Brooklyn* review. *New York Times*, April 19, 1946, 25.

_____. *Miracle of Morgan Creek* review. *New York Times*, January 20, 1944, 15.

_____. *Monsieur Verdoux* review. *New York Times*, April 12, 1947, 11.

_____. *Monsieur Verdoux* revisionist review. *New York Times*, July 4, 1964, 8.

_____. *My Favorite Brunette* review. *New York Times*, March 20, 1947, 38.

_____. *Road to Utopia* review. *New York Times*, February 28, 1946.

_____. "Those Marx Men." *New York Times*, August 18, 1946, Section 2:1.

_____. *To Be or Not to Be* review. *New York Time*, March 7, 1942, 13.

_____. "When Satire and Slapstick Meet." *New York Times Magazine*, August 27, 1944, 14–15.

"The Current Cinema: Charlie's Hitler." *The New Yorker*, October 26, 1940.

"Danny Kaye." In *Current Biography 1941*. Ed. Maxine Block. New York: H. W. Wilson, 1942.

"Danny Kaye." In *Current Biography 1952*. Eds. Anne Rothe and Evelyn Lohr. New York: H. W. Wilson Company, 1953.

Davis, Joe Lee. "Criticism and Parody." *Thought* (Summer 1951).

della Cava, Marco R. "Conan Brings a New Vibe to 'Tonight.'" *USA Today*, May 29–31, 2009, 2A.

"'Diddlebock' Sturges Antic Sparked By Return of Harold Lloyd." *Hollywood Reporter*, February 18, 1947, 3.

Duggan, Shirle. "Lloyd Film Laugh Makers." *Los Angeles Examiner*, November 27, 1950, section 2, 7.

"Eddie Bracken." In *Current Biography 1944*. Ed. Anna Rothe. New York: H. W. Wilson, 1945.

Eddy, Don. *Buck Privates* review. *American Magazine*, January 1943.

"Everybody's Favorite Hope." *Newsweek*, March 31, 1947, 92.

Farber, Manny and W. S. Poster. "Preston Sturges: Success in the Movies" (1954). In *Negative Space*. New York: Frederick Praeger, 1972.

Ferguson, Otis. *The Great Dictator* review. *New Republic*, November 4, 1940.

Fields, W. C. "The Mountain Sweepstakes." In the "W. C. Fields Papers" (copyrighted March 21, 1919). Library of Congress.

Fields for President review. *Newsweek*, April 22, 1940, 41.

Franklin, Nancy. "Conventional Wisdom." *The New Yorker*, September 15, 2008.

Gardiner, Reginald. "*The Great Dictator*: Charlie Chaplin's Gift of Humor and Satire to the Totalitarian State." *New York Herald Tribune*, September 16, 1940.

Gates, David. "The Visit." *New York Times*, May 17, 2009, Book Review section, 6.

Gehring, Wes D. "Chaplin and the Progressive Era: The Neglected Politics of a Clown." *Indiana Social Studies Quarterly* (Fall 1981), 10–18.

_____. Conversation with Eddie Bracken. Muncie, Indiana (October 5, 1982). Author's files.

_____. Conversation with Eleanor Norris Keaton, widow of Buster. Piqua, Kansas (late 1980s). Author's files.

_____. Correspondence with Larry Rhine, November 16, 1998. Author's files.

_____. *Nutty Professor* insert poster (Jerry Lewis, 1963). Author's collection.

"'Gold Rush' Plays to 306,000 In N. Y. Run." *Hollywood Reporter*, June 30, 1942, 1.

Grant, Jack. "That Nose of W. C. Fields." *Movie Classics*, February 1935.

Grant, Jack D. *Road to Utopia* review. *Hollywood Reporter*, December 5, 1945.

"The Great Dictator." *Sidney Morning Herald*, November 5, 1940, Women's Supplement section, 7.

The Great Dictator review. *Variety*, October 16, 1940.

Guernsey, Otis L., Jr. "'The Miracle of Morgan's Creek'—Paramount." *New York Herald Tribune*, January 20, 1944, 13.

_____. "The Playbill: Miss Lamour, Bing and Bob." *New York Herald Tribune*, April 2, 1944, 1.

Hale, Wanda. "Danny Kaye Musical Fine Holiday Fare." *New York Daily News*, April 19, 1946, 38.

Harmon, Melissa Burdick. "Noel Coward and His Jamaican Paradise." *Biography*, October 1998.

"Harold's Back Again." *Cue*, November 18, 1950.

"'Harold Diddlebock' Getting New Name." *Daily Variety*, May 26, 1947.

Harris, Mark. "Twilight of the Tummlers." *New York*, June 1, 2009.

"Hey Adolf! Millions Answer Call to Service. *PM*, October 16, 1940, 1.

Hift, Fred. *A Southern Yankee* review. *Motion Picture Herald*, August 7, 1948.

"Hope Springs Eternal in Road to Utopia." *Cue*, February 28, 1946, 14.

"Hughes Selects Miami For Lloyd Premiere." *Motion Picture Herald*, February 8, 1947.

"Jack Benny." In *Current Biography 1941*. Ed. Maxine Block. New York: H. W. Wilson, 1941.

Jonsson, Eric. "Preston Sturges and the Theory of Decline." *Film Culture* (Fall 1962).

Keaton, Buster, and Edward Sedgwick. *A Southern Yankee* "retakes" (April 20, 1948). In *Yankee* script material. Folder number 4. University of Southern California Cinema-Television Library. Los Angeles, California.

_____ and _____. *A Southern Yankee* "retakes" (April 27, 1948). In *Yankee* script material. Folder number 4. University of Southern California Cinema-Television Library. Los Angeles California.

The Kid from Brooklyn ad. *New York Journal American*, April 17, 1946, 15.

"The Kid from Brooklyn ... and Quite a Kid, Too." *Motion Picture Herald*, March 23, 1946.

The Kid from Brooklyn review. *Time*, April 22, 1946, 101.

The Kid from Brooklyn review. *Variety*, March 20, 1946.

"'Kid' Spectacular, Corny." *Hollywood Reporter*, March 20, 1946, 3.

Lane, Anthony. "Ants in His Pants: Preston Sturges ...." *The New Yorker*, September 14, 1998, 86.

_____. "Vanity Cases: 'Tropic Thunder." *The New Yorker*, August 25, 2008.

"Last of a Series." *Los Angeles Daily News*, December 21, 1943.

Lim, Dennis. "Unsettling Goofiness of the Divided Mind." *New York Times*, December 28, 2008, Arts & Leisure Section, 17, 20.

"Lloyd Slaps Suit Against Columbia." *Hollywood Reporter*, March 7, 1946, 1.

Lorentz, Pare. *Horse Feathers* review. *Vanity Fair*, October 1932.

Lubitsch, Ernst. "Mr. Lubitsch Takes the Floor for Rebuttal." *New York Times*, March 29, 1942, section 8, 3.

Manners, Dorothy. "'Buck Privates' Brings Riot of Laughs." *Los Angeles Examiner*, February 28, 1941.

Marshall, Jim. "The Marx Menace." *Colliers*, March 16, 1946, 71.

Marx, Groucho. Letter dated May 31, 1945. In "The Groucho Marx Papers." Box 1, Folder 3. Correspondence with Dr. Samuel Salinger, 1928–1938. State Historical Society of Wisconsin Archives. Madison, Wisconsin.

"Marx 'Casablanca' Riotous." *Hollywood Reporter*, April 15, 1946, 3.

Masters, Dorothy. "'Brooklyn Kid' Rates High." *Los Angeles Examiner*, July 5, 1946.

McCarten, John. "The Current Cinema: One Up For Kaye ...." *The New Yorker*, April 20, 1946, 85.

McCarter, Jeremy. "Method and Madness." *New York Times*, January 4, 2009, Book Review section, 12.

McGrath, Charles. "Mike Nichols, Master of Invisibility." *New York Times*, April 12, 2009, Arts & Leisure section, 1, 9.

McManus, John. "The Kid Wins by a Decision." *PM*, April 19, 1946, 6.

_____. "Mr. Sturges' Merry Miracle." *PM*, January 20, 1944, 24.

Miracle of Morgan Creek review. *Variety*, January 5, 1944.

Mishkin, Leo. *A Southern Yankee* review. *New York Morning Telegraph*, November 25, 1948.

Moffitt, Jack. "Back to Utopia." *Esquire*, April 1946, 63.

Monsieur Verdoux review. *Variety*, April 16, 1947.

Monsieur Verdoux review. *New York Daily Mirror*, April 12, 1947.

Mortimer, Lee. "'To Be or Not to Be' A Memorable Finale." *New York Mirror*, March 7, 1942, 19.

Mosdell, D. "Film Review: 'A Night in

Casablanca." *Canadian Forum*, September 1946, 138.
Mosher, John. "The Current Cinema: Charlie's Hitler." *The New Yorker*, October 26, 1940, 78.
_____. "The Current Cinema: Mahatma Fields." *The New Yorker*, December 14, 1940, 122.
"Mr. Chaplin Answers His Critics." *New York Times*, October 27, 1940, Section 9:5.
My Favorite Brunette review. *Commonweal*, April 4, 1947, 614.
My Favorite Brunette review. *Time*, March 31, 1947, 99–100.
My Favorite Brunette review. *Variety*, February 19, 1947.
"The New Pictures: A Night in Casablanca." *Time*, May 20, 1946, 89.
"The New Pictures." *Time*, December 30, 1940, 35.
"The New Pictures: To Be or Not to Be." *Time*, March 16, 1942, 90.
A Night in Casablanca review. *New York Sun*, August 12, 1946, 14.
A Night in Casablanca review. *Variety*, April 17, 1946.
Nugent, Frank. "Genius with a Slapstick." *Variety*, February 7, 1945, 2, 23.
Othman, Frederick C. "Hope Fades for Hope as He Sees Bear." *Hollywood Citizen-News*, January 29, 1944, 4, 5 .
Panama, Norman, and Melvin Frank. *The Spy*, August 12, 1947. In *A Southern Yankee* script material. Folder number 1. University of Southern California Cinema-Television Library. Los Angeles, California.
Parsons, Louella. "Old, New Chaplin in 'Dictator' Film." *New York Journal American*, January 29, 1939.
_____. "Skelton Gets Picture Break He Has Earned." *San Diego Union*, August 22, 1947.
Pelswick, Rose. "'Buck Privates' at Loew State." *New York Journal American*, February 14, 1941, 12.
_____. "Danny Kaye Film Opens." *New York Journal American*, April 19, 1946, 9.
_____. "Lubitsch Blends Farce, Drama Into Film." *New York Journal-American*, March 7, 1942, 14.
_____. "'M. Verdoux' At Broadway." *New York Journal American*, April 12, 1947, 6.
Poe, Edgar Allan. "Diddling: Considered as One of the Exact Sciences." In *The Complete Tales and Poems of Edgar Allan Poe*. New York: Random House, 1938.
"Preston Sturges." In *Current Biography 1941*. Ed. Maxine Block. New York: H. W. Wilson, 1942.
"Preston Sturges." *Look*, October 3, 1944, 64.
"Production Notes on 'Road to Utopia,'" Paramount *Road to Utopia* Press Kit, April 28, 1944. In the "*Road to Utopia* Clipping File." Margaret Herrick Library, Academy of Herrick Library, Academy of Motion Picture Arts and Sciences, Beverly Hills, California.
Pryor, Thomas M. *Mad Wednesday* review. *New York Times*, January 25, 1951, 21.
_____. *A Night in Casablanca* review. *New York Times*, August 12, 1946, 17.
"Radio Notes." *Newsweek*, September 24, 1945, 26.
Redelings, Lowell E. "Crosby and Hope Score Another Hit in 'Road to Utopia' Film." *Hollywood Citizen-News*, March 22, 1946.
Redway, Sara. "W. C. Fields Pleads for Rough Humor." *Motion Picture Classic*, September 1925.
"Right Up There: Red Skelton's Back on Top and Here Are [the] Reasons Why." *TV Guide*, April 28, 1956, 6.
Riley, Brooks. "Words of Hope." *Film Comment*, May-June 1979.
Road to Singapore review. *Hollywood Reporter*, February 21, 1940, 3.
Road to Utopia review. *Cue*, March 3, 1946.
Road to Utopia review. *New York Herald Tribune*, February 28, 1946.
Road to Utopia review. *Variety*, December 5, 1945.
Ross, George. "New Film at Rivoli Amusing." *New York World-Telegram*, March 7, 1942, 5.
Rowland, Richard. "American Classics." *Hollywood Quarterly*— now *Film Quarterly*, April 1947.
"Russell, Handless Vet, Wins 2 Movie 'Oscars.' *New York Post*, March 14, 1947, 4.
Sarris, Andrew. "Nostalgic Gamble." *Village Voice*, October 15, 1979.
Scheuer, Philip K. "'Buck Privates' Hilarious Comedy of Army Life." *Los Angeles Times*, February 28, 1941.
_____. "Harold Lloyd Back in 'Mad' Waggery." *Los Angeles Times*, November 27, 1950.

Schickel, Richard. "Frank Capra." In *The Men That Made the Movies*. New York: Antheneum, 1975.

———. "Nothing Stronger Than Gin Before Breakfast." *New York Times Book Review*, March 30, 2003, 11.

Sennwald, Andre. "W. C. Fields: Buffoon." *New York Times*, January 13, 1935, section 9, 5.

The Sin of Harold Diddlebock review. *Film Daily*, February 20, 1947.

The Sin of Harold Diddlebock review. *Variety*, February 19, 1947.

Sloan, Lloyd L. "Runyon Benefit Tops For Vaudeville Show." *Hollywood Citizen News*, March 20, 1947.

Smith, Darr. *A Southern Yankee* review. *Los Angeles Daily News*. In the *A Southern Yankee* file. Margaret Herrick Library, Academy of Motion Picture Arts and Sciences. Beverly Hills, California.

A Southern Yankee review. *Cue*, November 27, 1948.

A Southern Yankee review. *New York Times*, November 25, 1948, 47.

A Southern Yankee review. *Variety*, August 11, 1948, 8.

Stengel, Richard. "The Mark of Twain." *Time*, July 14, 2008, 4.

Tashlin, Frank. "*Son of Paleface* Went Thataway." *New York Times*, October 5, 1952, section 2, 5.

Thomas, Bob (syndicated Hollywood columnist). "Hollywood." *Burlingame Advance*, May 26, 1947.

———. "Ten Best Film Comics Picked by Joe E. Brown." *Long Beach Press Telegram*, May 26, 1947.

Thomas, Kevin. "'Bank Dick' in Fields Film Fest." *Los Angeles Times*, August 18, 1971.

———. "'Great Dictator' in Re-release." *Los Angeles Times*, June 23, 1972.

Thompson, Jack. *My Favorite Brunette* review. *New York Daily Mirror*, March 30, 1947, 16.

Thomson, David. "Danny Kaye." In *The New Biographical Dictionary of Film*. New York: Alfred A. Knopf, 2003.

Thurber, James. "The Secret Life of Walter Mitty." In his *My World—And Welcome to It*. New York: Harcourt, Brace and Company, 1969, 72–81.

Tinée, Mae. "Harold Lloyd's Latest Comedy Is Delightful." *Chicago Tribune*, March 7, 1936, 15.

To Be or Not to Be revisionist review/appreciation. *Cinemaphile*, April 1976, 3.

To Be or Not to Be review. *Variety*, February 18, 1942.

"'To Be or Not to Be' Very Funny Anti-Nazi Comedy." *Hollywood Reporter*, February 18, 1942.

"Top Notch Comedy Won't Miss at BO [box office]." *Hollywood Reporter*, August 6, 1948.

Tugend, Harry. *A Southern Yankee* script material (filed July 19, 1948). In *Yankee* script material. Folder number 1. University of Southern California Cinema-Television Library. Los Angeles, California.

"UA Double-Crosses Itself On Interview With Chaplin." *Hollywood Reporter*, April 11, 1947, 6.

"Universal's 'Buck Privates' Are More Musical Than Most." *PM*, February 14, 1941, 22.

Van Gelder, Robert. "Chaplin Draws a Keen Weapon." *New York Times Magazine*, September 8, 1940.

Warshow, Robert. "The Gangster as Tragic Hero" (1954). In *The Immediate Experience*, ed. Sherry Abel. New York: Atheneum, 1962.

———. "Monsieur Verdoux" (1947). In *The Immediate Experience*. 1962; rpt. New York: Atheneum, 1972.

Waterbury, Ruth. "'Utopia' Film Full of Fun." *Los Angeles Examiner*, March 22, 1946.

Watts, Richard, Jr. "On the Screen: 'The Milky Way'—Paramount. *New York Herald Tribune*, March 26, 1936, 15.

"W. C. Fields, Whose Funny Crimes Have Paid Him Well ... Will Be Seen as a Bank Dick in His New Picture." *PM*, December 8, 1940, 56–57.

Weaver, William R. *A Southern Yankee* review. *Motion Picture Daily*, August 6, 1948.

Wesolowski, Paul G. "Brother Against Brother." *The Freedonia Gaette*, Winter 1983, 4.

Winsten, Archer. *Monsieur Verdoux* review. *New York Post*, April 12, 1947.

———. "'To Be or Not to Be' Opens at the Rivoli Theatre." *New York Post*, March 7, 1942.

"Word of Mouth" *Miracle of Morgan's Creek* segment with Eddie Bracken. *Turner Classic Movies*, rebroadcast November 4, 2008.

"'Yankee' Verdict Is Generally Negative Among N. Y. Critics." *Hollywood Reporter*, December 1, 1948.

Documentaries

Telescope: Deadpan (Buster Keaton). CBS Canada, broadcast April 14, 1966. Video Collection of the Museum of Television and Radio. Beverly Hills, California.

The Tramp and the Dictator. BBC. A Kevin Brownlow Film, 2002.

INDEX

Numbers in ***bold italics*** indicate pages with photographs

Abbott & Costello 150, 179; *Buck Privates* and 46–47, ***48, 49, 50***, 51–58; "Who's on First?" 46, 58
Abel, Walter 104, 106, 107, 113
The Adventurer 44, 177
Agee, James 35, 43, 77, 87, 129, 130, 158, 168–169, 170–173, 178
Allen, Fred 61
Allen, Steve 61–62, 101, 110
Allen, Woody 11–12, 19, 32, 49, ***100***, 101, ***156***, 157, 160, 197
Andrews Sisters ***50***, 163
Arden, Eve 106, 107
Arsenic and Old Lace 87

Bainter, Fay ***113***
The Bank Dick 2, 30–32, ***33***, 34–39, ***40***, 41–43, ***44***, 45, 52, 84, 192, 193, 196
Barnum, P.T. 41, 120
Bazin, André 173, 174, 178
Benchley, Robert 34, 62, 75, 81, 91, ***92***, 129, 156
Benny, Jack 2, 3, 59–62, ***63***, 64–66, ***67***, 68–70, ***71***, 72–74, 127, 163, 192, 197
Bergman, Ingmar 126
Bergson, Henri 185
Bernheimer, Kathryn 57
Berra, Yogi 190, 192
Big Sleep 151, 162, 163
Blockade 20
Bogart, Humphrey 115, 117, ***118***, 128, 130, 151, 152–153, 156, 161, 162
Bonaparte, Napoleon 22, 168
Bracken, Eddie 2, 75–77, ***78***, 79, ***80***, 81–88, 135, 136, 142, 197
Bradbury, Ray 29
Bressart, Felix 70
Bringing Up Baby 139
Brooks, Mel 73, 160
Brownlow, Kevin 28

Buck Privates 46–47, ***48***, ***49***, ***50***, 51–58
Buckley, Christopher 5
Bunny, John 1, 30, 47
Buñuel, Luis 175
Burns, George 62

Cain, James 152, 154
Cantor, Eddie 40–41
Capra, Frank 51, 75, 77, 82, 83, 84, 87
Carrey, Jim 18, 88, 103, 104, 109
Casablanca 115, 116–117, 128, 130, 157
Catch-22 32, 176
Cawelti, John G. 158
Chandler, Raymond 151–153, 154, 161
Chaplin, Charlie 1, 10, 29, 57, 89, 95, 130, 133, 188, 190, 192, 194; *The Adventurer* 44, 177; *City Lights* 11, 14, 55, 108, 166, 171–172; *Easy Street* 10, 174; and Ernst Lubitsch 60, 64, 70, 72; *The Gold Rush* 21, 26, 74, 96, 98, 194; *The Great Dictator* ii, 3, 13–20, ***21***, 22–24, ***25***, 26–29, 30, 35, 56, 64, 65, 70, 74, 165, 174, 177, 196, 197; *Modern Times* 14, 134–135, 141, 171, 174; *Monsieur Verdoux* 165–168, ***169***, 170–174, ***175***, 176–178; *Shoulder Arms* 15, ***16***, 26, 53, 193; and W.C. Fields 37–38, 39, 42–45, 58, 193; *A Woman of Paris* 60, 165
Charade 145
Chinatown 155, 158, 162, 163
City Lights 11, 14, 55, 108, 166, 171–172
Cohen Brothers 187
Colgate Comedy Hour 58
Conlin, Jimmy 141–143
Coward, Noël 5
Crimes and Misdemeanors 160
Crosby, Bing 50, 89, ***90***, 91–98, ***99***, 100, 150, 160, 161, 179, 181
Crowther, Bosley 71–72, 130, 139, 157, 170, 178

223

Daniel, Henry *21*, 23
Demarest, William 76, *78*, 79, *80*, 81
Dickens, Charles 38, 39–42
Dr. Strangelove or: How I Learned to Stop Worrying and Love the Bomb 18, 26, 178
Donlevy, Brian 83–84, 87
Dumont, Margaret 127
Durant, Tim 19

Easy Street 10, 174
Emerson, Ralph Waldo 34–35
Errol, Leon 35

Farber, Manny 139–140
Ferguson, Otis 27
Ferrell, Will 106, 155
Fields, W.C. 1, 2, 37–38, 39, 42–45, 58, 77, 134, 193; *The Bank Dick* 2, 30–32, *33*, 34–39, *40*, 41–43, *44*, 45, 52, 84, 192, 193, 196
Fine, Sylvia 103, 110
Ford, John 20, 60
Frank, Melvin 94, 180–181, 188, 196, 197
Franklin, Joe 61
Frawley, William 47
The Fuller Brush Man 2, 129, 180

Gable, Clark 73, 181–182
Gehring, Emily v, 6
Gehring, Sarah (Sears) v, 6
The General 28, 98, 182, *183*, 193
Gilbert, Billy 22, 23, 24, 177
Goddard, Paulette *25*, 166
Going My Way 87, 97
The Gold Rush 21, 26, 74, 96, 98, 194
Goldwyn, Samuel 102–103, 106, 108, 111, 112, 114, 135
Good Morning, Vietnam 121
Gottlieb, Alex 47–48, 49, 51
Grant, Cary 125, 139, 145, 163
Grant, John 50–51, 53, 54
The Grapes of Wrath 20
The Great Dictator ii, 3, 13–20, *21*, 22–24, *25*, 26–29, 30, 35, 56, 64, 65, 70, 74, 165, 174, 177, 196, 197
Greene, Graham 152

Hamilton, Margaret 142
Hammett, Dashiell 151, 154
Hawks, Howard 139, 146
Hecht, Ben 64
Heller, Joseph 176, 177
Hitchcock, Alfred 20, 115, 125, 159–160, 162
Hope, Bob 2, 48–49, 50, 54, 61, 103–104, 129, 188, 197; *My Favorite Brunette* 150, *151*, 152–158, *159*, 160–164; *Road to Utopia* 89, *90*, 91–98, *99*, 100–101, 179, 180–181, 196
Howard, Shemp 36, 54
Huff, Theodore 26
Hughes, Howard 146–147, 164
Hutton, Betty 76, 77, *78*, 79, *80*, 81–85, 87, 91, 160, 163

Inglourious Basterds 20
It's a Wonderful Life 75, 82

Jones, Paul 180–181

Kafka, Franz 27
Kaye, Danny 2, 102–104, *105*, 106–112, *113*, 114, 135, 147, 163, 196, 197
Keaton, Buster 28, 95, 98, 106, 133, 179, 181, 182, *183*, 184–188, 190, 193
Kennedy, Edgar 140–141, 143–144
The Kid from Brooklyn 2, 102–104, *105*, 106–112, *113*, 114, 135, 196
Kiss Kiss, Bang Bang 162
Knipfel, Jim 109–110
Kovacs, Ernie 109

Ladd, Alan 152–153, 155, 157, 158
Lamour, Dorothy *90*, 91, 93–98, *99*, 100, 153, 155, 157, *159*, 161
Lane, Anthony 58
Lane, Conrad 6, 182
Langdon, Harry 55, 95, 133, 190
The Last Laugh 24
Laurel & Hardy 79, 95, 107, 117, 140, 168, 195, 197
Letterman, David 7
Lewis, Jerry 11, 54, 55, 78–79, 87, 103, 104, 107, 108, 129, 197
Lloyd, Harold 1, 88, 95, *148*; *The Milky Way* 103, 106, 107, *108*, 109, 114, 134–135; *Safety Last* 83, 133, *134*, 143; *The Sin of Harold Diddlebock* 133–136, 137, 138–149, 164, 193, 195
Lombard, Carole 62, *63*, *71*, 64–74
Lopez, Steve 5
Lorentz, Pare 130–131
Lubitsch, Ernst 60, 64, 70, 72
Lumet, Sidney 29
Lynn, Diana 76, 77, *78*, 79, 81, 83, 84, 87

Mad Wednesday see *The Sin of Harold Diddlebock*
The Major and the Minor 77
Maland, Charles J. 17, 21
Maltin, Leonard 42, 52, 58, 103, 131, 191
Martin, Dean 54, 55, 104, 129, 197

Marx, Chico 115–117, **119**, 120–122, **123**, 124–126, 128–129, **131**, 132, 141
Marx, Groucho 55, 66, 115–117, **119**, 120–122, **123**, 125, **126**, 128–130, **131**, 132, 134
Marx, Harpo 115, 117, **119**, 122, **123**, 125, **126**, 127–129, **131**, 132, 141, 194, 195
Marx, Zeppo 55
Marx Brothers 1, 55, 98, 141; *A Night in Casablanca* 2, 115–118, **119**, 120–122, **123**, 125, **126**, 127–130, **131**, 132, 192, 193, 194, 196, 197
M*A*S*H 177
Mast, Gerald 31, 57, 58
Match Point 32
Maupassant, Guy de 38
Mayo, Virginia **105**, 106, 113
McCarey, Leo 87, **108**, 109, 134, 146–147
Merkel, Una 41
The Milky Way 103, 106, 107, **108**, 109, 114, 134–135
The Miracle of Morgan's Creek 2, 75–77, **78**, 79, **80**, 81–88, 135, 136, 142, 195
Mr. Smith Goes to Washington 75, 82
Modern Times 14, 134–135, 141, 171, 174
Monsieur Verdoux 165–168, **169**, 170–174, **175**, 176–178
Monti, Carlotta 35–36
Mosdel, D. 130
Mosher, John 28, 43
My Favorite Brunette 150, **151**, 152–158, **159**, 160–164

Nairobi Trio 109
National Lampoon's Vacation 88
Network 176
Nichols, Mike 32, 176, 187
A Night in Casablanca 2, 115–118, **119**, 120–122, **123**, 125, **126**, 127–130, **131**, 132, 192, 193, 194, 196, 197
Notorious 115, 125

Oakie, Jack **21**, 22, 23
O'Brien, Conan 7, 11
Olsen & Johnson 47

Panama, Norman 94, 180–181, 188, 196, 197
Pangborn, Franklin 36–37, 38
Paradise Lost 97–98
Pendleton, Nat 53, 54
Poe, Edgar Allan 117–118
"Professor Backwards" 51

Ralph, Jessie 34
Raye, Martha 178
Riefenstahl, Leni 16, 74

Road to Utopia 89, **90**, 91–98, **99**, 100–101, 157, 160, 179, 180–181, 196
Rogers, Will 17, 62, 89, 150
Rooney, Mickey 41–42
Rowan & Martin's Laugh-In 47
Rumann, Sig 70, 123, 127–129
Runyon, Damon 163–164

Safety Last 83, 133, **134**, 143
Sailor Beware 55, 107, 109
Sandler, Adam 18
Sarris, Andrew 83, 145
Schickel, Richard 45, 136
Schlesinger, Arthur, Jr. 13, 29
Seidman, Steve 33–34
Sennwald, Andre 30
Shawn, Wallace 11
Shoulder Arms 15, **16**, 26, 53, 193
Simon, Neil 110
The Sin of Harold Diddlebock 76, 79, 133–136, **137**, 138–149, 164, 193, 195
Skelton, Red 2, 3, 7, 49, 54, 179–181, **182**, 183–186, **187**, 188–191, 193, 196
Slaughterhouse-Five 178
Slide, Anthony 1–3, 6
A Southern Yankee 2, 179–181, **182**, 183–186, **187**, 188–191, 193, 196
Stander, Lionel 106, 107
Stillwell, Edna 51
Stoppard, Tom 196–197
Stout, Clarence 185
Sturges, Preston 2, **86**; *The Miracle of Morgan's Creek* 75–77, **78**, 79, **80**, 81–88, 135, 136, 142, 195; *The Sin of Harold Diddlebock* 133–136, **137**, 138–149, 164, 193, 195
Sutton, Grady 36, 38, 40, 41

Tarantino, Quentin 20
Tashlin, Frank 79, 94, 128–129, 197
Thomas, Kevin 29
Thomson, David 50, 64, 108–109, 152, 188
"Three Stooges" 36, 52, 54
Thurber, James 33–34, 92, 95, 153–154
To Be or Not to Be 2, 3, 59–62, **63**, 64–66, **67**, 68–70, **71**, 72–74, 127, 192
The Tramp and the Dictator 28
Tropic Thunder 58
Twain, Mark 18, 40
Tyler, Parker 173, 174

Vonnegut, Kurt 178

Warner Brothers 116–117
Warshow, Robert 158, 171, 178
Welles, Orson 115, 117, 165, 173
West, Mae 42, 134

"Who's on First?" 46, 58
Wilde, Oscar 68, 139, 195
Wilder, Billy 77, 152, 154
Williams, Robin 121

Wilson, Owen 49
The Wizard of Oz 27, 41–42, 142
Wolfe, Bill 37
A Woman of Paris 60, 165

www.ingramcontent.com/pod-product-compliance
Ingram Content Group UK Ltd.
Pitfield, Milton Keynes, MK11 3LW, UK
UKHW041948140426
5217IPUK00014B/699